# THE WIND OF THE SPIRIT

## IN PERSONAL AND CORPORATE REVIVAL

# JOHN R. VAN GELDEREN

FORWARD BY DR. ED NELSON

**Preach the Word Ministries, Inc.**

*For the cause of revival and evangelism*

THE WIND OF THE SPIRIT
In Personal and Corporate Revival
John R. Van Gelderen

© 2003 Preach the Word Ministries, Inc.
   P.O. Box 242, Menomonee Falls, WI  53052

ISBN 0-9654935-5-5

Printed in the United States of America
Graphic Design: Mike Moreau/Harvest Media

Scripture quotations are from the King James Version of the Bible.

# FOREWORD

## THE NEED IS URGENT!

What is the need? The need in our fundamental churches is twofold: first, for individual believers to become acquainted with the Holy Spirit in a new and intimate way; second, for our churches to see the power and the fruits of revival. The two needs are definitely related.

## THE TIME IS NOW—THE NEED MUST BE MET!

Evangelist John R. Van Gelderen has met this great need in our fundamental churches by his writing this book, *The Wind of the Spirit*. I have just read the manuscript of the book. What a great blessing the book has proved to be in my own life! I was challenged by every chapter; often I received a new challenge on each page. He did develop the two needs I spoke of above, two needs that are definitely related: a personal acquaintance with the Holy Spirit and the application of that acquaintance, resulting in holy living and revival in our churches. I am looking forward to the publication of the book and to the privilege of ordering many copies to distribute among our own people.

Oh, how much we need the power of the Holy Spirit in our personal lives and also in the corporate life of the church. I am confident this book will be used to "stir up" the believers to have lives filled with the Spirit and to "stir up" pastors to lead their people in a hungering for real revival.

In *The Wind of the Spirit*, Evangelist Van Gelderen has given his readers excellent expositions of various passages in the Word of God. He has certainly done his homework well, quoting many authors. He has written with burden and conviction in developing his premise that believers must know the Holy Spirit and depend upon Him for the power to live godly lives. Very clearly he uses Scripture to reveal that if believers are to be empowered by the Spirit of God, they must turn from sin and seek the Lord and His power.

Line upon line; page upon page; chapter upon chapter—John R. Van Gelderen drives the truth home to our hearts. Personally, after reading the book, I was convicted to pray more and to live a life more dedicated to letting the Holy Spirit use me to see revival now. The book points out the need to deal with all sin in our lives, even the "little foxes that spoil the vines."

As I came to the closing sections of the book, I was thrilled with the historical illustrations of mighty outpourings of God's power. It was a blessing and a challenge to read of the personal experiences of Johnathan Goforth and of the revivals that came through his ministry. Another delight was to read of the revivals in Scotland, Wales, and Lewis. I closed the book and asked God to work in my life to see God's power in wonderful refreshing revival—even NOW.

I knew John's father, Dr. Wayne Van Gelderen, well. We were close friends. As I read the book, I saw the imprint of the father's burden and passion coming through the writing of his son. I know if he were still with us today, the senior Van Gelderen would be thrilled with the book his son has penned.

I do believe what Van Gelderen is saying in this book meets a supreme need in our fundamental churches today. I recommend the book to any who are interested in living a holy life and in seeing God's work in cleansing, purifying, soul-saving revival. And this book will work in our lives the fulfillment of Matthew 5:6: "Blessed are they which do hunger and thirst after righteousness: for they shall be filled." It will bring the results of Isaiah 44:3: "For I will pour water upon him that is thirsty, and floods upon the dry ground: I will pour my Spirit upon thy seed, and my blessing upon thy offspring." For those who are hungry and thirsty, this book can and will produce personal victory and corporate revival.

Dr. Ed Nelson
Pastor, Bethel Baptist Church
Tucson, Arizona

# TABLE OF CONTENTS

# PREFACE

Gray clouds nearly blanketed the sky. A damp, chilly ocean breeze briskly hurried in from the western shoreline approximately one hundred yards away, scampered through the fishing village, and skipped along across the peat bogs to the east. Though the day seemed dreary, my heart thrilled with joy and awesome wonder as I fixed my gaze on the village church in Barvas—a standing reminder of the mighty Spirit of Revival. It was mid-July of 2000. My wife and I were on the Isle of Lewis, located off the northwest coast of Scotland. Just fifty years before this brisk and windy but summer day, the Wind of the Spirit blew across the island. The Lewis Awakening began in December of 1949 in Barvas and continued into 1953 throughout the island. One cannot but think that if God has done it before, and is the unchanging Almighty, He can do it again!

I first became acquainted with the Lewis Revival by reading a brief article about it in the mid 1980s. Immediately my heart was quickened in reading of God's wonderful works. In the mid-90s I listened to an audiotape of Duncan Campbell whom God used as the primary declarer of truth during the revival. Again God stirred my heart deeply. Since then the Lord has virtually brought to me several books written by Duncan Campbell, more audiotapes of his preaching, a video of testimonies from the revival, Duncan Campbell's audio and written account of the awakening, and a biography of Campbell. So my wife and I, in God's gracious leading, took a trip to the Isle of Lewis as a part of a missions trip during the summer of 2000. Here God providentially led us to meet and fellowship with four people who were saved during the revival. The glow of God still shines in their countenances. God taught us much in those precious days.

Yet God had been preparing my heart especially in the eight years previous to this trip. After five years as an assistant to my father, Wayne Van Gelderen, Sr., I entered full-time evangelism in January of 1992. At the same time period, my father asked a group of young preachers to read the two-volume biography of Hudson Taylor, written by Taylor's son and daughter-in-law. God used the pen of Hudson

Taylor as he exposited certain Bible passages, along with an inductive study of Galatians and Ephesians, to open my eyes to life-changing truths. I saw the futility of flesh-dependence and the absolute necessity of God-dependence to access Spirit-enablement. Those truths budded and blossomed over the next few years. God cultivated faith in my heart during this rich spiritual pilgrimage.

Then on Christmas Day 1998—I'll never forget it—I began reading a Christmas gift from my wife, the book *By My Spirit* by Jonathan Goforth. Though the noise of Christmas festivities surrounded me, I could not put the book down. The printed preaching of Goforth highlighted overlooked promises in the Word of God. God burned in my heart the possibility of an access by faith for revival blessing. Noting that God used an intensive study on the Holy Spirit to bring Goforth to faith regarding revival, I began a similar study.

The impact has been revolutionary. Along the way, God deepened my understanding of God-dependence for Spirit-enabling. "Christ in you" became utterly real and life-changing. O I have failed—but He has never failed when trusted. The Spirit cultivated and is cultivating faith for personal and corporate revival.

This publication is a result of that study. The purpose of this book is to stir people to faith to access the ministry of the Spirit in personal and corporate revival. However, I believe one will readily see that any study of the ministry of the Holy Spirit is at the same time utterly Christ-exalting. In this regard, I was once a part of a conference in Myanmar (Burma) dealing with these truths of the Spirit. The comment from the preachers was that this is Christ-exalting preaching!

God has so fixed Scripture that you must have a seeking heart in order to find. A seeking heart is God-dependence. It is not a matter of simply uncovering facts, but rather discovering the spiritual realities that relate to those facts. This demands the illumination and convincement of the Holy Spirit. Some may consider this kind of study as "deep." Yet the truths are as profoundly simple, as they are seemingly deep. They are not intellectually deep; rather, they are spiritually deep. They demand the work of the Spirit to truly be understood.

Because of the desire to lay line upon line and precept upon precept, it may be advisable to read a full chapter at a sitting. This is more important in some chapters than others where the end of the chapter is built squarely on the foundation of the chapter's beginning. Also, each chapter clearly builds on all that precedes it. Occasionally, the grammar of the original language is referenced where the technical point seems to shed practical light.

It is not my desire to quibble over semantics. One may prefer to use different terminology than I have chosen. However, the bottom line is that the people of God stand in desperate need of the power of God! Will you humbly seek the Lord to enlighten you to all that is truly of

Him? It is my prayer that all that is not of God will fall to the ground, and all that is of Him, He will use by His mighty Spirit to once again lead His people into revival.

While standing in a Thomas Kinkade gallery one day, I was drawn to a new painting that centered on an old Dutch windmill. Because of my Dutch name, I stopped to admire the painting. I noticed that across some water stood an old church. As far as I could tell, it looked like a fundamental, Bible-preaching church! Then I leaned closer to read the name of the painting—*The Wind of the Spirit*. Sometime later, while musing over this imagery, the Lord moved me with the following words which my wife, Mary Lynn, has set to music.

As the ancient windmill stands
Holding out her bladelike hands,
Watching for the clouds to form,
Waiting for the windy storm,
When she moves with great delight,
Then made useful through her flight—
Spirit Who enables me,
So may I be filled with Thee.

Thou the Wind and I the mill,
I am useless standing still;
Without Thee, my life is death,
Blow upon me with Thy breath;
Thus enabled by Thy might
To revolve in useful flight—
Spirit Who enables me,
So may I be filled with Thee.

As the windmill by the seas
Ever moving with the breeze,
Wind of God, I look to Thee
Daily to enable me;
Make me useful in Thy cause,
For Thy praise, not man's applause.
Spirit Who enables me,
So may I be filled with Thee.

May the Wind of the Spirit once again fill a God-dependent people, and thus restore the people of God to spiritual life. This is awakening to the Spirit of life in Christ Jesus. This is the essence of revival!

—John R. Van Gelderen
Autumn, 2001

# PART I

## POTENTIAL REVIVAL: THE INHERITANCE OF THE SPIRIT

CHAPTER ONE

# LIVING UP TO YOUR INHERITANCE

Revival, in short, is a restoration to life. The question is: What life? The answer is Christ's life, or the Spirit-filled life. This is living up to your inheritance. As we begin, will you ask God to open the eyes of your heart to understand His truth and to create in you a hunger for all that He desires to give you?

# GALATIANS 4:4-7

Is the reality of God supreme in your daily experience? Anything less than this is subnormal to the norm of New Testament living. However, if you are unaware of the real norm God intends for life in Christ, you will not know what you are missing.

The story is told of a poor Civil War soldier who had been severely injured in the war. After being sent home, eventually he received a letter from Abraham Lincoln. However, he was illiterate, so he could not read the contents of the letter. He simply was told that the letter was from Abraham Lincoln. This man, in his poverty, dressed in rags. Although he would boast of receiving a letter from Abraham Lincoln, people did not take him seriously. Some would laugh in disbelief. After a number of years, a man who heard him boast of this asked to see the letter. Upon opening it, he found it to be a healthy pension from the government because of the man's war injuries. It was signed by Abraham Lincoln.

Here was a poor man who had been given a healthy pension, but he was not using it because he did not know what he had. Whether this story is true or not, I do not know; but it does illustrate a point. Every child of God possesses a phenomenal inheritance in Christ, yet many do not use it because they do not know what they have, or they do not know how to access it. The tragic outcome is a substandard, subnormal life that does not match up to the promises of God in the New Testament. The powerlessness to gain victory over sin, the ineffectiveness in pointing people to Christ, the disintegration of many marriages and homes, the compromises with the world—all indicate a substandard, subnormal Christianity which does not match up to the inheritance which believers have in Christ.

Galatians 4:4-7 "But when the fulness of the time was come, God sent forth His Son, made of a woman, made under the law, To redeem them that were under the law, that we might receive the adoption of sons. And because ye are sons, God hath sent forth the Spirit of His Son into your hearts, crying, Abba, Father. Wherefore thou art no more a servant, but a son; and if a son, then an heir of God through Christ."

Notice God's two great gifts. The first gift is that *God sent forth His Son*. This is God's great gift to the world. "For God so loved **the world**, that He **gave** His only begotten Son, that whosoever believeth in Him should not perish, but have everlasting life" (John 3:16). This "gift of God is eternal life through Jesus Christ our Lord" (Romans 6:23). Have you received this gift? Are you rightly related to Jesus Christ?

The second gift is that *because ye are sons, God hath sent forth the Spirit of His Son into your hearts*. This is God's great gift to the church. This "gift of the Holy Spirit" (Acts 2:38) is given to the child of God. Have you recognized and received this gift? Are you rightly related to the Holy Spirit? This second gift unfolds the blessed and personal ministry of the Holy Spirit—the wind of the Spirit. Yet somehow the ministry of the Holy Spirit is often overlooked, and He is both quenched and grieved.

What are the implications of using this gift? The benefit of the first gift— *To redeem them that were under the law*—is for the benefit of the second gift: *that we might receive the adoption of sons*. The keyword is *adoption*. Notice that it says *adoption of sons*. The word *sons* does not refer to an infant, but rather to a mature son. The adoption does not emphasize being placed into the family of God. Rather, adoption emphasizes that when you are born into God's family, you are also adopted as a mature son with full rights to access the inheritance—the inheritance of a son of God! Verse 7 says, "Wherefore thou art no more a servant, but a son; and if a son, then an heir of God through Christ." **Are you living up to your inheritance?**

With the inheritance of a prince, is it not foolish to live as a pauper? Yet, what is this inheritance? Why would believers with a rich spiritual inheritance live impoverished lives? How can you access your inheritance? Fair questions. The book of Galatians reveals six dynamics involved in living up to your inheritance in Christ. This chapter provides an overview of the biblical truths inherent in personal revival. The six dynamics regard being properly related to the Holy Spirit and His ministry. We will seek to unfold these dynamics in more detail in later chapters, but for now let us see the big picture by way of overview.

## ENDOWMENT: THE PROMISE OF THE SPIRIT

Galatians 3:14 states, "That we might receive the promise of the Spirit through faith." The term *promise* becomes a connecting word in the remainder of Galatians 3. Verse 18 speaks of "the inheritance . . . by promise." Verse 29 says, "and if ye be Christ's [if you are saved], then are ye . . . heirs according to the promise." Although other truths are also involved, we do, at least, see a connection between the word *promise* and *the Spirit, the inheritance,* and *heirs.* "Heirship" is then expanded in our text in Galatians 4.

*God sent forth His Son . . . to redeem . . . that we* [the redeemed] *might receive the adoption of sons* (Galatians 4:4-5). At the heart of this adoption is the indwelling Spirit: *And because ye are sons, God hath sent forth the Spirit of His Son into your hearts, crying, Abba, Father* (Galatians 4:6). The emphasis of sonship is then seen as heirship. Galatians 4:7 says, *Wherefore thou art no more a servant, but a son; and if a son, then an heir of God through Christ.* The *Wherefore* of verse seven reveals that heirship is directly related to the ministry of the indwelling Spirit mentioned in verse six.

The potential of this ministry of the indwelling Spirit is powerful, for in Luke 24:49 Jesus says, "I send the **promise . . .** be endued with **power** from on high." Acts 2:33 explains that when Jesus ascended into heaven, He was "exalted" to "the right hand of God," and "having received of the Father the promise of the Holy Spirit," He then sent the Spirit. This momentous event launched the age of the Spirit—the age of power. For the "Sent Spirit" is not technically the Spirit of the earthly Christ, but rather the Spirit of the glorified Christ on the throne of power. If you are a child of God, the Spirit who lives in you connects you to Christ on the right hand of the throne of God, which Jesus called "the power of God" (Luke 22:69). Thus, you are seated together with Christ in heavenly places (Ephesians 2:6). You are connected by the Spirit of Christ to the triumphant, victorious Christ on the right hand of the Father, the throne of power! This is *power from on high!*

Is this not an amazing inheritance? The believer's position in Christ is powerful. Christ is Life, and the Spirit is the Life-giver. O the riches of His grace to which every believer has access rights, through adoption, is beyond our full comprehension. This is New Testament Christianity. In contrast, "the heathen religions were feeble and poor as beggars for they bring no rich endowment of spiritual treasures."[1] We have an endowment: the promise of the Spirit. Our inheritance in Christ is given to us through the ministry of the Holy Spirit. Then why are so many Christians powerless?

## ENFEEBLEMENT: THE PROBLEM OF UNBELIEF

Our opening text in Galatians 4 continues with verse 9: "But now, after that ye have known God, or rather are known of God, how turn ye again to the weak and beggarly elements, whereunto ye desire again to be in bondage?" Paul under inspiration asks the Galatians, in essence,

"Now that you are saved, which was by forsaking flesh-dependence and trusting Christ alone, how can you turn back again to the *weak and beggarly elements* of works-dependence?" No wonder he exclaims in Galatians 3:1, "O foolish Galatians, who hath bewitched you, that ye should not obey the truth, before whose eyes Jesus Christ hath been evidently set forth, crucified among you." You were saved by looking to Jesus. Why did you stop looking unto Jesus? Verse 2 asks, "This only would I learn of you, Received ye the Spirit by the works of the law, or by the hearing of faith?" Of course, the answer is *the hearing of faith*. The point is then emphasized in verse 3: "Are ye so foolish? having begun in the Spirit [by faith], are you now made perfect by the flesh [through works]?" The argument is simply that your flesh did not help save you, and your flesh will not help you grow either. So keep depending on God for everything in the Christian life for "the flesh profiteth nothing" (John 6:63). Flesh-dependence, even for the goal of Christian living, enfeebles you because it is *weak and beggarly*. This unbelief prevents you from accessing your inheritance as the power for the Christian life. This explains why so many Christians are up and down in their experience.

Though flesh-dependence for the goal of holiness and service seems noble, it actually detracts from "the offence of the cross" (Galatians 5:11) by giving credit to man's ability. The reason that the cross is an offense is because you must identify with it in order to die to yourself. This is where lost men trip up regarding salvation and where saved men trip up regarding sanctification and service. Andrew Murray suggested that the Reformation was good as far as it went—justification by faith but it did not go far enough. Sanctification is also by faith.

This lesson must be learned in order to be effectively used by God. In D. L. Moody's early years as a Christian, he was a hard worker. He was full of activity for God. But something was still missing. Two godly ladies told him that they were praying that he would receive the power of the Spirit. This produced a hunger in his heart, which eventually led to his accessing the power of the Spirit by faith. He testified that he preached the same sermons, but, whereas before, there were little results, now there were great results. May each of us allow the enfeeblement of unbelief to produce a hunger in our hearts for the power of God.

## ENTITLEMENT: THE PROVISION OF CHRIST

Having seen the problem of unbelief, let us refocus on the provision we have in Christ. Galatians 3:26 says, "For ye are all the children of God by faith in Christ Jesus." You were saved by faith. Now see the glorious provision you have in Christ. Verse 27 explains, "For as many of you as have been baptized into Christ have put on Christ." We will study this more fully later, but, for now, simply note the twofold provision. When you were saved, you were both baptized into Christ and clothed with Christ. The reality of *have put on Christ* ought to make a radical difference in our lives.

Galatians 5:24 states, "And they that are Christ's have crucified the flesh with the affections and lusts." What a statement—*have crucified the flesh with the affections and lusts!* You might say, "But my flesh is very much alive with its affections and lusts!" However, do you see that this is what the Scripture says? Now you are faced with a choice: focus on your experience and continue in unbelief, or focus on the promise and access a new experience. The provision of Christ struck a deathblow to your flesh.

Galatians 6:14 declares, "But God forbid that I should glory, save in the cross of our Lord Jesus Christ, by whom the world is crucified unto me, and I unto the world." Did you notice that amazing statement *by whom the world is crucified unto me, and I unto the world?* You might say, "But the world is alive to me, and I am alive to the world!" However, do you see what the Scripture says? Again you are faced with a choice: focus on your experience and continue in an enfeebled condition, or focus on the promise of provision and access a new condition. Christ's cross-work also struck a deathblow to the world. John 16:11, stating "the prince of this world is judged," indicates that Satan received a deathblow as well. What a mighty provision we have in the finished work of Christ! May the Spirit grant us a fresh vision of the cross. When Jesus cried, "It is finished" after three hours of darkness during the Crucifixion at what seemed the darkest hour, in essence Jesus shouted, "Victory!"

Galatians 1:3b-4 teaches, "our Lord Jesus Christ, Who gave Himself for our sins." Why? Certainly to save us from our sins and give us eternal life. But notice what this verse says: "that He might deliver us from this present evil world." Deliverance now from *this present evil world!* What a glorious provision! This is the provision necessary for holiness and service. How do we access this abundant provision?

## ENTHRONEMENT: THE PRESENTATION AND PRACTICE OF SURRENDER AND FAITH

This is the imagery of Romans 12:1. We are urged as believers to present (presentation) our bodies a living (practice) sacrifice. When we thus "surrender," which is dependence on God, the Spirit who lives in our spirit now possesses our bodies and reigns as Lord and Life.

We see indications of this enthronement in Galatians 3. Verse 13 says, "Christ hath redeemed us." Why? Verse 14 says "that the blessing of Abraham might come on the Gentiles through Jesus Christ [cf. v. 8:

justification by faith].” Why? Verse 14 continues, “That we might receive the promise of the Spirit through faith.” When you were saved, you received the indwelling Spirit (Galatians 3:2) so that you *might receive the promise of the Spirit,* which emphasizes the Spirit's power rather than His person. This is done *through faith.* This reception through dependence correlates to the *presentation* of Romans 12:1. How about the practice of surrender and faith?

Galatians 3:5 explains, “He therefore that ministereth [lit., is supplying] to you the Spirit, and worketh miracles among you, doeth He it by the works of the law, or by the hearing of faith?” Just as you receive the person of the Spirit by faith (Galatians 3:2) and just as you receive the promise (power) of the Spirit by faith (Galatians 3:14), you keep receiving the power of the Spirit by faith (Galatians 3:5). The verb tense of Galatians 3:2 and 14 speak of an event (the former salvation, the latter presentation). However, the verb tense of Galatians 3:5 speaks of a practice (lit., He who is supplying to you the Spirit and works miracles). All of this occurs by faith. The point is that God desires the practice of our lives to be marked by the Spirit working *miracles!* Anything less than a miraculous life is substandard to the provision we have in Christ! More will be seen later, but we begin to see that the access to the power of the Spirit is through the presentation and practice of surrender and faith.

## ENABLEMENT: THE POWER OF LIVING

The enthronement opens the way for Spirit-enablement, which is Christ being formed in you and thus living in you. Galatians 4:19 says, “My little children [Notice that believers are addressed], of whom I travail in birth again.” How can that be since you can only be born again once? Notice the remainder of the verse “until Christ be formed in you.” It does not say “until Christ be in you.” That occurred at regeneration. It says *until Christ be **formed in you.*** This is the ministry of the Spirit conforming us into the image of Christ (II Corinthians 3:18). This is true spiritual growth. This also is the reality of Galatians 2:20: “I live; yet not I, but Christ liveth in me.”

If Christ lives in you, this ought to make a radical difference! Remember, however, that without faith, we miss out on the impact. With faith, the self-life is exchanged for the Christ-life. This is what Hudson Taylor termed “the exchanged life.”

After preaching on this truth once, the next day a man said to me, “I used to think I lived by myself, but I realized I have a Partner. Would He want to live here? I had to do some cleaning up.” The implication was both physical and spiritual.

I remember as a boy we visited some friends on a Colorado ranch. It was the time for branding their cattle. How well do I remember the change of the branding iron when it was put into the fire, to prepare it for branding. Before it was put in the fire, it was cold and blackened. But when it remained in the fire, it became hot and red. As the branding iron remained in the fire it exchanged its characteristics for the fire's characteristics. When the iron moved into the fire, the fire moved into the iron. Though technically separable, practically there was a oneness. Then the branding iron became useful. So it is with us. Without the reality of Christ in us, we are cold spiritually and darkened with sin. But when we depend on Christ, we exchange our characteristics for Christ's. When we depend on our position in Christ, He manifests His reality in us. Though technically separable, practically there is a oneness. This is when we become useful in God's cause. O the wonder of *not I, but Christ!*

## ENTRUSTMENT: THE PURPOSE OF USEFULLNESS

The enablement is for the purpose of usefulness. The Spirit enables us to be holy so that we can serve God. This exchanged life invests us with a trust. What is it? Galatians 1:15b-16 explains, "by His grace [Spirit-enabling], to reveal His Son in me [not I, but Christ], **that I might preach Him among the heathen.**" When Christ is living through you, He is seen, and He is heard. This is what makes witnessing powerfully effective!

In the early part of the twentieth century, Duncan Campbell was born in the Scottish Highlands. Though his parents were saved when he was a boy, he grew up still lost. One night, while playing the bagpipes at a dance, he came under deep conviction of sin. Though now a young man on his own, he decided to return home that night. Later, he arrived and was surprised to see the light on. He entered the house to find his mother praying—for him. As he poured out his heart to her, she explained simply the way of salvation and suggested he go out into the barn and tell God what he had told her. That night he was marvelously converted.[2]

Soon he witnessed unashamedly for Christ. He was a zealous new Christian. However, he was drafted into service during World War I. Injured on a battlefield, he thought he was going to die. A Canadian soldier put him on the back of his horse to take him for help. Ashamed of his little service for God and the darkness of his own heart, he prayed the prayer of Robert Murray McCheyne, which his father prayed, "Lord, make me as holy as a saved sinner can be." The power of the Spirit came mightily upon him with all His cleansing power. Campbell said, "At that moment I felt as pure as an angel." When being treated medically, he began to sing in Gaelic. He also quoted Psalm 103 in Gaelic. The praises of God burst forth from his lips. The presence of God became powerfully real, and at least seven Canadians trusted Christ![3]

Returning home, he received Bible training. Early in his ministry he saw repeated visitations of the Spirit in real revival. Then upon leaving the itinerate ministry as an evangelist, he pastored several churches. He still preached at conferences. However, something was missing. He referred to those years as "seventeen years in a barren wilderness, baffled and frustrated in Christian work and witness."[4] After a confrontation from his sixteen-year-old daughter as to why he was not seeing revival anymore, he, the conference speaker of revivals of the past, was smitten with conviction. Soon, in new despair, he sought a meeting with God through the nighttime hours.[5] God graciously visited him again, and he "came to know the recovering power of the blood of Christ."[6] Shortly after this, God led him to the Isle of Lewis. He thought he was going for a ten-day mission. But God poured out His Spirit, and he preached there for the next three years! The remainder of his life was marked by revivals and the power of God.

Perhaps you once knew the joy and power of God as a new believer. However, somehow and somewhere you lost this blessing. Now is the time to again access the power of the Spirit. Are you living up to your inheritance?

---

[1]Fritz Rienecker and Cleon L. Rogers, *Linguistic Key to the Greek New Testament* (Grand Rapids: Zondervan, 1980), p. 512.

[2]Andrew A. Woolsey, *Channel of Revival: A Biography of Duncan Campbell* (Edinburgh: The Faith Mission, reprint 1982), pp. 26-33.

[3]Ibid., pp. 50-53.

[4]Duncan Campbell, *The Price and Power of Revival* (Vinton, Va.: Christ Life Publications, reprint n.d.), p. 30.

[5]Duncan Campbell, *The Nature of a God-Sent Revival* (Vinton, Va.: Christ Life Publications, reprint n.d.), pp. 23-25.

[6]Campbell, *The Price and Power of Revival*, p. 30.

# CHAPTER TWO

# ENGINE TRUTHS

Before we move ahead in applying "living up to your inheritance" personally, we will take the time to lay down basic foundational truths, which we will refer to throughout this book. These truths permeate the Bible. I have come to call these truths the "engine truths." Will you ask the Lord to internalize in you this foundation?

# ROMANS 5:1-5

When I was a boy, my brother and I built an electric train set equipped with landscaping and buildings. Sometimes I would back an engine up to a line of railroad cars to connect them. Then I would switch the engine to move forward. Occasionally, the engine would move ahead, but the cars sat still because they were not actually connected. This pictures the lives of many believers. They are not moving ahead for God. Knowing something is amiss, they may opt for polishing the cars so at least they look better. But still, there is no forward progress. Some may opt to add more cars to the railroad train—more duties to their Christian activity—yet, without the engine, they sit still. Something is obviously wrong. The key is to be rightly related to the engine power of "Christ in you" to pull the railroad train of holiness and service.

In view of this picture, we need to recognize the "engine truths." These are basic truths to a life that dynamically moves forward for God. Romans 5:1-5: "Therefore being justified by faith, we have peace with God through our Lord Jesus Christ: By whom also we have access by faith into this grace wherein we stand, and rejoice in hope of the glory of God. And not only so, but we glory in tribulations also: knowing that tribulation worketh patience; And patience, experience; and experience, hope: And hope maketh not ashamed; because the love of God is shed abroad in our hearts by the Holy Ghost which is given unto us." Notice after *being justified by faith*, there is *also access by faith into this grace.* This is grace for the glories of verses 2-5. Before we proceed in the following chapters with a progression of truth regarding the ministry of the Holy Spirit, first **we need to understand the foundational engine truths.** What are these engine truths? The engine truths are based on two biblical words that permeate the Scriptures—*grace* and *faith.* Both of these terms are found in our text.

# THE ABILITY OF GRACE

Romans 5:2 states, *By whom also we have access by faith into this grace wherein we stand.* What is grace? During my elementary school years in the church my father pastored, we had Training Union before the Sunday evening service. In those days, if asked the question, "What is grace?" I could promptly raise my hand and answer, "Grace is unmerited favor." Certainly this is a good traditional and correct answer. Yet if someone would have then asked, "What is unmerited favor?" I would have been stumped. The "unmerited" part obviously means that which is not deserved, but what is the "favor"? By investigating the usage of the word *grace* in Scripture, we can determine a fine-tuned understanding of this vital engine truth.

## Grace Is a Gift

First, grace is a gift. Speaking of salvation, Ephesians 2:8 says it "is the gift of God." Ephesians 3:7, speaking of grace for Christian service, says, "the gift of the grace of God." If a gift is truly a gift, it is unmerited by the recipient. It is not deserved or earned. Rather, a true gift to the recipient is absolutely free. So grace, whether for salvation or the Christian life, is a free gift.

## God Is the Giver of Grace

Second, God is the Giver of grace. Notice again Ephesians 2:8 and 3:7 respectively: *the gift of God* and *the gift of the grace of God.* Therefore, in the biblical sense, grace is not that which man produces. Rather, God is the Giver of grace.

## Grace Is Supernatural Enablement

Third, grace is supernatural enablement. For example, Paul states under inspiration in Ephesians 3:7, "Whereof I was made a minister, according to the gift of the grace of God given unto me by the effectual working of His power." Notice the defining phrase *by the effectual working of His power.* Whatever the *effectual working* is, it is of God's *power.* Therefore, it is supernatural and miraculous. The phrase *effectual working* translates from the Greek term *energeia.* The transliteration of this term sounds like the English word *energy.* Transliterations do not always mean what they sound like. However, *energeia* means "energy, working, or operation."[1] *The grace of God given unto* Paul was by the energy or operation of God's power. Is this not clearly supernatural enablement? Other passages like Galatians 2:8-9 and I Corinthians 15:10, to name a few, unfold this same understanding. Grace is supernatural enablement.

## The Agent Is the Holy Spirit

Fourth, the agent is the Holy Spirit. Hebrews 10:29 refers to "the Spirit of grace." The Spirit is the One who enables. It is significant that Ephesians 1:2, like so many of the Epistles, says in its greeting, "Grace be to you, and peace, from God our Father, and from the Lord Jesus Christ." Why is the Spirit not listed? Because He is implied in the word *grace*. The agent of supernatural enablement from God and Christ is the Spirit.

## The Purpose Is to Do God's Will

Finally, the purpose is to do God's will. Paul, under inspiration, follows up Ephesians 3:7, which I have referred to already, with verse 8: "Unto me . . . is this grace given, that I should preach among the Gentiles the unsearcheable riches of Christ." God enabled Paul to preach, which was God's will for Paul's life. The same is seen in Galatians 2:8. In Romans 6:14, grace is stated as the power to free one from the "dominion" of sin. In Titus 2:11-12 grace is seen as the enablement to "live soberly, righteously, and godly, in this present world." Hebrews 4:16 teaches us that we may "come boldly unto the throne of grace" to "find grace to help in time of need." Repeatedly, whether it is for enablement in victory over sin or power in service, the purpose of grace is that we might be enabled to do God's will.

Based on these five aspects of usage, we can discern the "favor" of grace. Simply put, grace is the supernatural enablement through the Holy Spirit to do God's will. In short, grace is Spirit-enabling. This is the first engine truth. The ability (for both salvation and the Spirit-filled life) is grace. The focus is not on the ability of man, but rather on the ability of God.

Without this understanding, many are frustrated in attempting to live the Christian life. To obey the commands "Be ye holy" (I Peter 1:16), "Preach the gospel to every creature" (Mark 16:15), or "love thy neighbor as thyself" (Matthew 19:19) is impossible without supernatural enablement. If you are attempting to walk this high and holy road without grace, then you will have to either resign yourself to a defeated life, or lower the standard. Sadly, many are the saints which think that though they are eternally secure, life this side of heaven will only be a struggle with regular defeats. Also, tragically many are the saints that lower the standards of the Christian life down to a level attainable without God's power. This compromise may ease their conscience, but it is the wrong kind of relief. What we desperately need is the supernatural enablement through the Holy Spirit not only for salvation, but also to walk the high and holy road of the Christian life. It is only the power of the Spirit that is able to pull the many cars of the railroad train of holiness and service. But how is this power accessed?

## THE ACCESS OF FAITH

Romans 5:2 in our text plainly teaches: *By whom* [Christ] *also we have access by faith into this grace wherein we stand.* Faith accesses grace. But what is faith? Faith is not mere acknowledgement of facts, nor is it simply mental assent. Faith is not wishful thinking, positive thinking, or an unsteady hoping. What then is faith? Consider several key issues.

## The Essence of Faith

First, consider the essence of faith. The word *faith* used in the New Testament means "trust."[2] The verb form in the religious sense means "believe (in), trust."[3] Notice it does not mean to believe *about* but to believe *in.* This is the difference between acknowledgement and dependence. The essence of faith is dependence. Therefore, the essence of unbelief is lack of dependence. Disbelief is denial; unbelief is a lack of dependence. When it comes to the Bible, we may not disbelieve it through denial, but we are often unbelieving through a lack of dependence on it.

## The Education of Faith

Second, consider the education of faith. Hebrews 11:1 explains, "Now faith is the substance of things hoped for, the evidence of things not seen." The emphasis of *substance* is "reality," and the emphasis of *evidence* is "convincement."[4] Hebrews 11:1 teaches us that faith is depending on the reality of things we are hoping for, being convinced of those very unseen things. How can you be so convinced as to depend on the reality of that which you cannot see?

Romans 10:17 clarifies, "So then faith cometh by hearing, and hearing by the word of God." The foundation for faith is *the word of God.* Here we must take note that *the word* is not *logos,* a larger term often referring to the whole of Scripture, but rather *rhema* (pronounced RAY-mah), referring to a specific part of the whole.[5] The significance of this is monumental. The foundation for faith is not general, but rather it is specific. It is because God specifically says so. The foundation for faith is specific truth. This will be emphasized in further chapters. Notice, too, that God gives us the *rhemas* because the foundation for faith is *the rhema of God.* If we do not depend on God's words, we are placing man's words, thoughts, and reasonings on a higher plane. Is this not a wicked sin?

Based on our "education" of faith thus far, we can now define faith as the simple choice to depend on the reality of the words of God—

before the reality is humanly visible! Faith is the choice to depend on the reality of God's words. Yet could not one argue that the object of faith is God or Jesus Christ? Yes, but this is not a contradiction, for Jesus is *the Word* in John 1. There is a mystery of oneness between the incarnate Word and the inscribed Word. When you depend on the living words of God [Scripture], you are depending on the living Word of God [Christ]. Several years ago I saw some unique paintings. At first glance the paintings looked like colors splattered around with no distinct image to be viewed. However, when looked at in a certain way, a clear image or scene could easily be observed. Likewise, sometimes when we first look at Scripture passages, we may see only confused statements. But when seen with Holy Spirit illumination, we see Christ's image beyond the words. Instead of seeing just facts, we see the realities that relate to those facts.

In this light, Hebrews 12:2 teaches us as to how we are to be regularly educated to faith. "Looking unto Jesus [who is at oneness with the Word], the author [divine convincement by the Spirit's illumination] and finisher [divine enablement by the Spirit's power] of our faith." As you meditate on the Word of God, the Spirit convinces you of those words. This is the gift of faith (Ephesians 2:8-9). The gift of faith is not something that is bestowed as an alien outside element, but rather it is by becoming so convinced of the worthiness of the object of faith, you now place your confidence in that object. In the physical realm, if you are seriously ill and a friend convinces you of the worthiness of a certain doctor so that you begin to depend on that doctor's care, he has given you the gift of faith in that doctor. The same is true spiritually.[6] As you meditate on the words of God, the Spirit through illumination convinces you of the worthiness of those words. This is authoring faith. As you then choose to depend on the reality of those words, the Spirit then enables you in accordance to the words on which you are depending. This is finishing faith. Yet it is *our faith*. God is not the one depending; man is. However, it is God-centered because the object of faith is God.

Since the object of faith is *the Word of God*, we must be *looking unto Jesus*. The focus of faith must not be our faith, but the object of faith. A double focus produces blurred vision. In the context of the statement "But let him ask in faith, nothing wavering" (James 1:6), the Scripture says, "A doubled minded [lit., double souled] man is unstable in all his ways" (James 1:8). The soul which vacillates between taking the lead from the body versus taking the lead from the spirit, where the Spirit guides based on truth, is *unstable*.

The education of faith enlightens us to the definition and cultivation of faith. Faith is cultivated by the Spirit as we look unto Jesus by meditating on His words. We then are responsible to choose to depend on the reality of the words of God. This is biblical faith. In short, faith is God-dependence.

## The Elements of Faith

Third, consider the elements of faith. Faith can be likened to a three-legged chair. In order for a chair to be stable enough for you to rest your entire weight on it, it must have at least three legs. Faith is like one chair with three legs. The first leg is *understanding*, which involves the intellect. The second is *agreement*, which involves the affections. The third leg is *dependence*, which involves the will. *Dependence* presupposes *understanding* and *agreement*, but *understanding* and *agreement* without *dependence* is not faith.

For example, in salvation one may understand he is a sinner, that he deserves hell, and that Christ is the only Savior. One may even agree with all this. Yet to stop here is only acknowledgment, or "easy believe-ism." It is not faith and, therefore, is not salvation. It is not until one moves beyond believing that God *can* save him to depending on God *to* save him that faith exists. The result is faith for salvation. There must be a transfer of dependence to Christ alone for salvation from sin and hell.

A preacher friend of mine said he led a man to Christ. While witnessing, he had explained the three angles to "saving faith." After trusting Christ, the man said, "Up to this point in my life, my life has been like a two-legged stool." My friend replied, "What do you mean?" The new convert said, "I already understood these things and agreed with them, but it was not until today that I depended on Christ to save me." Thus, the "three-legged chair" illustration of biblical faith came into being.

## The Exercise of Faith

Fourth, consider the exercise of faith. In a passage addressed to "my brethren," James 2:26 says, "For as the body without the spirit is dead, so faith without works [exercise] is dead also." In other words, understanding and agreement without dependence is dead faith. Just as living faith for salvation must depend on Christ to "receive" forgiveness of sins, credited righteousness, and eternal life, so living faith for sanctification and service must depend on the Spirit to "do" right, which is enabled righteousness. Faith not connected to the steps of obedience [exercise], is not dependence. It is acknowledgement to say, "I believe God can enable me to victory over sin." It is faith to actually depend on God for the enablement to do so. It is acknowledgement to say, "I believe God can enable me to witness." It is faith to actually depend on God to witness. Faith without exercise is not faith. You do not have faith for the steps of obedience without taking the steps. This also will be emphasized in later chapters.

# The Endurance of Faith

Finally, consider the endurance of faith. Our text in Romans 5:1-5 delineates a progression: *faith* (v. 2), *tribulations* (v. 3), *patience* (v. 3), *experience* (v. 4), and *hope* (v. 4). *Faith* must be tested. If it is not tested, it would be sight and not faith. These *tribulations* produce *patience*. James 1:2-4 teaches the same truth. *Patience* is a compound word meaning "endurance." More literally, it means enduring abiding or enduring dependence. This is how faith is increased on a given issue. Certainly faith can be increased for the number of areas in which it is exercised. Also, there is an aspect of increase regarding faith for a more difficult purpose. But on a given application of dependence, the nature of the increase is not quantitative but rather in term (i.e., short-term vs. long-term) or duration. This understanding is important because if you think you have to "believe harder," or somehow you have to muster up more faith, then you are depending on yourself, when the correct object of faith is God based on His words. *Faith*, tested by *tribulations*, produces *patience* or enduring dependence. Endurance produces *experience*. The promises are realized in fulfillment. Then *experience* produces *hope*, which is confident expectation.

Let me illustrate. I was born in Colorado on the western slope of the Rocky Mountains in the old cowboy town of Durango. When I was four years old, we moved from there to the city limits of Chicago. My boyhood and teen years were spent in Chicago, most of which were in the suburbs of Chicago. As a result, I am not a cowboy but, more accurately, a "city-slicker."

Several years ago I was back in Durango for a meeting at the church my father used to pastor. While there, some friends invited me to go horseback riding. Now I had heard of a horse before! Although I was not familiar with riding horses in the open range, I had ridden a horse on trail rides a few times. So I went with two true cowboys riding on a 3,000-acre ranch. It was a beautiful clear day. The temperature was comfortably cool. Off in the distance you could see the breathtaking snow-covered La Plata Mountains in the San Juan Range.

Eventually we came to a place where a ledge went around the curvature of a mountain. The next thing I knew, the first cowboy took his horse out on that ledge, then the next cowboy went, and I followed. I remember becoming uncomfortably aware of my environment! When I looked to my left, I could nearly reach out and touch the mountainside as it continued to ascend upwards. That gave some comfort. When I looked to my right, I could see nothing—unless I looked down! Upon doing so, I noticed huge rocks in a river down below. Later we came to a place where not only could you look to the right and see nothing unless you looked down, you could also look to the left and see nothing unless you looked down!

Then, at a place where there was still a steep slope to the right though no river at the bottom, the cowboy who worked on that ranch moved the reigns of his horse to the right and, to my astonishment, led his horse straight down that steep slope. It was so steep that the hind legs of the horse tucked up under itself, and the horse skidded downward! Then it would regain its footing. Then it would skid some more. I remember thinking, "That guy is crazy!" Then, to my horror, the next cowboy did the same thing. Obviously I was supposed to follow. Fortunately, there was one old cowboy word that I remembered, and I yelled it right out—"Whoa!" Thankfully the horse was an obedient horse and stopped.

When the cowboy below me heard me yell, he looked back up and said, "John, what's wrong?" I do not remember what I said, but obviously revealed that I was petrified. He then said, "Just loosen up on the reigns, and the horse will take you down." That is exactly what I was afraid of!

Finally, I loosened up on those reigns, and I *depended* on that horse to take me down that slope, which it safely did. However, may I hasten to say that while I was in the process of depending, my feelings were not in line with my dependence! Do you see the difference between faith and feeling? Many are derailed because they look for a feeling that they equate with faith, but faith is not a feeling.

To clarify, my dependence was a "clinging dependence"—I was hanging on for dear life! However, the other two cowboys just leaned back to get in line with gravity and rested on their horses to do what they knew, from experience, they would do. Theirs was a "resting dependence." Clinging faith is depending against your feelings. Resting faith is depending with your feelings in line with your faith. What takes you from clinging dependence to resting dependence? Experience. In fact, when I reached the bottom of that slope, I thought, "You know, I could do that again!" Experience then produces a confident expectation. You know from experience the faithfulness of your object of dependence.

It is resting faith, which allows you to be in a position where you can help others. So cling to the promises even through difficulties, and that enduring dependence will bring you to experience which, in turn, brings you to confident expectation. But if you "bail out" during the trial of faith, you miss out on the blessing of faith.

It works like this. God stirs you to lay hold of an exceeding great and precious promise. You plant your feet on that promise. Then everything seems to go opposite! Get excited—that is the test of faith (James 2:2-3). Keep on depending and, through enduring dependence, God will bring you to experience. Hebrews 10:36 says, "For ye have need of patience [enduring dependence], that, after ye have done the will of

God, ye might receive the promise." Experience then gives you that confident expectation. This is the progression we see laid out in Romans 5:1-5.

Faith accesses grace. God-dependence accesses Spirit-enabling. This connects you to the power of God to pull the train of the Christian life. These are the "engine truths."

---

[1]Stewart Custer, A *Treasury of New Testament Synonyms* (Greenville, S.C.: Bob Jones University Press, 1975), p. 27.

[2]William F. Arndt and F. Wilbur Gingrich, A *Greek-English Lexicon of the New Testament*, 2d. ed. (Chicago: University of Chicago Press, 1979), p. 662.

[3]Ibid., p. 661.

[4]I have written a more detailed discussion of this in *Engine Truths* (Menomonee Falls, Wis.: Preach the Word Ministries, Inc., 1999), pp. 7-8.

[5]Custer, p. 82.

[6]Handley G. C. Moule, *The Holy Spirit* (Great Britian: Christian Focus Publications, reprint 1999), pp. 69-74.

# PART II

## PERSONAL REVIVAL:
## THE FILLING OF THE SPIRIT

# CHAPTER THREE

# THE PROMISE OF THE SPIRIT— THE PROMISE OF POWER

**Endowment: The Promise of the Spirit**
Enfeeblement: The Problem of Unbelief
Entitlement: The Provision of Christ
Enthronement: The Presentation and Practice of Surrender and Faith
Enablement: The Power of Living
Entrustment: The Purpose of Usefulness

Now let's unfold a progression of truth regarding the ministry of the Holy Spirit. To do this, we will follow the overview seen in chapter one. This entire part seeks to address the ministry of the filling of the Spirit. Also, as we move forward, remember the engine truths: God-dependence for Spirit enablement. May the Spirit convince us of all that we have in Christ.

# ACTS 2:32-33

By the gracious movement of the hand of God in the last quarter of the nineteenth century, there was an awakening among some of God's children to a truth that had lain dormant. As this spiritual rediscovery gained strength, special conferences were held to proclaim this great truth. One of the preachers, named Evan Hopkins, wrote a book articulating these truths. However, not all openly received this teaching.

Handley G. C. Moule, principal of the Theological College of Ridley Hall at Cambridge and a respected theologian, had heard some negative reports. In response to the new book, he wrote four lengthy, critical, but anonymous, articles which were published in a Christian periodical. Yet at the same time, he sensed there were possessions that he had not yet possessed. He was dissatisfied with his present Christian experience.

In God's divine providence, Moule made a visit to relatives the following autumn. That same time period, they were hosting a conference on their estate regarding these very truths. Although Moule did not desire to attend, he felt out of courtesy he must. The first evening, he left critical and yet with internal conflict. The second night the first preacher spoke from Haggai. In Moule's own testimony, the message took "to pieces the Christian life which is not satisfied, and piercing into the reasons why it is not satisfied, all more or less reducible to our letting the self-life intrude itself into the work of God; the man feeling himself, afterall, well-nigh as important in Christian work as his master." Moule continues, "Somehow or other that address, under the Spirit's good guidance, pulled me to pieces with a second conviction of sin, the sin of the converted life, the sin of the professing Christian man." Now humbled and no longer the critic, Moule recognized the truthfulness of the message.

The second address of that evening was by Evan Hopkins. As he stood to preach, he, of course, was unaware that his anonymous critic was before him. Again Moule's own testimony describes the message as having "all the power of spiritual conviction in it. It was one long ordered piling up of the promises of God to the soul that will do two things toward Him—surrender itself into His hands, and trust Him for His mighty victory within . . . It was as if there were two great weights in my balance. One was down heavily on the ground, loaded with the sins of my converted life and its grievous secret or open failures. Into the other balance the speaker now put promise after promise, aimed precisely at this, not for the unconverted man flying for refuge to the city where the guilty shall be safe under the protection of the high-priest, but the promises to that same fugitive, now dwelling in the city of refuge, who is starving there, and wretched, and miserable, because of himself. And as these promises were recited, grace enabled me to take them as meant, not to take them as read, but to take them as meant; to realize that they were meant to act; that I was to step on them with both feet, and to see if they did not bear."

Moule went home in faith now conscious he was in the hand of an "absolute Master" as well as a "Liberator . . . Who would, so long and so much as I used Him, make me more than conquerer." Moule's life began to change. Others at Cambridge noticed it. Soon he began and for the rest of his life continued to preach these wonderful truths.[1]

What was the truth which gripped him so that his life experience was transformed from being regularly defeated and surprised by victory to being regulary victorious and surprised by defeat! What was the truth which had lain dormant and now some were awakened to it? It was simply the ministry of the Holy Spirit based on the promises of the Word of God! O that we would spiritually apprehend all that is included in "the promise of the Holy Spirit."

Jonathan Goforth learned the life of faith for grace early in his ministry. God's hand clearly was upon him. Yet he testifies:

> Upon returning to China in the fall of 1901, after having recuperated from the harrowing effects of the Boxer ordeal, I began to experience a growing dissatisfaction with the results of my work. In the early pioneer years I had buoyed myself with the assurance that a seed-time must always precede a harvest, and had, therefore, been content to persist in the apparently futile struggle. But now thirteen years had passed, and the harvest seemed, if anything, farther away than ever. I felt sure that there was something larger ahead of me, if I only had the vision to see what it was, and the faith to grasp it. Constantly there would come back to me the words of the Master: "Verily, verily, I say unto you, he that believeth on Me, the works that I do shall he do also; and greater works than these shall he do . . ." And

always there would sink deep the painful realization of how little right I had to make out that what I was doing from year to year was equivalent to the "greater works."

Restless, discontented, I was led to a more intensive study of the Scriptures. Every passage that had any bearing upon the price of, or the road to, the accession of power became life and breath to me. There were a number of books on Revival in my library. These I read over repeatedly. So much did it become an obsession with me that my wife began to fear that my mind would not stand it. Of great inspiration to me were the reports of the Welsh Revival of 1904 and 1905. Plainly Revival was not a thing of the past. Slowly the realization began to dawn upon me that I had tapped a mine of infinite possibility.[2]

What was this "mine of infinite possibility"? According to his wife,

> Mr. Goforth became more and more absorbed in his intensive study of the Holy Spirit. Not that his regular work was ever neglected, but every possible moment, when free to do so, he gave himself to this work, rising before six, sometimes five, in order to get unbroken time at his Bible. I became anxious and one day when entering his study I found him on his knees with Bible and pencil before him. I said, "Jonathan, are you not going too far with this? I fear you will break down!" Rising, and putting his hands on my shoulders, he faced me with a look I could never forget. I can openly describe it as "glorious" and yet sad, as he said, "Oh, Rose, even you do not understand! I feel like one who has tapped a mine of wealth! It is so wonderful! Oh, if I could only get others to see it!" From that time on I could only step aside, as it were, and watch to see "whereunto this thing would grow."[3]

Soon Goforth began to see mercy drops of real revival and by 1908 saw the mighty outpouring of the Spirit of God in revival in Manchuria. Goforth regularly saw "greater works" throughout the rest of his ministry. The "mine of infinite possibility" is the ministry of the Holy Spirit. O that we would spiritually apprehend all that is included in "the promise of the Holy Spirit"! Do we understand this beyond academic theoretical affirmations? Goforth claimed "the majority of Christian people are living on a plane far below what our Master planned for them. Only the few really seem to 'possess their possessions.' Nothing can clothe with victorious might but the baptism with the Holy

Ghost."[4] But what is "the baptism with the Holy Spirit"? That question brings us to "the promise of the Spirit."

Our text introduces us to this biblical phrase: Acts 2:32-33: "This Jesus hath God raised up . . . Therefore being by the right hand of God exalted, and having received of the Father the promise of the Holy Spirit, He hath shed forth this . . . "

This grand text records that when Jesus, as the resurrected Savior, ascended into heaven, He was exalted to the Father's right hand. He received the promise of the Spirit, and He sent the Spirit. This marvelous event launched the age of the Holy Spirit—the age we live in right now!

What is the background text that led up to this impacting event?

## BACKGROUND TEXT

## What?

Acts 1:1 states, "The former treatise have I made, O Theophilus, of all that Jesus began both to do and teach." Consider what *Jesus began . . . to do*. Imagine being in the crowd when Christ fed the five thousand. Imagine actually seeing Christ walking on water. Imagine beholding Christ making blind eyes to see, deaf ears to hear, mute tongues to speak, being there when Christ spoke the word, and those who were lame were healed and began to leap for joy. Imagine literally watching Christ when He gave the command and raised Lazarus from the dead. O consider all that *Jesus began . . . to do—and teach*.

Imagine being in the audience that day when Jesus preached the sermon on the mount. Being there with the multitudes, not in an auditorium, not in a stadium, but in the open air listening to Christ preach the gospel of the kingdom. Think of the thrill of seeing many *believe*—a greater miracle than all of the physical miracles!

## How?

How did Jesus do it? We might answer that He is God, and, therefore, that is how He did it. But can we get a more specific answer? Acts 1:2 states, "He through the Holy Spirit"—that is how He did it! Technically, Acts 1:2 refers to His post-resurrection ministry. What about before this death and resurrection?

Let's let *the former treatise* of the Gospel of Luke, which is the chronological account, aid our understanding. Speaking of the birth of Christ in Luke 1:35, the angel explained to Mary, "The Holy Spirit shall come upon thee, and the power of the Highest shall over shadow thee." So that according to Matthew 1:20 in the angel's explanation to Joseph, "that which is conceived in her is of the Holy Spirit." Did you ever stop to consider that Jesus Christ was indwelt by the Spirit at conception? As we are indwelt by the Spirit at salvation, Christ was indwelt by the Spirit at conception. In simple terms, this is the Spirit *in* Christ.

Let's consider the first thirty years of Christ's life on earth, often called the "silent years." Luke 2:52 records, "And Jesus increased in wisdom and stature, and in favor with God and man." To increase *in favor with God* obviously refers to His humanity. Yet to do so demands the work of the Spirit. It would be fair to say that Christ was filled with the Spirit—He was led and enabled by the Spirit—during those first thirty years. In simple terms, this is the Spirit *through* Christ.

Now we come to the three years of public ministry. Did anything significant regarding the ministry of the Spirit occur? The baptism of Jesus marked the beginning of His public ministry, and Luke 3:21 records "that Jesus also being baptized, and praying, the heaven was opened." What was He praying? Verse 22 records the answer: "And the Holy Spirit descended in a bodily shape like a dove upon Him." (Interestingly, not like fire as in Acts 2 for there was no sin to purge.) Christ was already indwelt by the Spirit at conception. For thirty years He was perfectly filled with the Spirit. Yet now another dimension takes place—the Spirit also came *upon Him*. In simple terms, this is the Spirit *on* Christ.

The next recorded event is the temptation of Christ found in Luke 4:1-13. "And Jesus being full of the Holy Spirit . . . Being forty days tempted of the devil . . . the devil . . . departed." Christ's victory over temptation is explicitly connected to His *being full of the Spirit*. This is an amazing fact. His power for personal holiness was the power of the Spirit.

The very next event is recorded in Luke 4:14-15: "And Jesus returned in the power [*dunamis*] of the Spirit into Galilee . . . and He taught." Christ's ministry of teaching is also explicitly tied to His being *in the power of the Holy Spirit*. This is another amazing fact. His power for public service was the power of the Spirit.

The power of Christ's ministry is summed up by His own testimony when He read from the book of Isaiah in the synagogue in Nazareth recorded in Luke 4:18: "The Spirit of the Lord is upon me, because He hath anointed me to preach the gospel . . . " Acts 10:38 confirms, "How God anointed Jesus of Nazareth with the Holy Spirit and with power [*dunamis*]."

Now here is the point: If Jesus, because of having taken on the limitations of a human body at the incarnation, needed the ministry of the Spirit, how much more do we!

# Therefore . . .

Having considered *what* Christ did—*all that Jesus began both to do and teach* (Acts 1:1) and *how* He did it—*He through the Holy Ghost* (Acts 1:2), let's consider the *therefore*. Acts 1:4 records that "being assembled together with" the apostles, He commanded them to "wait for the promise of the Father, which, saith He, ye have heard of Me." This is the promise of the Spirit spoken of in our opening text. When did the apostles hear Christ teach of this *promise*? Forty-three days earlier on the day Christ was betrayed, Christ taught His disciples regarding the blessed ministry of the Holy Spirit in the precious Paschal Discourse recorded in John 14-16. Repeatedly He says that although He is leaving He is sending "another Comforter." On occasion He says the Father was sending the Spirit and sometimes He says that He was sending the Spirit. We already noted in Acts 2:33 that when Christ was exalted to the right hand of the Father He received from the Father the promise of the Spirit and sent Him. So both were involved in the sending of the Spirit.

How is this *promise* described in Acts 1? In verses five and eight Christ explains "For John truly baptized with water; but ye shall be baptized with the Holy Spirit . . . Ye shall receive power [*dunamis*] . . . the Holy Spirit . . . upon you: and ye shall be witnesses unto Me both in Jerusalem, and in all Judea, and in Samaria, and unto the uttermost part of the earth."

Note that the *promise* is equated to being *baptized with the Holy Spirit*. Many run from this phraseology because of the excesses some hold with these terms. Yet remember this phraseology is from the words of Christ. As He meant them, we must embrace them. Significantly, in the original language the definite article *the* is absent before the name *Holy Spirit*. English translations include it because it would seem awkward in English without it. However, the presence of the definite article emphasizes the person, while the absence of the article emphasizes the operation or power of that person. Jesus is simply stating that *the baptism with the Holy Spirit* is *the baptism with the power of the Holy Spirit!* Literally, He says *ye shall be baptized with Holy Spirit*. Then in Acts 1:8 Christ incorporates the definite article indicating that the *power* which *ye shall receive* is the person of power: *the Holy Spirit*. So far we have noted that Christ says *wait for the promise*, and here is how you will know it when it comes—you will be *baptized with the power of the Holy Spirit*.

Luke 24:47-49 provides a parallel passage: "And that repentance and remission of sins should be preached in His name among all nations . . . And ye are witnesses of these things." How would these defeated disciples be *witnesses* to *all nations*? "And, behold, I send the promise of My Father upon you: . . . be endued with power [*dunamis*] from on high." Luke 24:49 equates the *promise* with being *endued with power from on high.* We found similar wording in Luke 1:35: *the power of the Highest overshadowing Mary.* There this expression is an appositive of the *Holy Spirit* coming upon her. Therefore, *power from on high* is the power of the Holy Spirit. *Be endued* means "to sink into (clothing), put on, clothe oneself."[5] *Power* is the Greek word *dunamis,* which "signifies 'power' or 'strength', with a root meaning of 'being able.' "[6] It implies "a miracle."[7] Often with Christ *dunamis* is translated as "mighty works" (e.g., Matthew 11:20). *Dunamis* emphasizes miraculous, supernatural power. It is truly **power from on high!** So Jesus says *tarry* for the promise, and here is how you will know it when it comes—you will *be endued with power from on high.*

Jesus describes *the promise* in Acts 1:5, 8 as being *baptized with the power of the Holy Spirit,* and in Luke 24:49 as being *endued with power from on high.* Do you see the parallel? Being baptized [immersed] with the power of the Holy Spirit is the same as being endued [sinking into / being clothed] with power from on high.

## FINAL CONCLUSION

**The promise of the Spirit is a promise of power!** When Jesus sent the promised Spirit, He launched the age of the Spirit—the age of power. Hallelujah! This is the age we live in right now! This glorious fact ought to make a significant difference. For the promise of the Spirit is a promise of power!

---

[1]Steven Barabas, *So Great Salvation* (Westwood, N.J.: Fleming H. Revell Company, 1952), pp. 171-74.

[2]Jonathan Goforth, *By My Spirit* (Elkhart, Ind.: Bethel Publishing, 1983), p. 19.

[3]Rosalind Goforth, *Goforth of China* (Minneapolis: Bethany House Publishers, 1937), pp. 180-81.

[4]Jonathan Goforth, p. 13.

[5]Wigram-Green, *The New Englishman's Greek Concordance and Lexicon* (Peabody, Mass.: Hendrickson Publishers, Inc., 1982), p. 290.

[6]Stewart Custer, *A Treasury of New Testament Synonyms* (Greenville, S.C.: Bob Jones University Press, 1975), p. 33.

[7]Wigram-Green, p. 188.

CHAPTER FOUR

# THE PROMISE OF THE SPIRIT— THE REASONS FOR POWERLESSNESS

**Endowment: The Promise of the Spirit**
Enfeeblement: The Problem of Unbelief
Entitlement: The Provision of Christ
Enthronement: The Presentation and Practice of Surrender and Faith
Enablement: The Power of Living
Entrustment: The Purpose of Usefulness

In our progression of truth regarding the ministry of the Holy Spirit, especially as it relates to the Spirit-filled life, we have seen so far that the promise of the Spirit is a promise of power. Yet why, if we are honest, are we often anemic rather than empowered? As we seek to answer this question in the following chapter, will you ask the Spirit of God to search you thoroughly as to where you are in relation to the reasons for powerlessness?

# ACTS 2:32-33

In the last chapter we learned that the promise of the Spirit is a promise of power. Yet this very truth begs a sincere question: **Why are many believers so powerless?** Why do so many Christians live in defeat surprised by victory instead of victory surprised by defeat? Why do so many Christians practice the so-called lesser sins of impatience, irritation, short tempers, abrasive speech, pride, jealousy, envy, and many others? Why the lack of real victory over "secret" sins which, if brought out of the closet, would cause painful shame? Why the lack of power in witnessing for Christ? Why is there so often the disparaging difference between the high road of the Christian life as seen in Scripture and the low road of the defeated life as seen in experience? Should not our experience match up to the reality of the promises of God? Why are we often powerless? The Scripture articulates three reasons for powerlessness.

## MISUNDERSTANDING WHEN THE PROMISE OF THE SPIRIT IS BESTOWED

When is the promise of the Spirit bestowed? We have already seen in the last chapter that the promise of the Spirit is equated to the baptism with the Spirit. By investigating the passages relative to Spirit-baptism, we discover three types of passages regarding the baptism with the Spirit. Through comparing the passages we find the answer to the question of when the promise of the Spirit is bestowed.

## Prophetical

The prophetical passages are found in the Gospels and Acts (Matthew 3:11; Mark 1:8; Luke 3:16; John 1:33; Acts 1:5). The wording of all the passages except John includes the word *shall*, and all five passages point forward to a future baptism with the Holy Spirit.

## Historical

This is the book of Acts. The first baptism of power occurred in Acts 2 on the Day of Pentecost. When Christ "shed forth" the "promise of the Holy Spirit" (2:33), many manifold blessings relating to the Spirit simultaneously occurred: the filling of the Spirit (2:4), the outpouring of the Spirit (2:17), and the gift of the Spirit (2:38-39). Though all a part of the promise or baptism, each blessing is not necessarily equivalent to the other as the epistles later clarify. Also, though other manifestations took place in God's master plan which were for a specific time and purpose, we must not lose sight of the fact that there was a baptism of power ultimately resulting in the salvation of three thousand souls. Acts 8:14-17 indicates the Spirit-baptism moved beyond the Jews to the half-Jews, or Samaritans. Acts 10:44-48 and 11:15-17 record the Spirit-baptism including Gentiles. This occurs again in Acts 19:1-6. The book of Acts simply records the empowerment of the church during the beginnings of the church-age in which we are still. From Acts 2 to Acts 19 approximately twenty-five years elapsed. The age of the Spirit's power goes beyond the Day of Pentecost to the entire church age.

## Instructional

The instructional passages are the epistles (Romans 6:3-4; I Corinthians 12:13; Galatians 3:26-27; Ephesians 4:5; Colossians 2:12). Here we find the verb tenses relating to Spirit-baptism point backward to when one believes in Christ for salvation.

In summary, the prophetical passages point forward to fulfillment. The historical passages record the beginnings of the age of the Holy Spirit. And the instructional passages point backward to fact. Ultimately, the epistles teach that the fact of the baptism with the Spirit is connected to the fact of salvation (e.g., Galatians 3:26-27). Therefore, the promise of the Spirit is bestowed factually at salvation. Then why are we often powerless?

### Misunderstanding What the Promise of the Spirit Includes

What does the promise of the Spirit include? Scripturally, we find that it includes two directions and three dimensions.

# Two Directions

## Baptism by the Spirit into Christ

The first direction simply stated is that at the moment you believe in Christ for salvation, the Spirit baptizes you into Christ. I Corinthians 12:13 states, "For by one Spirit are we all baptized into one body." Also Galatians 3:26-27 says, "For ye are all the children of God by faith in Christ Jesus. For as many of you as have been baptized into Christ have put on Christ." Both verses proclaim the baptism by the Spirit into Christ. This is "positional" truth. However, neither of the verses quoted stop with what we have just noted.

## Baptism by the Son with the Spirit

The second direction simply stated is that when the Spirit baptizes you into Christ at salvation, Christ baptizes you with the Spirit. I Corinthians 12:13 ends by stating " . . . and have been made to drink into one Spirit." Interestingly, the term *into* is from the Greek word *en* which, in all five prophetical passages cited earlier, is translated "with." Galatians 3:27 carefully states both directions with "For as many of you as have been baptized into Christ **have put on Christ**." The three words *have put on* come from the same word translated *be endued* in Luke 24:49, which is parallel to *baptized* in Acts 1:5. Therefore, theologically Galatians 3:27 could read like this: "For as many of you as have been baptized into Christ have been baptized with Christ." Just as when a sponge is placed into water, the water is placed into the sponge. Similarly, when the Spirit places you into Christ, Christ places His Spirit into you. The same two verses which proclaim the baptism by the Spirit into Christ also proclaim the baptism by the Son with the Spirit. This is "powerful" truth.

Tragically, this second direction is often overlooked, and therefore, the enduement, or clothing of power, is neglected.

# Three Dimensions

## Positional Power:
## The Indwelling of the Spirit When He Moves Into You

To be "in Christ" (Ephesians 1:3) is to have "Christ in you" (Colossians 1:27). This new position is a position of power. The Spirit of the glorified Christ is now in you because you have been baptized into Christ. Notice, it is not the Spirit of the earthly Christ but the Spirit of the glorified Christ who finished His work at the cross and won the victory—it is the Spirit of the victorious, triumphant Christ who lives in you! Christ now sits on what He called "the right hand of the power of God" (Luke 22:69). This is Christ's position of power. Yet, we are *in* Him and *with* Him positionally. This is a position of an heir (Galatians 3:29; Ephesians 3:6), adopted in as a mature son (Galatians 4:4-7; Ephesians 1:5), with all the rights to this grand inheritance (Galatians 3:18; Ephesians 1:11, 14, 18; Colossians 1:12), blessed with all spiritual blessings in heavenly places in Christ (Ephesians 1:3), raised and made to sit together in heavenly places in Christ (Ephesians 2:6). This is the believer's new position. It is a powerful position!

## Practical Power:
## The Filling of the Spirit When He Moves Through You

Positional power is the necessary platform for practical power. The indwelling of the Spirit is the necessary platform for the filling of the Spirit. From the fountain that is now in you, the Spirit can flow through you (John 7:38-39). The Spirit of grace (supernatural enabling) is able to make you a practical partaker of your inheritance. II Corinthians 9:8 declares, "And God is able to make all grace abound toward you; that ye, always having all sufficiency in all things, may abound to every good work." Notice the superlative promises in that grand text. The Spirit-filled life is power for holiness as the Spirit enables you to be what you ought to be and power for service as the Spirit enables you to do what you ought to do. The goal of "Christ in you" (Colossians 1:27) is that "Christ be formed in you" (Galatians 4:19) through Christ living through you (Galatians 2:20). The purpose of the new position is a new practice.

This is powerful living because of a powerful position.

## Paramount Power:
## The Outpouring of the Spirit When He Moves On You

Practical power is the necessary platform for paramount power. Not only is it possible to experience the Spirit working through you but also on or outside of you. This is what A. T. Pierson called "attestation."[1] The principle involved is the Spirit powerfully attesting outside of a man as well as through a man. Remember we saw the concepts already of the Spirit *in* Christ, *through* Christ, and *upon* Christ. This reality allows an individual to have supernatural, miraculous impact. Duncan Campbell once said, "We are the ambassadors of eternity in the courts of time, and it is our business to permeate the courts of time with the atmosphere of eternity."[2]

This principle manifested in a corporate way is revival. Until the overreaction to the excesses of the Charismatic movement beginning in the 1960s, orthodox people often defined revival as the outpouring of the Spirit of God. History records of revival are replete with examples from many centuries and cultures of the terminology of the outpouring of the Spirit in reference to revival. Revival is the powerful spiritual manifestation of the presence of God, which leads believers to a restoration of the Spirit-filled life for holiness and service and leads unbelievers to the convincement of sin, righteousness, and judgment for salvation. As the Spirit moves through a yielded vessel, He can also attest to this reality by moving on (or outside) of a man.

For example Duncan Campbell testifies regarding the Lewis Awakening (1949-53) in the Hebrides Islands of Scotland:

> Perhaps the greatest miracle of all was in the village of Arnol. Here, indifference to the things of God held the field and a good deal of opposition was experienced but prayer, the mighty weapon of the revival, was resorted to and an evening given to waiting upon God. Before midnight God came down, the mountains flowed down at His presence, and a wave of revival swept the village: opposition and spiritual death fled before the presence of the Lord of life. Here was demonstrated the power of prevailing prayer, and that nothing lies beyond the reach of prayer except that which lies outside the will of God. . . . in a matter of minutes following this heaven-sent visitation, men and women were on their faces in distress of soul.[3]

The issue here is not the sensational element. The issue is the powerful spiritual manifestation of God's presence and its impact. According to Campbell's biographer, "He pronounced the benediction immediately and walked out to find the community alive with an awareness of God. A stream of blessing was released which brought salvation to many homes during the succeeding nights."[4] This is the power of Acts 1:8, "But ye shall receive power . . . the Holy Spirit . . . upon you: and ye shall be witnesses unto Me . . . unto the uttermost part of the earth." This is the power necessary to fully fulfill the Great Commission.

One of the most classic examples of this is when God poured out His Spirit on the village church of Herrnhut in Saxony in 1727. The godly leader, Count Zinzendorf, and the people, the Moravians, experienced such an immersion of power that within twenty-five years this one church sent out over 100 missionaries long before William Carey ever sailed for India.[5] By Zinzendorf's death in 1760, the Moravian Church had sent out no fewer than 226 missionaries around the world.[6] It was the Moravian missionaries who were used of God in the conversions of John and Charles Wesley, who were used of God to shake several nations. Literally, one village church, because of the outpouring of the Spirit, fulfilled Acts 1:8 in their generation! Is this not paramount power?

When Jesus promised in John 14:12, "He that believeth on Me, the works I do shall he do also; and greater works than these shall he do . . ." He then explains why. ". . . because I go unto My Father." What did He do when He went to the Father? In John 14:16 He further explains, "And I will pray the Father, and He shall give you another Comforter, that He may abide with you forever." This is the event recorded in our text in Acts 2:33. Christ sent the promised Spirit. He is the power for greater works.

In summary, positional power is the reservoir, or fountain, of Christ *in* you. Practical power is the rivers, or flowing, of the Spirit *through* you. Paramount power is the rain, or floods, *on* you. You may have the indwelling of the Spirit without the filling, but you never have the filling without first of all being indwelt. Also, you may have the filling without the outpouring, but you never have the outpouring without someone being filled who, by the faith of intercession, accesses the promise. The promise of the Spirit includes two directions and three dimensions. Yet why are so many still powerless?

## MISUNDERSTANDING HOW THE PROMISE
## OF THE SPIRIT IS ACCESSED

How is the promise of the Spirit practically accessed? We must note that there is a difference between what is factual (positional) and what is functional (practical). For instance, a carpenter may factually possess tools for carpentry work, but he must depend on those tools by using them for the function of carpentry. Even so, a believer factually possesses the promise of the Spirit, but he must depend on the Spirit for the function of holy living and powerful serving. Faith (dependence) is the necessary link between the factual (the promises) and the functional (the experience).

Galatians 3:2 asks, "Received ye the Spirit by the works of the law, or by the hearing of faith?" The answer of course is *by . . . faith*. Verse 3 continues: "Are ye so foolish? having begun in the Spirit [by faith], are ye now made perfect by the flesh [through works, which is flesh-dependence]?" The answer again is obvious. *Having begun in the Spirit* by faith at salvation, now live in the Spirit *by faith*. These Scriptures clearly teach that the Spirit is *received* by faith factually at salvation.

What about the function? More details will be given in a later chapter, but for now note Galatians 3:5 in this same context: "He therefore that ministereth [present tense, lit. *is supplying*] to you the Spirit, and worketh miracles among you, doeth He it by the works of the law, or by the hearing of faith?" The answer again is *by . . . faith*. In contrast to the aorist tense [fact of an action] of having *received* the Spirit by faith at salvation is the present tense [continuous action] of, by faith, regularly coming back to the Spirit so that God *is supplying to you the Spirit to work miracles.* This is the function, or experience, based on the facts.

Although it is certainly possible to "happen" into this in moments of desperation, which cause us to depend on God, it is easy to "happen" out of this when we do not feel so desperate. However, when one consciously, through scriptural understanding, begins to depend on the Spirit, he is entering into a life of surrender. This conscious entrance is the emphasis of the Romans 12:1 "presentation." Galatians 3 alludes to this when it states that "Christ hath redeemed us . . . " (3:13), "That the blessing of Abraham might come on the Gentiles through Jesus Christ [justification (cf. v. 8)] that we might receive the promise of the Spirit through faith" (3:14). Notice the two occurrences of *that*, or "in order that." Christ redeemed us so that we might be justified (first event) so that we might receive the promise of the Spirit (second event). Both can occur at salvation if there is basic understanding, but for many the surrender to the Spirit occurs later. The factual reception of the Spirit at salvation must be functionally received. When this reception (surrender/dependence) occurs, the effect is powerful because now the facts become function. We could say this is the experiential Spirit-baptism based on the factual Spirit-baptism.

Dormant facts accessed by faith into function constitute the "likeness" of re-birth. Galatians 4:19 says, "My little children, of whom I travail in birth again until Christ be formed in you." Simply put, when a believer who has turned back to flesh-dependence for living the Christian life begins to depend on the Spirit for a holy life and powerful service, the experience that follows is "like" getting saved in its impact.

What *is* regarding the promise of the Spirit must be accessed by faith *to be experienced.* Galatians 3:27 states, "For as many of you as have been baptized into Christ have put on Christ." Yet Romans 13:14 commands, "But put ye on the Lord Jesus Christ." Why does Romans command believers to do what Galatians says has already been done? *Have put on [enduo]* is an aorist tense, middle voice, indicative mood verb used in Galatians 3:27. Whereas *put . . . on [enduo]* is an aorist tense, middle voice, imperative mood verb used in Romans 13:14. The grammar helps us understand the enigma. Romans commands [imperative mood: potential reality] what Galatians claims [indicative mood: reality], indicating believers are responsible to access their inheritance, the result of which is like to "awake out of sleep" (Romans 13:11). The middle voice indicates that you initiate the action [choice of faith], and then participate in the results. The ten passages where *enduo* is used in a spiritual sense, all use the aorist middle.

This explains the historical confusion of terms regarding the baptism with the Spirit. Factually, one is baptized with the Spirit once-for-all at salvation when one believes for salvation. Functionally (experimentally), one is baptized with the Spirit when one believes for Spirit-empowered living (this can occur at salvation, but for most it occurs later and could occur more than once if there is more turning back to flesh-dependence). The "experiences" may vary greatly. The old term *experimentally* was used not to discover if something was true, but to demonstrate that something *is* true. Like a science teacher "experimenting" in class not to discover but to demonstrate something, *experimental religion* is not discovery as much as it is demonstration. Are we not in desperate need of *the demonstration of the Spirit?*

Evangelist James A. Stewart from Scotland provides some clarifying statements in his classic book *Heaven's Throne Gift:* "It cannot be too strongly stated that the fullness of the Spirit is not something apart from Christ, but in Him, so that in seeking His fullness, we are but seeking to know experimentally, what is already ours potentially."[7] "There is no once-for-all baptism for power that ignores daily renewals."[8] "There is no stereotyped experience of being filled with the Spirit, just as there is no stereotyped case of conversion."[9]

The evangelical writer D. A. Carson in his book entitled *Exegetical Fallacies* makes an interesting observation:

> Or how about "baptism in the Spirit?" Charismatics tend to want to make all occurrences of the expression refer to a post conversion effusion of Spirit; some anticharismatics contemplate I Corinthians 12:13 ("For we were all baptized by one Spirit into one body—whether Jews or Greeks, slave of free—and we were all given one Spirit to drink." NIV) and conclude; with equal fallacy, that all New Testament references are to the effusion of Spirit all Christians receive at their conversion. The problem is complicated by the uncertain syntax of I Corinthians 12:13; but the worst problem is the assumption on both sides that we are dealing with a *terminus technicus* that always has the same meaning. There is insufficient evidence to support that view; and the assumption makes it exceedingly difficult to handle the five passages (one in each Gospel and one in Acts) that stand in most urgent need of being treated carefully and evenhandedly as references to a step in the progress of redemption. Interestingly, the Puritans adopted neither extreme. Apparently detecting in the phrase *baptism in Holy Spirit* no consistent, technical meaning, they took it to mean "effusion in Spirit" or "inundation in Spirit" and

felt free to pray for revival in the terms, "Oh, baptize us afresh with thy Holy Spirit!"[10]

In summary faith for the indwelling of the Spirit is the necessary platform to exercise faith for the filling of the Spirit; faith for the filling of the Spirit is the necessary platform to exercise faith for the outpouring of the Spirit, whether personally or corporately. Faith for the filling of the Spirit is a matter of depending upon the reality of what is (e.g.,"My grace [Spirit-enabling] is sufficient for thee" II Corinthians 12:9); faith for the outpouring of the Spirit is a matter of depending upon the reality of what is to come (e.g., "for it is time to seek the Lord, till He come and rain righteousness upon you" Hosea 10:12).

## Final Observations

1. The indwelling of the Spirit is a constant reality for believers (I Corinthians 6:19—"Holy Spirit which is in you").

2. The filling of the Spirit is to be a constant reality (Ephesians 5:18—lit., "keep on allowing yourselves to be filled with the Spirit").

3. The outpouring of the Spirit is to be in regular seasons (Acts 3:19 "times of refreshing . . . from the presence of the Lord").

4. The normal Christian life is to be the experience of practical power. NOTE: The power is for God's will and purpose, not man's. James Stewart said, "Many have been keenly disappointed because they have not received a sudden acquisition of power to do the work which God has assigned to someone else. God only fills us so that we may have power to do that which He has appointed for us to do."[11]

5. The normal church life is to be the seasonal experience of paramount power.
   NOTE: "Thomas Charles, who saw revival in Bala, North Wales, in 1791, said: 'Unless we are favored with frequent revivals, and strong and powerful works of the Spirit of God, we shall in a great degree degenerate and have only a name to live; religion will soon lose its vigor, the ministry will hardly retain its luster and glory, and iniquity in consequence will abound.' "[12] "Between 1762 and 1862 there were at least fifteen outstanding revivals in Wales."[13] This is an average of a revival every seven years! Is this not "seasons of refreshing"?

6. What Jesus began in His earthly ministry He continues through His heavenly ministry—this is *the ministry of the Spirit of the glorified Christ.*

In Acts, Christ's work in His body through the Spirit is on the level of paramount power. Note the following biblical indications of power of the Spirit in Acts:

a. Acts 2• "the **multitude** came together" (6) • "Then they that gladly received His word were baptized: and the same day there were **added** unto them about **three thousand** souls. And they **continued** steadfastly" (41-42) • "the Lord **added** to the church daily" (47)

b. Acts 3 • Lame man healed • Peter's sermon • Acts 4 • "**many** . . . believed . . . **five thousand**" (4) • "when they had prayed, the place was shaken . . . spake . . . with **boldness**" (31) • "with **great power** [*dunamis*] gave the apostles witness . . . **great grace** was upon them all" (33)

c. Acts 5 • "believers were the more **added** to the Lord, **multitudes**" (14) • persecution • "daily . . . ceased not to teach and preach Jesus Christ" (42)

d. Acts 6 • "And the word of God **increased**; and the number of the disciples **multiplied** . . . **greatly**" (7a) • "**a great company** of the priests were obedient to the faith" (7b) • Acts 7 • Stephen martyred

e. Acts 8 • Persecution • Dispersion • Philip in Samaria • "the people with one accord gave heed" (6) • **great joy** in that city" (8) • "they believed" (12) • "they received the Holy Spirit" (17) • Eunuch believed (26-40)

f. Acts 9 • Saul's salvation (1-22) • Peter at Lydda—Aeneas healed • "**all** that dwelt at Lydda and Saron . . . **turned** to the Lord" (35) • Tabitha raised • "**many** believed" (42).

g. Acts 10 • Cornelius • "**the Holy Spirit fell** on all them which heard the word" (44)

h. Acts 11 • Antioch "a **great number** believed" (21) • Barnabas • "**much people** was **added** unto the Lord" (24)

i. Acts 12 • James martyred • Peter arrested and delivered • "But the word of God **grew** and **multiplied**" (24)

j. Acts 13 • Pisidian Antioch ". . . **came almost the whole city** together to hear the word of God" (44) • "**many** . . . believed" (48) • "And the word of the Lord was published throughout all the region" (49) [**Note:** no signs and wonders]

k. Acts 14 • Iconium "**a great multitude** both of the Jews and . . . Greeks **believed**" (1) [**Note:** no signs and wonders] • Lystra • man healed • Paul stoned • Derbe "taught [made disciples] **many**" (21)

1. Acts 15 • Debate over circumcision • Acts 16 • "churches . . . **increased** in number **daily**" (5) • Macedonia vision • Philippi • Lydia saved • cast out demon from girl • riot or near riot • jail • earthquake • "all here" (28) • jailer saved (29-34)

m. Acts 17 • Thessalonica for three Sabbaths • "And some of them [Jews] believed . . . and of the devout Greeks a **great multitude**, and of the chief women **not a few**" (4) [**Note:** no signs and wonders] • riot • "These that have turned the world upside down" (6) • Berea • "**many** of them believed; also of honourable women which were Greeks, and of men, **not a few**" (12) • riot or near riot • Athens • "certain men clave unto him, and believed" (34)

n. Acts 18 • Corinth • "And Crispus, the chief ruler of the synagogue, believed on the Lord with all his house; and **many** of the Corinthians hearing **believed**" (8) • "then spake the Lord to Paul . . . I have **much people** in this city" (9-10)

o. Acts 19 • Ephesus • "**All** they which dwelt in Asia **heard the word** of the Lord Jesus" (10) • "the name of the Lord **Jesus** was **magnified**" (17) • "**many**" burned books (19) • "So **mightily** grew the word of God and **prevailed**" (20) • riot

p. Acts 20 • Ephesus • Acts 21 • Jerusalem • riot • Acts 22-26 Paul gives gospel before councils, governors, and kings • Acts 27 • shipwreck • Acts 28 • people healed (8-9) • Rome "there came many [Jews] to him . . . to whom he expounded and testified . . . some believed" (23-24) • "the salvation of God is sent unto the Gentiles, and . . . **they will hear it**" (28) • Paul . . . "received all that came in unto him, Preaching . . . the Lord Jesus Christ, with all confidence, no man forbidding him." [**Note:** When great power was displayed, the result was either great blessing or great resistance and sometimes both. The more Christ is powerfully manifested, the greater the draw to Him or the greater the offense. We must be willing for either or both.]

7. The Epistles speak regularly of *dunamis* [miraculous] level power in Christ by the Spirit.

8. The Epistles speak often of *putting on* [*enduo*] Christ, referring to accessing by faith the promise of the Spirit of power.

9. The church of Jesus Christ should match the power of Jesus Christ.

a. James A. Stewart: "As long as the blessed Holy Spirit, Himself the great standing miracle, abides and works on the earth, the Church's potential is the same as it was in the apostolic days."[14]

b. James A. Stewart: "A sub-normal and backslidden church is an insult and a disgrace to a holy, powerful God."[15]

c. Wayne Van Gelderen, Jr: "We are the body of Christ and to limit this to an anemic state is blasphemy!"

# Conclusion

If we are powerless, it is either because of a lack of understanding (Matthew 22:29 "Ye do err, not knowing the scriptures, nor the power [*dunamis*] of God") and/or because of a lack of faith (Matthew 13:58 "And He [Jesus] did not many mighty works [*dunamis*] there because of their unbelief.") Faith presupposes understanding and agreement, so ultimately the issue is faith. May it not be said of us, "Ye do always resist the Holy Spirit."

---

[1] A. T. Pierson, *The Acts of the Holy Spirit* (Harrisburg, Penn.: Christian Publications, Inc., reprint 1980), p. 53.

[2] Andrew A. Woolsey, *Channel of Revival: A Biography of Duncan Campbell* (Edinburgh: The Faith Mission, reprint 1982), p. 64.

[3] Duncan Campbell, *The Lewis Awakening* in *Heritage of Revival* by Colin N. Peckham (Edinburgh: The Faith Mission, 1986), pp. 169-70.

[4] Woolsey, p. 133.

[5] John Greenfield, *When the Spirit Came* (Minneapolis: Bethany Fellowship, 1967), p. 26.

[6] "A Christian History Time Line," *Christian History*, ed. W. Carey Moore, vol. 1, no. 1 (Worcester, Penn.: Christian History Magazine, 1982), p. 12.

[7] James A. Stewart, *Heaven's Throne Gift* (Asheville, N.C.: Revival Literature, reprint n.d.), p. 185.

[8] Ibid., p. 153.

[9] Ibid., p. 189.

[10] D. A. Carson, *Exegetical Fallacies* (Grand Rapids: Baker Book House, 1984), p. 46.

[11] Stewart, p. 190.

[12] Stanley C. Griffin, *A Forgotten Revival* (Bromley, Kent, England: Day One Publications, 1992), p. 109.

[13] Eifion Evans, *Revival Comes to Wales* (Bryntirion, Bridgend, Mid Glamorgan, Wales: Evangelical Press of Wales, reprint 1995), p. 10.

[14] James A. Stewart, *Opened Windows* (Asheville, N.C.: Revival Literature, reprint 1999), p. 89.

[15] Ibid., p. 92.

CHAPTER FIVE

# THE FLESH-LIFE VS. THE SPIRIT-LIFE

Endowment: The Promise of the Spirit
**Enfeeblement: The Problem of Unbelief**
Entitlement: The Provision of Christ
Enthronement: The Presentation and Practice of Surrender and Faith
Enablement: The Power of Living
Entrustment: The Purpose of Usefulness

We have seen that the promise of the Spirit is a promise of power. Yet unbelief is the reason for powerlessness. It is like a disease that is hindering the normal growth of the body. This unbelief manifests itself with the symptoms of a fleshly life. May the Spirit reveal any unbelief, which has enfeebled us, that we might respond in confession and faith and be restored to spiritual health.

# GALATIANS 5:16-25

During the last quarter of the nineteenth century when England was being blessed by the renewed emphasis on the ministry of the Holy Spirit, another preacher helped by this truth was J. Elder Cumming from Scotland. "Moody had thought him the 'most cantankerous Christian I had ever met.' A shattering bereavement had thickened his skin, he was a fearsome theologian who delighted in shrivelling opponents, yet could look back on a genuine evangelical conversion and ruled himself, he thought, with strictest rectitude."[1] In the summer of 1882, he was drawn to attend a conference where Evan Hopkins was preaching. In his own words he later testified:

> I cannot tell you what pain and misery I experienced during the first three days—first, something like indignation; secondly, something like perplexity, for my theological chart seemed to have certain things laid clearly down, and I did not see how other things could be put in without disarranging the former. I cannot tell how the arrow of God's Word was going home. I passed a very miserable time during the first days of that week. Then the way the Lord dealt with me was this. He told me, while on my knees in my solitude of this, and this, and this. In perfect simplicity and innocence I said, "Lord, these are not sins." The answer that came by His Spirit was, "Whatever they are, are they worthy of a son of God?" And at once I had to say, "No!" "Are you willing to put them away?" "Yes, Lord." I should have to go home to settle some of them. I took pencil and paper, and marked everything down and said, "Now, Lord, I promise that by Thy grace I will." It was all alone in the solitude of my room.[2]

J. Elder Cumming simply embraced the teaching of sanctification by faith. So excited was he that he began a conference in Glasgow to proclaim this freshly discovered old truth. "Moody returned to Glasgow in 1891. 'Whatever has happened to Cumming?' he asked. 'I have never seen a man so altered, so full of the love of God.'"[3] J. Elder Cumming stepped from the flesh-filled life to the Spirit-filled life, and as he depended on the ministry of the Holy Spirit, the Spirit transformed him from the inside out.

Galatians 5:16-25 distinguishes between the flesh-life and the Spirit-life: "This I say then, Walk in the Spirit, and ye shall not fulfil the lust of the flesh. For the flesh lusteth against the Spirit, and the Spirit against the flesh: and these are contrary the one to the other: so that ye cannot do the things that ye would. But if ye be led of the Spirit, ye are not under the law. Now the works of the flesh are manifest, which are these; Adultery, fornication, uncleanness, lasciviousness, Idolatry, witchcraft, hatred, variance, emulations, wrath, strife, seditions, heresies, Envyings, murders, drunkenness, revellings, and such like: of the which I tell you before, as I have also told you in time past, that they which do such things shall not inherit the kingdom of God. But the fruit of the Spirit is love, joy, peace, longsuffering, gentleness, goodness, faith, Meekness, temperance: against such there is no law. And they that are Christ's have crucified the flesh with the affections and lusts. If we live in the Spirit, let us also walk in the Spirit."

Did you notice our text commences and concludes with the phrase *walk in the Spirit*? **Are you walking in the Spirit, or are you walking in the flesh?** How do you know? For years I knew that the Spirit-filled life was the answer, but I really could not explain exactly what it was and how you could "get there." How do you move from the pathway of walking in the flesh to the pathway of walking in the Spirit? Our text provides explanations of each walk and how to exchange one walk for the other.

## EXPLANATIONS

In investigating the explanations of walking in the flesh, versus walking in the Spirit, in this chapter we will focus predominantly on the former and will focus on the latter in chapters six and seven and the following chapters.

## Walking in the Flesh

Galatians 5 unveils both the evidences of the flesh-filled walk and the engine for it.

### Evidences: Works of the Flesh (Galatians 5:19-21)

Verse 19 states, *Now the works of the flesh are manifest.* They are evident. So we can research the *works of the flesh* listed and discover if we are walking in the flesh. It is a biblical "test." The scriptural list is stated in three categories.

First listed are the moral sins given in verse 19. Four are specifically mentioned. *Adultery* refers to extramarital affairs. The emphasis is on a married person who goes outside the boundaries of his marriage in an affair-type relationship. Toward the end of a particular meeting, I remember a pastor once telling me, as we looked over the congregation before a service, that there were six church discipline cases in his church at the time. From the context of the conversation, it appeared that these cases were not yet dealt with. If that was so, may I kindly say that that is probably why there were six cases. "A little leaven leaveneth the whole lump" (I Corinthians 5:6). He proceeded to explain that one partner from one married couple was involved in an affair with another partner from another couple, all in the same congregation! Is this not wicked? It is the flesh!

The next word listed is *fornication*, a broader term involving any sexual deviation including premarital affairs, sodomy, and incest. A survey I came across several years ago stated that 43% of evangelical teenagers had lost their purity by the age of eighteen. Is this not tragic? Beyond that, the number of incest cases even in Bible-preaching churches is shockingly not much different from secular society. Is this not wallowing in the flesh?

The next word is *uncleanness.* This term is broader, yet refers to the impurities which lead to the acts of sexual sin. For example, when the average rock singer openly states that rock music is "sex," would it not be fair to say that the rock genre of music is what the Bible calls *uncleanness*? When the rock culture states that the power which makes their music sensual and sexual is not so much the lyrics, but rather the kind of rhythm they use—the rock beat—would it not be fair to say that music which uses the same rock beat like much of Contemporary Christian Music is also what the Bible labels *uncleanness*? When country and western artists openly boast that their music contributes to the moral decline in the United States, would it not be accurate to say that the Bible calls this musical genre *uncleanness*? It is plainly walking in the flesh.

The last word listed among the moral sins is *lasciviousness*, which means licentiousness. It is license, or the disregarding of restraints. The idea is lewdness and unbridled indecency.

These four words evidence walking in the flesh. Even if you are not personally involved in the acts of moral sin, are you participating in them through the eye-gate or ear-gate, and thus gratifying the flesh? What about television, cable TV, videos and so forth? Though these forms of media can be used for good, would it not be fair to say that much of what is produced today by entertainment industries is saturated with *adultery, fornication, uncleanness,* and *lasciviousness?* When you consider innuendos, double meanings, immodesty, and sensual plots, much of what is produced wallows in the works of the flesh.

What about the Internet? Again, although it can be used for good, many Internet tragedies have occurred through sensual addictions and improper relationships, leading to scarred minds and broken marriages. What about literature, magazines, and novels? Is it right to romanticize about someone who is not your spouse? Are not many wallowing in the flesh through these and other avenues?

The second scriptural category is religious sins. Verse 20 mentions two. *Idolatry* is first and significantly the first sin listed after the moral sins. *Idolatry* is not just worshipping a wood or stone pot-bellied image on a shelf. Any concept of God which is not true to that which God revealed about Himself in His Word is not God! Consider how man thinks. Every time we sin, we think that God somehow will not see, or that God will not care. We think somehow we will get away with it as if God does not mind. This is *idolatry!* God sees, and God cares. I'm convinced that the commandment broken more than any other commandment by both unsaved people and saved people alike is the first commandment. How many Christians think God will not mind their half-hearted Christianity; yet God minds!

Also, *idolatry* is revealed by wrong objects of dependence. For example, some depend on music which gives an emotional high to lift their spirits instead of looking to God for the joy of the Lord. What about material things and wealth? Why did Jesus say that it is easier for a camel to go through the eye of a needle than it is for a rich man to enter heaven? Riches are not intrinsically evil. But what is a rich man used to trusting? His riches. Yet salvation comes only through trusting Christ. Many in materialistic societies, perhaps unwittingly, are depending on comforts and conveniences for satisfaction and happiness, when they ought to be looking to God for true fulfillment and joy.

The next word listed is *witchcraft.* This word means "sorcery" and can even include drug use. If you use horoscopes, you are walking in the flesh. If you can dabble around with Satanic games, you are playing a dangerous game.

The third scriptural category is social sins. Ten are listed. *Hatred* means hostility. Many are the homes where the words "I hate you!" wound and hurt. Is this not fleshly living?

*Variance* means strife or contentions. O the bickering, arguing, and word wars between the saints! Bitterness, grudges, resentment, and an unwillingness to forgive plague many congregations. Gossip, tale-bearing, and backbiting often rule the day. Irritability describes the demeanor of so many. What about abrasive speech? What about being easily offended? Tragically is this not an accurate picture of many homes and churches?

*Emulations* means jealousies. Self-promotion motivates this work of the flesh. As silly as it may seem, there are church people who are watching to see if the pastor or evangelist spends more time with so-and-so or shakes so-and-so's hand but not theirs. Musicians take notice of who gets to sing more or play the piano more, desiring "fair" time. Whatever happened to being servants in God's cause? A test to see whether or not you have a problem with jealousy is this: Are you glad and do you rejoice when God blesses—someone else? If your cause is the cause of Christ, you will rejoice. If your cause is yourself, you won't.

*Wrath* refers to outbursts. This is the idea of losing your temper or "blowing your stack." Isn't it amazing what people do when they lose their temper? Some men punch holes in the wall. Now they have to fix it. I heard about a teen guy who became so angry that he started punching a tree—and broke his wrist! Isn't it incredible what becomes airborne during fits of rage?

I remember losing my temper at my younger sister when I was a young boy. I verbally let her have it. Later I felt badly and went to check on her in her room. It was winter, and she often wore tall black boots. When I looked in her room, her boots were sticking out from underneath the bed skirt at the bottom of the bed. Thinking I had crushed her and so demolished her feelings that she had crawled underneath the bed, I began to apologize profusely. After no response, I eventually looked under the bed only to find her boots! All that apologizing to no avail! Isn't it a tragedy when these outbursts still occur as adults?

*Strife* means selfishness. This selfishness often leads to disputes motivated by selfish ambitions.

*Seditions* or dissensions follow.

*Heresies*, meaning schisms or factions, are often the sad result. The dissensions lead to "divisions organized into factions."[4] Obviously, this implies unscriptural divisions since there is a proper biblical separation.

*Envyings* refers to another fleshly desire. While the word for jealousy in verse 20 "refers to the desire of being as well off as another," this word "refers to the desire to deprive another of what he has."[5] It is that cut-throat mentality which waits to pounce on another, especially when a competitive spirit enters in, seeking to bring him down at every opportunity and consequently push yourself up.

*Murders* sadly speaks of the full outgrowth of hatred.

*Drunkenness* pictures outwardly what is true inwardly—being out of control because you are under some other influence.

*Revellings* means carousing. It describes the "party" mentality and lifestyle of our day.

Then the Scripture says *and such like*. Many today try to say that if the Bible does not explicitly name something as sin, then it is all a matter of preference (as if it is wrong to apply the principles of Scripture). *And such like*, however, indicates that God means for us to apply His ways based upon His words.

The list now concluded, verse 21 continues with a startling statement: *of the which I tell you before, as I have also told you in time past, that they which do such things shall not inherit the kingdom of God.* What does this mean? Remember, this passage begins and ends with the instruction to *walk in the Spirit.* So is this passage written to saved or unsaved people? Obviously it is written to the saints. The point is that lost people go to hell for their sin. Although saved people have eternal life, they had better realize that no one gets away with sin. Interestingly, Galatians speaks of *inherit the kingdom of God* while John 3 speaks of "see" and "enter the kingdom of God." Perhaps the emphasis is different.

An unsaved elderly man once asked a pastor if murderers could go to heaven. Instead of listing an example such as Paul before he was saved, the pastor opened his Bible to several passages, including this one, and pointed to the word *murders* and the result. The man responded by saying, "I thought so," thinking murderers cannot *ever* be saved. Then the pastor pointed to the word *envyings*, one word to the left of *murders* in verse 21. The man came under conviction, realizing his self-righteousness was faulty. The pastor then led him to Christ.

This reveals how we unwittingly and carnally divide between types of sins. The "carnal" categorization includes "grosser sins" and "lesser sins." We might say "grosser sins" and "the glossed-over sins." Grosser sins would be the moral sins like *adultery* and *fornication*, the religious sins of *idolatry* and *witchcraft*, and the worst of the social sins such as *murders, drunkenness,* and *revellings.* Often Christians think that the people who do such things probably are not saved.

But we gloss over the "lesser sins" like *hatred, variance* [contentions], *emulations* [jealousies], *wrath* [outbursts], *strife* [selfishness], *seditions* [dissensions], *heresies* [factions], and *envyings.* We gloss over bitterness, irritability, abrasive speech, gossip, slander, malice, unforgiveness, worrying, fretting, fickleness, laziness, boasting, and so forth. Is this a fair categorization? Perhaps if the "lesser sins" were listed last after all the "grosser sins," a case could be made. However, what we think of as "lesser sins," the Holy Spirit sandwiches between the terms *witchcraft* and *murders!* Although the consequences of sins vary, sin is sin. The *works of the flesh* are all wicked and grieve the Spirit of God.

To think that certain sins are signs of being unsaved and other sins are necessary baggage for most believers is a deception. This leads believers into being content with the sins of the converted life. In reality, it is all walking in the flesh. Are you walking in the flesh?

### Engine: Strength of the Flesh

Galatians 5:1 says, "Stand fast therefore in the liberty wherewith Christ hath made us free, and be not entangled again with the yoke of bondage." The emphasis of Galatians is that since you were saved by faith, not works [flesh-dependence], keep believing on Christ for victory, and do not go back to the bondage of works [flesh-dependence]. The strength of the flesh is what Jeremiah 17:5 calls "the arm of the flesh." Those who live in the sins or works of the flesh are obviously depending on the flesh. Yet it is possible to be seeking to live for God, to be going through the right motions outwardly, and still be depending on the strength of the flesh. It is possible to have the "form of godliness" but be "denying the power thereof." This too is flesh-dependence. It is "works" without the power of the Spirit. This is the "good heart" that still is powerless to obey (Romans 7:15–24).

Someone has rightly called this "struggle theology." Struggle theology says that if you are saved, then some day you will get to heaven and be free from the presence of sin, but down here, you just struggle along while doing the best you can. The idea is to grit your teeth and try to do right. And if you fall, get up and try harder the next time. Notice the emphasis of struggle theology is on what *you* do. It is no different than unsaved disciplined moralists! This is not to say we never have struggles. But the struggles of trials are much different than struggling along, defeated and discouraged because of flesh-dependence. Struggle theology is simply flesh-dependence to live the Christian life.

This is not New Testament teaching; in fact, the New Testament warns against depending on the strength of the flesh even for good and proper goals. Consider the following three realities regarding flesh-dependence.

First, flesh-dependence is profitless. John 6:63 says, "It is the Spirit that quickeneth [gives life]; the flesh profiteth nothing." We all know the works of the flesh *profit nothing*, but have we considered that the strength of the flesh also *profits nothing*? It is possible for you to try to be the right kind of spouse, parent, or Christian worker; it is possible for you to try to get victory over sin and live for God—but that's the problem—it's "you trying." And *the flesh profits nothing*! It is "wood, hay," and "stubble" which will be incinerated at the Judgment Seat of Christ.

Second, flesh-dependence is counterproductive. II Corinthians 3:6 says "for the letter [of the law] killeth, but the Spirit giveth life." Even the exact rendering of the law deadens apart from the life-giving Spirit. This is a sobering truth. You can have correct doctrine, you can have right position, you can have orthodoxy—but if it is without the Spirit who gives life, it is dead orthodoxy! No wonder Paul said to the church at Thessalonica in I Thessalonians 1:5, "For our gospel came not unto you in word only, but also in power, and in the Holy Spirit." *Word only* preaching deadens. *Word only* witnessing kills. If you have never considered this biblical truth before, it may come as an alarming discovery! Perhaps this sheds light on perplexed parents who brought their children to church regularly, placed them in a Christian school or home-schooled them, had good rules and standards, and yet their children rebelled against God. Perhaps the parents were orthodox, but it was dead orthodoxy, and the letter of the law without the life of the Spirit kills. O how vital is the life of the Spirit!

Third, flesh-dependence is sinful. Romans 14:23 states, "For whatsoever is not of faith is sin." If we are not depending on God and His word, what are we depending on? Man, the flesh. Man has never yet and will never meet God's standard of perfection on his own. Isaiah 64:6 boldly says, "All our righteousnesses are as filthy rags" in God's sight. Man's righteousness—whether unsaved man's righteousness or saved man's righteousness—is as a dirty rag in God's sight. It is self-righteousness, which is not righteousness. Only as we are brought into union with Christ are we acceptable in God's sight. Enabled righteousness, which is Christ's righteousness through you, based on credited righteousness, which is Christ's righteousness to you, is the only righteousness God accepts. Only Christ's righteousness produces "gold, silver," and "precious stones" through the believer in dependent union with Christ. All else, as good as it may outwardly look, is *wood, hay,* and *stubble.* Just as wood, hay, and stubble can make a building look nice, yet when put to the test of fire, it goes up in smoke; likewise, flesh-dependent "Christian" living can make someone look "good," yet at the Judgment Seat of Christ, it will be destroyed as that which is of man (I Corinthians 3:11-15).

You may be trying to gain victory over sinful habits, you may be trying to be the right kind of spouse, parent, or Christian worker, but if it is just "you trying," flesh-dependence is profitless, counterproductive, and sinful. These are realities regarding the engine of the strength of the flesh.

A young married lady, who is involved with her husband in full-time Christian ministry, once wrote my wife and me after we had been at her church for meetings. She wrote, "We have believed that if we did everything we were supposed to (taught to) do then we would be doing what we were supposed to be doing. Unfortunately, the operative word here is *we* and not *Him*." She then asked for prayer for the Holy Spirit to produce in them lasting fruit. She understood the futility of the flesh.

Another college young lady who had been in church all her life said to me during a meeting, "I used to think that when it comes to the various matters of the Christian life, 'I can do this.' Now," she said, "I realize *I* can't." She realized that the form of godliness without the power for godliness is not godliness.

The evidences of the works of the flesh and the engine of the strength of the flesh reveal the sad experience of so many Christians—walking in the flesh.

## Walking in the Spirit

We will focus on this truth in greater detail in the following chapters, but our text does emphasize what it is to be walking in the Spirit. We will briefly note the text's emphasis.

### Evidences: Fruit of the Spirit (Galatians 5:22-23)

*But the fruit of the Spirit is love, joy, peace, longsuffering, gentleness, goodness, faith, meekness, temperance.* Notice it says *the fruit*, not "the fruits," *of the Spirit.* The singular indicates that when one is walking in the Spirit, all of these Christian graces evidence themselves. If you say, "I've got this one down, and this one and this one, but I still have a problem with this one and this one," you don't have any of them! It is not the fruit of you, but rather *the fruit of the Spirit.*

### Engine: Power of the Spirit

Both Galatians 5:16 and 25 challenge us to *walk in the Spirit.* Both times the definite article *the* is absent, therefore emphasizing the power or operation of the Spirit. Walk in the power of the Spirit is the command of verse 16 and the exhortation of verse 25. It is possible to *live* [be made alive] *in the Spirit* and yet not *walk in the Spirit,* or verse 25 would not exhort us as it plainly does. The engine for the Spirit-filled life is the power of the Spirit. An elderly lady once said to me during a meeting when I was preaching on the ministry of the Holy Spirit, "I've tried so hard to walk in the Spirit"—then with anguish she exclaimed, "but I can't do it!" I replied, "That's the whole point—it's not your power, but the Spirit's."

## EXCHANGE

Having investigated the explanations of each walk, how do you exchange the flesh-filled walk for the Spirit-filled walk? Again, we will return to this thought repeatedly in the following chapters, but our text does begin to point up the exchange. Both Galatians 5:16 and 25 say **walk in the Spirit.** How do you *walk in the Spirit?* Let's shorten the question for a moment. How do you walk? What is walking? Walking is simply reiterated steps. So what is walking in the Spirit? It is reiterated steps in the Spirit.

Let Colossians 2:6 explain: "As you have therefore received Christ Jesus the Lord . . ." How did you receive Him? By faith. Colossians 2:6 then teaches, " . . . so walk ye in Him." So how do you walk? By faith. Herein lies a revolutionary truth. Does not II Corinthians 5:7 say, "For we walk by faith"? Remember that faith is the simple choice to depend on the reality of the words of God. So walking in the Spirit is simply depending on the Spirit, one promise at a time. As you depend on the Spirit, He enables you according to the promise on which you are depending.

Now return to our initial question. How do you exchange the flesh-filled walk for the Spirit-filled walk? The answer is by one step of faith. This shocks many as they think it is a long upward struggle before they might enter "spiritual" living. One lady in a meeting said to me, in effect, "I used to think that it would be twenty or thirty years before I could be truly spiritual, but now I see I can be spiritual now by depending on the Spirit." She understood. You step from the pathway of the flesh-filled life to the pathway of the Spirit-filled life by a step of faith. The exchange is switching your dependence from self to the Spirit. You exchange flesh-dependence for the flesh-filled life to Spirit-dependence for the Spirit-filled life. It is one step of faith one direction, and, by the way, it is one step of unbelief back in the other direction. There is no mixture. We are either walking in the flesh, or we are walking in the Spirit. Experience reveals we often go back and forth.

However, the point is that you step into the Spirit-filled life. If it was a long struggle, new converts could not obey the command to *walk in the Spirit*. It is true that there is growth once you start walking in the Spirit (which some new Christians do without understanding all the principles involved). That is true spiritual growth. New and good acquired habits form good character as you depend on/walk in the Spirit, just as bad acquired habits formed bad character as you depended on/walked in the flesh. We are not saying that once you step into the Spirit-filled life, you "grow up" spiritually all at once. We are saying that it is only in the moment of faith that we can truly grow spiritually. This is why, as my father used to say, some Christians will think they lived for God for forty years, yet in God's record book, it will only be a year and a half! But as we believe, we access grace and grow spiritually. Certainly there is spiritual growth as the power of the Spirit changes you into the image of the Lord from glory to glory (II Corinthians 3:18). But let us not forget that though we grow in grace, it is only one step of faith to access the grace or Spirit-filled life!

## Conclusion

If you are defeated in certain areas of life, if you find yourself anemic as to effective service for God, if weakness prevails—let us remember the true nature of the case. Isaiah 59:1-2 boldly declares, "Behold, the Lord's hand is not shortened, that it cannot save, neither His ear heavy that it cannot hear: But your iniquities have separated between you and your God, and your sins have hid His face from you, that He will not hear." Will you ask the Spirit to search you, to test your thoughts, to see if there is any wicked way in you? Will you then confess it at once and look to the Holy Spirit to lead you into the way everlasting?

---

[1]J. C. Pollock, *The Keswick Story* (Chicago: Moody Press, 1964), p. 60.

[2]Steve Barabas, *So Great Salvation* (Westwood, N.J.: Fleming H. Revell Company, 1952), p. 164.

[3]Pollock, p. 61.

[4]Fritz Rienecker and Cleon L. Rogers, *Linguistic Key to the Greek New Testament* (Grand Rapids: Zondervan, 1980), p. 517.

[5]Ibid.

CHAPTER SIX

# THE MAGNA CARTA
# OF CHRISTIAN VICTORY

Endowment: The Promise of the Spirit
Enfeeblement: The Problem of Unbelief
**Entitlement: The Provision of Christ**
Enthronement: The Presentation and Practice of Surrender and Faith
Enablement: The Power of Living
Entrustment: The Purpose of Usefulness

Thus far, we have searched the treasures of our endowment: the promise of the Spirit. Yet we have discovered that which hinders us from accessing our inheritance, and thus enfeebles us: the problem of unbelief. Now let's resume our spiritual treasure hunt by focusing on our entitlement: the provision of Christ. What a glorious provision it is! To do this, first we will study the concept of "identification" with Christ. Ask the Spirit to make what could otherwise be an intellectual exercise a spiritual feast.

# ROMANS 6:1-14

"The Magna Carta Memorial at Runnymeade stands in a meadow southwest of London, England. King John approved historic Magna Carta on this site in 1215. The granite shaft inside the circular stone structure bears the inscription, 'To Commemorate Magna Carta—Symbol of Freedom Under Law.'"[1] Some have referred to Romans 6 as the Magna Carta of Christian victory. After five chapters which carefully instruct regarding the doctrine of justification, the Apostle Paul, under inspiration, provides a theological treatise on sanctification in chapters 6-8.

Sanctification involves a past (positional), present (practical or experimental), and future aspect. Positionally at justification the believer is set apart to God from sin. Yet practically this must be worked out this side of heaven. Ultimately this will be fully borne out when we see Christ for "we know that, when He shall appear, we shall be like Him; for we shall see Him as He is" (I John 3:2). How is sanctification to be worked out in the present? Is it automatic? Is it inevitable? Can it be hindered by unbelief? Can it be liberated by faith? Romans 6:1-14 provides the answers to these questions.

Romans 6:1 asks, "What shall we say then? Shall we continue in sin, that grace may abound?" The question here is a present tense subjunctive which gives the sense of "May we or should we be continuing in sin . . .?" The term *that* is the term *hina*, indicating a purpose clause. "Should we be continuing in sin in order that grace may abound?" The very question reveals that chapters 1-5 teach justification by faith alone without any human merit. This teaching is so clear that the Apostle knows some might think that justification is too free. Yet he does not go back and restate how one is justified. Rather, he begins to teach sanctification responsibility now that justification is settled. Verse 2 says, "God forbid. How shall we that are dead to sin, live any longer therein?" Paul indicates we are dealing with a knife-edge truth. Free salvation is a right conclusion; license to sin is a wrong conclusion. He emphasizes, in essence, "How shall we who died to sin [sin's claim and penalty] live any longer in it?" The purpose of justification is not license to sin, but victory over sin. New life, which is free by faith, looks forward to new living, which is also free by faith. Verses 3-14 back up the answer of verse two with solid proof.

Before we detail this proof, notice several identification phrases in this passage: "buried with Him" (v. 4), "crucified with Him" (v. 6), "dead [died] with Christ" (v. 8), and "live with Him" (v. 8). *With* is an identification word that is key to understanding this grand text. The implication is **identify with Christ to access His victory**. Yet how do you identify with Christ, practically speaking? Romans 6:1-14 reveals three elements of identification involving the intellect (understanding), the affections (agreement), and the volition (transfer of dependence).

## KNOW THE RIGHT FACTS (VERSES 3-10)

The first element of identification emphasizes you must get your facts straight! Verses 3-10 delineate three concepts you must know or understand. Three times the word *know* is used (vs. 3, 6, and 9), yet three different words provide a fine-tuned explanation of the facts.

## Concept 1: Death with Christ Accesses the Possibility of Christ's Life (vs. 3-5)

Verse 3 asks, "Know ye not" from *agnoeo*, meaning "not to know, ignorant."[2] Used in the present tense, the sense is "Are you not knowing?" or "Are you being ignorant of?" Then inspiration lays out a logical progression of a fact, a purpose, and a reason.

### Fact (verse 3)

"Know ye not, that so many of us as were baptized into Jesus Christ were baptized into His death?" Galatians 3:26-27 says, "For ye are all the children of God by faith in Christ Jesus. For as many of you as have been baptized into Christ . . . " When you believed in Christ, you were *baptized into Christ*. Since this is true, Romans 6:3 emphasizes if you were baptized into Christ at salvation, you *were baptized into His death*. So the fact at hand is **union with Christ in death**.

### Purpose (verse 4)

"Therefore we are buried with Him by baptism into death: that [*hina* means *in order that*] like as Christ was raised up from the dead by the glory of the Father, even so we also should walk in newness of life." Notice *should walk* is a subjunctive verb which is the mood of probability, indicating what might or should happen. This implies the action is not necessarily true at the present. The fulfillment of this purpose then is not automatic or inevitable, rather it is conditional. However, the point made is that there is a real purpose for our first fact: *that . . . we also should walk in newness of life*. This new life is Christ's life now in the believer. The purpose of union with Christ in death is **union with Christ in life.**

### Reason (verse 5)

"For [indicating the reason] if we have been planted together in the likeness of His death, we shall be also in the likeness of His resurrection." Notice *planted together*, or "united together", defines for us the "baptism" in this context. Therefore, the baptism of Romans 6 is referring to spiritual baptism, not physical baptism; although, physical baptism pictures spiritual baptism. Verse five clarifies that one identification of necessity leads to another identification. Missionary Ruth Paxson explains, "Co-crucifixion opens the door to co-resurrection."[3] Co-death with Christ opens the way for co-life with Christ. The fact is union with Christ in death. The purpose is union with Christ in life. The reason is **identification with Christ's death of necessity leads to identification with Christ's resurrection life.**

The logic of verses 3-5 supports the first concept we must know and understand: Death with Christ accesses the possibility of Christ's life.

## Concept 2: Death with Christ Cancels the Authority of Sin's Claim (vs. 6-8)

Verse 6 begins with the second word for *know* in this passage. "Knowing" from *ginosko* means "I know by experience" or "I discern with the implication of acquired knowledge."[4] The present tense indicates continually knowing (based on the experience of salvation). Again we see a logical sequence of a fact, a purpose, and a reason, this time with a reminder.

### Fact (verse 6a)

"Knowing this, that our old man is [aorist tense, therefore "was"] crucified with Him." The aorist tense emphasizes the fact of an action. The old man is your unregenerate spirit. Before salvation this old man was dead to God, but alive to sin. Ephesians 2:1 explains that this unregenerate spirit was "dead in trespasses and sins." Not annihilated or non-existant, for this old man is reveling *in trespasses and sins*. At salvation this old man, which was alive to sin, was crucified with Christ. The old man was then raised with Christ a "new man, which after God is created in righteousness and true holiness" (Ephesians 4:24). This new man is the regenerate spirit where the Spirit of the glorified Christ also dwells. I Corinthians 6:17 says, "But he that is joined unto the Lord is one spirit." What an amazing union! So the old man and the new man do not dwell together in the same body. Rather the old man became the new man which is now alive to God and dead to sin. Although the old man is now gone, the new man still lives in "the body of sin." But the fact is **your old man was crucified with Christ.**

## Purpose (verse 6b)

"That [*hina* in order that] the body of sin might be destroyed, that henceforth we should not serve sin." Notice that *might be destroyed* is a subjunctive verb indicating again probability as opposed to actuality. The action is conditional. *Destroyed* means "to render inoperative, to make inactive."[5] The idea is to cancel out or be cancelled. Perhaps a clarifying term would be "counteracted." We will expound on this concept in the next chapter. This does not mean we have no responsibility to "watch and pray." Rather, *the body of sin*, where the flesh tendency is downward, is now potentially in abeyance as the ruling power. Why is *the body of sin . . .* cancelled? The present tense infinitive [*that* is not *hina*] clarifies with "to no longer be being slaves to sin." As Evan Hopkins said, "Your old master, sin . . . may assert its power, but it has no authority."[6] Sin as a master has been cancelled. It lost its legal claim and penalty at the cross. As Charles Wesley exclaimed:

> He breaks the power of cancelled sin,
>   He sets the prisoner free;
> His blood can make the foulest clean,
>   His blood availed for me.

The fact is your old man was crucified with Christ. The purpose is **freedom from an old master.** Because the Spirit now lives in the new man, the body of sin can be counteracted and overcome. Formerly the soul (mind, affections, will) was sandwiched between two negative pressures: the old man and the body of sin. Now the soul is sandwiched between the new man and the body of sin. This is why James 1:8 warns against being "double minded," which is literally double-souled.

### Reason (verse 7)

"For he that is dead [has died] is freed from sin." The first verb is an aorist tense indicating the fact of an action. The second verb is a perfect tense indicating the fact of an action in the past with continuing results into the present. The essence is "For he who has died has been freed from sin." Therefore, the freed one is presently free from sin's claim of guiltiness and penalty of judgment. The fact is your old man was crucified with Christ. The purpose is freedom from an old master. The reason is **death obtained freedom from sin's claim and penalty.** "The wages of sin is death" (Romans 6:23). But the believer died in Christ. Therefore sin's claim is gone. Sin's penalty has been met in Christ!

### Reminder (verse 8)

"Now if we be dead [died] we Christ, we believe that we shall also live with Him." Death with Christ frees you from sin's legal bondage. Life with Christ frees you from sin's moral bondage. Verse 8 reminds us of our first concept: Death with Christ accesses life with Christ.

In review, the first concept teaches that death with Christ accesses the possibility of Christ's life. The second concept teaches that death with Christ cancels the authority of sin's claim. One of the best illustrations of these truths is the Emancipation Proclamation which President Abraham Lincoln declared during the Civil War. Legally, the slaves were set free from their masters. Their masters had no more claim on their lives. Some masters asserted their former power, but they had no legal right to do so because the slaves were set free as a matter of legal fact. This is the case with every true child of God. Legally we are set free from our old master, sin. Sin has no more legal claim on our lives. What blessed facts! Our identification with Christ emancipates us from sin's claim and penalty.

## Concept 3: Christ's Death to Sin Is a Once-for-All Event, and His Living to God Is a Continual State (vs. 9-10)

Another synonym for *know* introduces our third concept. Verse 9 uses "knowing" from *oida*, which "denotes 'I know' in the full absolute sense."[7] Here, *knowing* is in the perfect tense indicating "having known." This time, only a fact and a reason are given.

### Fact (verse 9)

"Knowing [having known] that Christ being raised [having been raised] from the dead dieth no more; death hath no more dominion over him." Death's dominion has been cancelled in Christ. Christ died, but He arose! The fact is **Christ conquered death.**

### Reason (verse 10)

"For in that He died, He died unto sin once [once-for-all]: but in that He liveth [is living], He liveth [is living] unto God." Christ died to sin's claim and penalty once for all, and He is living to God. The fact is Christ conquered death. The reason is two-fold: **First, Christ died to sin's claim and penalty once for all (an event); second, Christ is living to God forevermore (a continual state).**

In review, the first concept teaches death with Christ accesses the possibility of Christ's life. The second concept teaches death with Christ cancels the authority of sin's claim. The third concept teaches Christ's death to sin is a once-for-all event, and His living to God is a continual state. These are the facts with which every child of God must identify. We have died with Christ that we might continually live with Christ. Identify with this union with a glorious Savior! The first element of identification involves the intellect (understanding): Know the right facts. The second element of identification involves the affections (agreement). True identification demands a heartfelt "I agree" with the facts!

## COME TO THE RIGHT CONCLUSION (VERSE 11)

"Likewise reckon ye also yourselves to be dead indeed unto sin, but alive unto God through Jesus Christ our Lord." The key word is the verb *reckon*. This same verb is translated in Romans 3:28 as "conclude." Based on the right facts, the emphasis, therefore, is to come to the right conclusion. *Reckon* here is a present tense imperative. Therefore, we have a responsibility, as a matter of obedience, to continually do this. The command is followed by a present tense infinitive and participle. The essence is "conclude yourselves to being dead in very truth to sin (as a master), but being alive to God (as a new Master) through [in dependence on] Christ Jesus our Lord." Ruth Paxson beautifully said, "To be 'in Christ' is to be what Christ is. Christ, the Head of the body, and the Christian who is a member of that body have one life."[8] Handley Moule theologically stated, "What He did and does, as such, was done and is done by those who are 'in Him' as their Head."[9] Moule also wrote, "The new creation is such that the member and Head are 'One Spirit'          (I Corinthians vi. 17), and the member derives from the Head spiritual force and faculty profoundly altering the conditions and possibilities of deliverance from sin's 'reign' (ver. 12), and so of holy obedience."[10] This is God's conclusion. We are to reckon according to God's reckoning. We are commanded to come to the conclusion that God concludes. **Conclude yourself to being dead to sin as a master and being alive to God as a new Master.** This flows from the facts of your identification with Christ in His crucifixion, death, burial, and resurrection life. If you do not identify with that union with Christ, you miss out on many of the blessings of that union. Death to sin is only realized through our union with Christ. This is not a mere activity of the mind but, beyond that, a heartfelt embracing of these facts involving the affections, by coming to the right conclusion.

The first element of identification involves the understanding: Know the right facts. The second element of identification involves agreement: Come to the right conclusion. Now the third element of identification involves a surrendered transfer of dependence. This activates the volition or will.

## MAKE THE RIGHT CHOICES (VERSES 12-13)

Verses 12-13 give three imperatives in succession. Since verse 12 begins with "Let not . . . " indicates this is the first appeal to the will directly. The first two commands are negative, and the final command is positive.

## Commands of Cessation (Verses 12-13a)

Both commands, "Let not sin . . . reign" and "Neither yield," are present tense imperatives with a Greek negative. The grammar "demands the cessation of an action already in progress." In contrast, "the aorist subjunctive in a prohibition is an exhortation against doing a thing not yet begun."[11]

### Cease Allowing Sin's Rule (verse 12)

"Let not sin therefore reign in your mortal body, that ye should obey it in the lusts thereof." As already noted, the force of the present tense command with the negative is "Stop letting sin reign!" The term *in* applied to *your mortal body* implies sin's presence as a defeated master still seeking to usurp from God the throne of leadership. This explains the battle in our experience. Moule explains that *your mortal body* is the "special field for the action of sin."[12] The last phrase is a present tense infinitive, indicating "to be obeying it in its lusts."

Again, quoting Evan Hopkins, "Your old master, sin . . . may assert its power, but it has no authority."[13] The force of the command, *Stop let-*

*ting sin reign*, implies it is possible as a believer to *let* sin rule in one's life. This, however, does not have to be allowed. Since sin is no longer our master, we must stop allowing sin to rule as if it were.

### Cease Aiding Sin's Agenda (verse 13a)

"Neither yield [translated as "present" in Romans 12:1] ye your members as instruments [or "weapons"] of unrighteousness unto sin." Again the force of the present tense command with the negative is "Stop presenting your members as weapons of unrighteousness to sin." In other words, "Stop aiding sin as an old master by surrendering your members *to* it to be used as weapons of unrighteousness."

During the time of the Emancipation Proclamation, there were, to my understanding, situations where slaves were kept in bondage through ignorance. These slaves legally were set free, but they did not know the right facts (the Emancipation Proclamation). Therefore, they made wrong conclusions (slavery). Consequently, they submitted to cancelled masters. Does this not illustrate many of God's people today? Though former bond slaves to sin, believers are legally set free in Christ. Yet many do not really know the right facts. Therefore, they make wrong conclusions. Consequently, they submit to a cancelled master. What an unnecessary tragedy! But this bondage to sin need not continue.

# Command of Activation (verse 13b)

"But yield [present] yourselves unto God, as those that are alive [as being restored to life] from the dead, and your members as instruments [weapons] of righteousness unto God." From the center (*present yourselves . . . to God*) to the circumference (*present . . . your members . . . to God*) we must *yield . . . to God*. The double emphasis *yield . . . to God* articulates the concept of surrender which, properly understood, is an expression of faith. When you surrender all, from center to circumference, *to God*, you are transferring your dependence *to God*. The expression of verse 13 marks a clear transfer of dependence. On the one hand, do not hand over your members into the hand of sin as weapons to use for unrighteousness. On the other hand, do hand over your members into the hand of God as weapons to use for righteousness. The *yield* of the positive command interestingly switches to the aorist tense. The grammatical change indicates that this presentation is to be a directional turning point. The grammar "calls for an immediate decisive new action as a break from the past."[14] This is not to say there is no more responsibility, as Romans 6:16 uses *yield* in the present tense, indicating "keep yielding." The first yielding is, however, a directional turning point and, therefore, an event. Romans 12:1 incorporates this same progression from the fact of an action to continuous action as we will see more fully in a later chapter.

Identify with Christ to access His victory. How do we "identify"? Know the right facts. Come to the right conclusion. Make the right choices. When we understand, agree, and depend, verse 14 grants a glorious promise: "For sin shall not have dominion over you: for ye are not under the law, but under grace." When you transfer your dependence all to God, you access *grace*, which is Spirit-enabling. Romans 5:2 states, "We have access by faith into this grace wherein we stand." Your new Master is God, and when He is surrendered to, which implies He is depended on, He enables you. He, by His Spirit, empowers you to victory over sin!

Romans 7:1–4 teach the same emphasis as Romans 6 but through a picture. Verse 1 gives a binding regulation: "the law hath dominion over a man as long as he liveth." Verses 2 and 3 give by way of example a physical illustration: "For the woman which hath an husband is bound by the law to her husband so long as he liveth; but if the husband be dead, she is loosed from the law of her husband. So then if, while her husband liveth, she be married to another man, she shall be called an adulteress: but if her husband be dead, she is free from that law; so that she is no adulteress, though she be married to another man." Then the next verse brings home the spiritual application: "Wherefore, my brethren, ye also are become dead to the law by the body of Christ; that ye should be married to another, even to Him who is raised from the dead, that we should bring forth fruit unto God." Since this verse speaks of being *married to another*, it implies that before you were saved, you were married to sin. Your unregenerate spirit was in union with the sin principle within the body and soul levels of your being. But when you got saved, you died with Christ unto sin (Romans 7:4a; 6:6a, 7, 11). Therefore, the marriage with sin is over! Also you were raised with Christ unto God (cf. Romans 6:5; Ephesians 2:6). Now you are married to Christ. Verse 4 says *that ye should be married to another, even to Him who is raised from the dead*. Your regenerated spirit is now in union with the Holy Spirit. I Corinthians 6:17 says, "He that is joined unto the Lord is one spirit." Now based on that union with Christ, it is possible to *bring forth fruit unto God*. Walking in the Spirit and, thus, the fruit of the Spirit is based on a union with the Spirit.

Simply put, before you were saved you were dead to God and alive to sin. You were separated from God and joined to, or in union with, or "married" to sin. Through salvation you are now dead to sin and alive to God. You are separated from sin and joined to, or united with, or "married" to God. When you died to sin the "marriage" with sin was legally over. When you were raised to new life the "marriage" with Christ was begun. Sin did not die to you; you died to sin. The union between your inner man and the sin principle was broken. A new union of your new inner man and the Holy Spirit was begun. So the old man (unregenerated spirit) and the new man (regenerated spirit) are not in the same body.

The old man, through death and resurrection with Christ, became the new man who lives in the body of sin. The sin principle, or flesh, still resides in your body, but now you are no longer in union with it. Rather you are in union with the Spirit. Thus the battle is not between the old man and the new man. The battle is between the flesh or sin principle and the Spirit. When a regenerated person yields to sin, it is like a married person yielding to adultery. But when a regenerated person yields to the Spirit, it is nothing for the power of the Holy Spirit to overcome the power of the flesh. The flesh and the Spirit are by no means equal entities. So depend on the Spirit whom you are united with in the inner man, and He will counteract and overcome the flesh!

After discussing the frustration of attempts to Christian victory without reliance on the Spirit in Romans 7:7–25 where the Spirit is not mentioned once, inspiration explains in Romans 8 that the victory of Christ (7:25) is accessed through dependence on the Spirit (Romans 8:2). Two-thirds of all the mentions of the Spirit in the Book of Romans are in Romans 8. Romans 8:2 speaks of "the law of the Spirit" as much greater than "the law of sin." In other words, as the single-souled believer yields to the leadership and enablement of the Spirit in the new man, the Spirit counteracts and overcomes the body of sin. Flesh-dependence is depending on the body of sin for victory. This is destined not to work. However, the one who depends on the Spirit accesses the life of Christ, therefore, the victory of Christ, and freedom from sin's reign. This is part of the believer's glorious inheritance! Romans 6:14 alludes to this but states, in essence, that the God-dependent believer is *not under the law* of sin, but under the law of *grace*, or the Spirit. The law of grace frees you from the law of sin. This is Christian liberty: not the license to do as you please (cf. vs. 1), but the freedom or enablement to do right and, thus, *sin shall not have dominion over you*. The law of sin brings death, but the law of the Spirit brings life (cf. Rom. 8:2, 6). This is the Magna Carta of Christian victory: "freedom under law"—the law of grace, which is the law of the Spirit.

Think of it. The old man died with Christ and was raised with Christ a new man. That new man is "created in righteousness and true holiness" (Ephesians 4:24). Not only that, the Spirit of the triumphant, glorified Christ moved into the regenerated spirit. Before salvation, the soul (mind, affections, will) was pressured to do evil from both the old man and the body of sin. Now the soul is pressured to do right by the Spirit in the new man and pressured to do wrong by the flesh (body of sin and even soulish level of mere intellect alone, emotions alone or mere willpower). Notice the battle is not between the old man and your new man. The old man is gone! The battle is between the Spirit and the flesh. The adversaries are not equal (black dog/white dog). If you will but yield to the Spirit, He will easily counteract and overcome the flesh. Ask the Spirit to take each temptation to the cross for fresh application of Christ's finished victory. Resurrection life necessarily follows. Spirit-dependence accesses Spirit-dominance. This is glorious spiritual victory! (Note: For graphical illustrations and further explanations of the truth of this chapter, see Appendix H.)

[1]*The World Book Encyclopedia*, 1975 ed., s.v. "Magna Carta."

[2]William F. Arndt and F. Wilbur Gingrich, *A Greek-English Lexicon of the New Testament* (Chicago: University of Chicago Press, 1979), p. 11.

[3]Ruth Paxson, *Rivers of Living Water* (Chicago: Moody Press, 1930), p. 59.

[4]Stewart Custer, *A Treasury of New Testament Synonyms* (Greenville, S.C.: Bob Jones University, 1975), p. 112.

[5]Fritz Rienecker and Cleon L. Rogers, *Linguistic Key to the Greek New Testament* (Grand Rapids: Zondervan, 1980), p. 36.

[6]Steven Barabas, *So Great Salvation* (Westwood, N.J.: Fleming H. Revell Company, 1952), p. 90.

[7]Custer, p. 112.

[8]Paxson, p. 62.

[9]Handley G. C. Moule, *Studies in Romans* (Grand Rapids: Kregel Publications, reprint 1977), p. 116.

[10]Ibid., p. 268.

[11]Kenneth S. Wuest, revised by Donald L. Wise, *The Practical Use of the Greek New Testament* (Chicago: Moody Press, 1946, 1982), p. 42. Those with theological views which favor no real possibility of the carnal man, and tend to fatalism, seek to challenge these grammatical implications. But to do so, years of Greek grammar have to be condemned. The theological prejudice as a motivation for this change certainly seems suspect.

[12]Moule, p. 117.

[13]Barabas, p. 90.

[14]Rienecker and Rogers, p. 362.

CHAPTER SEVEN

# THE REALITY
# OF THE SPIRIT-FILLED LIFE

Endowment: The Promise of the Spirit
Enfeeblement: The Problem of Unbelief
**Entitlement: The Provision of Christ**
Enthronement: The Presentation and Practice of Surrender and Faith
Enablement: The Power of Living
Entrustment: The Purpose of Usefulness

In addition to Romans 6, Galatians 2:20 encapsulates
our marvelous provision in Christ and translates it into
practical living. Will you pray that the Spirit of wisdom and revelation will reveal to you not just the facts
of His Word, but the spiritual realities which relate to
those facts? These spiritual realities can make a familiar text emanate with fragrant freshness. When
embraced by faith, the truth of Galatians 2:20 can
make the wilderness of one's life a fruitful field.

# GALATIANS 2:20

In the early years of Jonathan and Rosalind Goforth's ministry in China, Rosalind overheard a conversation of Chinese workers. Unaware that she was on the other side of a thin wall, they were talking about Rosalind. Admitting she obviously loved them and was a zealous worker, they begrudged her impatience and quick temper. Then one said, "If she only would live more as she preaches!" This cut deeply in Rosalind's heart. At first angered, she knew that it was far too true. Grieved, she fled to her room knowing her life lacked usefulness if she could not even live Christ before the Chinese workers.[1]

A little later in their ministry at Changte, they had a house built. To dispel vicious rumors about the "foreign devils," they allowed their house to be an open house for weeks so the curious Chinese could investigate. Once when a small group of Chinese women entered, one exclaimed loudly, "Oh, these foreign devils, the smell of their home is unbearable!" Rosalind tells the story of her response in her autobiography Climbing:

> My temper rose in a flash and, turning on her with anger, I said, "How dare you speak like that? Leave the room!" The crowd, sensing a "storm," fled. I heard one say, "That foreign devil woman has a temper just like ours!"
>
> Now, I had not noticed that the door of my husband's study was ajar, nor did I know that he was inside, until, as the last woman disappeared, the door opened and he came forward, looking solemn and stern. "Rose, how could you so forget yourself?" he said. "Do you realize that just one such incident may undo months of self-sacrificing, loving service?"
>
> "But Jonathan," I returned, "you don't know how she—"

But he interrupted, "Yes, I do; I heard all. You certainly had reason to be annoyed; but were you *justified*,
with all that is hanging in the balance and God's grace
sufficient to keep you patient?"

As he turned to re-enter his study, he said, "*All* I
can say is *I am disappointed!*"

Oh, how that last word cut me! I deserved it, yes,
but, oh, I did so want to reach up to the high ideals he
had. A tempestuous time followed alone in our inner
room with my Lord.[2]

Many would desire to reach these "high ideals." But how? How do
you obey? Is it sheer grit and duty?

Later, when on furlough in Canada, a friend took Rosalind to the
Nigara-on-the-Lake Bible Conference. Charles G. Trumbull spoke at a
session which Rosalind attended. She was seated in the very front of the
auditorium. God used this time as the beginning of what became the
major turning point in Rosalind's spiritual walk with the Lord. She
humbly tells the story:

[Trumbull] drew simply but vividly, first a picture
of an ordinary, all too common Christian life. If he had
drawn the picture from my everyday life experience, he
could not have given it other than he did—sometimes
on the mountaintop with visions of God and His
mighty power; then the sagging, the dimming of
vision, coldness, discouragement, even definite disobedience and a time of downgrade experience. Again
through some sorrow or trial, there would come a
return and seeking of the Lord, with again the higher
Christian experiences. In a word, the speaker pictured
an up-and-down life of intermingled victory and
defeat.

The speaker then asked all who truly sought for
God's highest and best, yet who knew the picture he
had drawn was true of their Christian life and experience, to hold up their hands. Being in the front seat
and realizing many behind knew who I was, and that
they thought of me as a "good missionary," I kept my
hand down. It was too humiliating to acknowledge *that*
picture was representing me! But the Spirit of God
strove with me. "If you keep your hand down, you are a
hypocrite! If you truly want God's best, humble yourself." So up went my hand.

Then the speaker drew another picture: it was the Christian life as God had not only *planned* it for His children but had made abundant provision for their living it. He described it as a life of victory, not defeat, of peace and trust, not struggle and worry. All through his address, I kept thinking, "Yes, it's wonderful, but I've tried so often and failed; I doubt if it is possible." Then the speaker ended by urging us to go over the texts listed on a slip of paper to be given free at the close of the meeting. He emphasized the importance of standing on God's Word.

The following morning I rose early, as soon as it was light enough to see. On my knees, I read from the list I have mentioned all the texts given. But before I had gone halfway down the list, I saw clearly that God's Word taught, beyond the shadow of a doubt, that *the overcoming, victorious life in Christ is the normal life God has planned for His children.* In the two days that followed clearer light came, with a dawning hope that this life might be possible for me. . . .

The day after reaching home, I picked up the little booklet, *The Life That Wins,* and, going to my son's bedside, I asked him to allow me to read the booklet aloud, as it was the personal testimony of Charles G. Trumbull, editor of the *Sunday School Times,* the man who had been a great blessing to me at the conference.

As I began to read, quite a number gathered around, listening with deep interest. I read on till I came to the words: "At last I realized that Jesus Christ was actually and literally within me." I stopped amazed. The sun seemed suddenly to come from under a cloud and flood my soul with light! How blind I had been! I saw as in a flash the secret of victory. *It was just Jesus Christ Himself!*[3]

The sufficiency for victory is Christ in you. This reality "God in man" ought to make a radical difference! The impact of Rosalind's depending on the indwelling Christ to live through her is seen in the following account:

Many months (I forget just how long) had passed after our return to our Changte station when one evening one of our leading evangelists came in just when my husband was about to start for the street chapel. The evangelist showed plainly he wished to speak to my husband alone, so I left the room. When he had gone, I returned to find my husband standing by the table with a strange look on his face. He seemed deeply moved, yet glad. I exclaimed, "Whatever is the matter?"

"Rose," he said, "you could never guess what he came for. He came as a deputation from the other evangelists and workers, yes, and servants, too, to ask what is the secret of the change in you. Before you went home, none of the servants wanted to serve you, but now they all want to be your servants."[4]

What a miraculous transformation! Rosalind was experiencing by faith the reality of Spirit-filled living.

Galatians 2:20 says, "I am crucified with Christ: nevertheless I live; yet not I, but Christ liveth in me: and the life which I now live in the flesh I live by the faith of the Son of God, who loved me, and gave Himself for me."

This grand verse teaches us that **the reality of the Spirit-filled life is the Spirit of Christ living the life of Christ through the believer in Christ.** Please do not read this merely as pious-sounding rhetoric. True spiritual victory over sin and power in service is the Spirit of the glorified Christ living the divine victorious, triumphant life of Christ through your vessel of clay! How can the Spirit of Christ live the life of Christ through the believer in Christ? Galatians 2:20 teaches us three truths which reveal this marvelous reality.

## THE AUTHORITY FOR THE SPIRIT-FILLED LIFE IS THE CROSS

The grounds, basis, provision, all that is truly necessary for a life of holiness (to be what we ought to be) and service (to do what we ought to do) is the finished work of Jesus Christ on the cross. The Apostle Paul under inspiration testifies what the reality is for every true believer, "I am crucified with Christ." We often picture Christ on the cross, but have you ever pictured yourself there *with* Him? Yet only Christ died for sins. How can we be *crucified with Christ?* It is in the sense of dying unto sin. It is the Romans 6 concept of being dead to sin. Co-crucifixion means we are dead to sin's claim. Sin may assert its power, but it no longer has any authority. We have a new Master. What an amazing identification! Ephesians 2:5 also proclaims that we are made alive "with Christ."

When we consider the finished work of Christ, certain promises relating to salvation immediately come to mind. The Scripture promises that when one depends on Christ to save him from sin and hell, his sins are forgiven (Acts 10:43), the righteousness of Christ is credited to his account (Romans 10:4), and he is given eternal life (John 6:47). These are glorious promises! However, so much more is actually provided through the shed blood of Christ on the cross.

Just as the authority for our justification freeing us from the penalty of sin is the cross, so the authority for our sanctification emancipating us from the power of sin right now is also the finished work of Christ on the cross. Galatians 1:3b-4 says, "Our Lord Jesus Christ, who gave Himself for our sins, **that He might deliver us from this present evil world.**" When we read *who gave Himself for our sins*, we often conclude "for our salvation," and rightly so. However, this verse teaches us that the cross is also so *that He might deliver us from this* **present** *evil world.* No wonder I Corinthians 1:30 states: "Christ Jesus . . . is made unto us . . . sanctification." Not only is Christ our redemption, He is our sanctification. As the provision of all that is necessary for our salvation to free us from the penalty of sin is the cross, so in the cross there is the provision of all that is necessary for our sanctification to free us from the power of sin right now!

Duncan Campbell of the Lewis Awakening, in his book *The Power and Price of Revival*, records, "I want to bear testimony that it was the realization of this glorious truth that revolutionized my life and my ministry. . . . After spending seventeen years in a barren wilderness, baffled and frustrated in Christian work and witness, I suddenly came to realize that God had made provision for clean hands and a pure heart. And on my face in my own study at five o'clock in the morning I came to know the recovering power of the blood of Christ."[5]

*God had made provision*, and God has for you, too. Can you relate with being, perhaps for years, *baffled and frustrated in Christian work and witness*? By spiritual apprehension you, too, can come *to know the recovering power of the blood of Christ*. It is no accident that this realization came to Duncan Campbell with impact before his usefulness in the Lewis Awakening.

The authority for the Spirit-filled life (of holiness and service) is the cross. May we spiritually apprehend this foundational truth. What then is the nature of this victory? The second truth of our text unfolds this vital point.

## THE AGENT OF THE SPIRIT-FILLED LIFE
## IS THE SPIRIT

It seems like this should go without saying, yet this is often the very truth people miss. People try to live "the Spirit-filled" life in their own power. You may say, "The Spirit-filled life is the answer so I am going to live the Spirit-filled life." But you can't. You are not the agent; the

Spirit is. After testifying *I am crucified with Christ*, Galatians 2:20 further declares *nevertheless I live; yet not I, but Christ liveth in me*. Repudiating the *I myself* life of Romans 7, the apostle, under inspiration, speaks of the *not I, but Christ* life. Acts 2:33 explains that when Christ was exalted to the right hand of the Father, He "received of the Father the promise of the Holy Spirit" and sent the Spirit. Therefore, when the text says *Christ lives in me*, we know it is referring to the Spirit of the glorified Christ. Not just Christ in His earthly ministry, but Christ who finished His work and was exalted to the right hand of power. It is the Spirit of the glorified Christ in power who now lives in us. What a powerful connnection! As the authority of the Spirit-filled life is the cross, so the agent of the Spirit-filled life is the Spirit. Notice two facts regarding this truth which are intrinsically connected.

## A Life: The Life of Christ

Galatians 2:20 literally speaks of the life of Christ in the believer. Duncan Campbell said, "What we call a presence, in reality is a life."[6] The Scripture explains *Christ lives in me*. It is not just that He takes up residence there because the believer's body is the temple of the Holy Spirit, He *lives* there! In other words, Christ lives through me—through my spirit, soul, and body.

Consider the literalness of this truth in Philippians 1:21, "For to me to live is Christ." It does not say, "For to me to live is to try to be like Christ." That reveals flesh-dependence, and God does not accept the strength of the flesh. It does not say, "For me to live is to attempt Christ-likeness." Again, that is flesh-dependence. The flesh cannot be Christ-like. "The flesh profiteth nothing" (John 6:63). It says, "For to me to live is Christ." The impact is "For to me to live is Christ living through me." Duncan Campbell explains, "It is not my struggling, not my trying, but Jesus in me expressing Himself through me. . . . Let us discover the secret that all the resources of the Christian life are in Christ Himself, as He lives in me, by His Spirit."[7] The life is not the *I myself* life but *Christ's life* through your spirit, soul, and body. As new life in Christ is Christ's life in you, so new living in Christ is Christ living in you. This is simply the manifestation of "Christ in you, the hope of glory" (Colossians 1:27). True Christ-likeness is Christ's likeness. It is Him in me. What a miraculous union. The Christ-life is Christ's life in me.

How can *I live; yet not I, but Christ*? Consider, by way of analogy, the reality of inspiration. Who really wrote the Bible? II Peter 1:21 explains that "holy men of God spake as they were moved by the Holy Spirit." The Holy Spirit is the author, yet He used forty human authors. Just as the Holy Spirit authored the Scripture through forty penmen using their personalities, their faculties, and their vocabularies, and yet it is the Word of God, likewise the Spirit can live divine life through your faculties, your mind, and your body, yet it is Christ's life. Though the Spirit authored Scripture through men, they were not robots. He wrote through their vocabularies and so forth. Likewise, when the Spirit lives through believers, we are not robots. All of us do not look alike. Yet there is a similar look. My father used to say, "Spirit-filled people are attracted to each other, and the attraction is Christ." This directs us to a second fact for consideration.

## A Law: The Law of the Spirit

Romans 8:2 connects the law of the Spirit to the life of Christ by stating, "For the law of the Spirit of life in Christ Jesus hath made me free from the law of sin and death." Notice what this verse does not say. It does not say that the law of the Spirit of life in Christ Jesus eradicates my sin nature. Any honest person knows well that he still has a sin nature. It does not say that the law of the Spirit of life in Christ Jesus means that there is no more tendency to sin. Even the aged saint who has walked with God for decades still has the tendency to sin.

What does this text say? It says, "For the law of the Spirit of life in Christ Jesus **hath made me free** from the law of sin and death." It does not mean there is no more law of sin and death. It plainly teaches *in Christ* we are made *free from the law of sin and death.* This is the principle of counteraction. One law counteracts and overcomes another law.

For example, physically we know of the law of gravity. There is a constant tendency downward toward planet Earth. However, it is possible for another law to counteract the law of gravity. Consider, in simple terms, the law of hot air rising. Hot air balloons apply this law to overcome the law of gravity. When a hot air balloon soars upward seemingly without effort, it appears that there is no more law of gravity. Yet we know that the law of gravity is still in place. It is simply being counteracted.

Suppose you were to step into the basket of a hot air balloon for a ride. When the balloon soars skyward, you do as well because you are in the basket. The law of hot air rising would take you up because you are in the hot air balloon. After a long ride, you might think that you are no longer affected by the law of gravity and step out of the basket. Immediately you would experience the tendency downward of the law of gravity. So what is the key? Stay in the basket! Keep depending on the basket. Keep abiding in the basket. For every moment that you are depending on the basket, not just some or most, the law of hot air rising counteracts and overcomes the law of gravity.

Likewise, spiritually we know of the law of sin and death. The law of sin can be likened to the law of gravity being the constant tendency downward to sin. However, the law of the Spirit can be likened to the law of hot air rising as the ability to counteract and overcome the law of sin. The law of sin is still there but can be overcome by the law of the Spirit. The basket can be likened to Christ.

When you abide in Christ by depending on Christ's life, the law of the Spirit counteracts and overcomes the law of sin. This is true power for victory. More than likely, since the time of your salvation there have been moments when in desperation you looked to Christ, and the Spirit worked. But often because we do not understand the spiritual dynamics involved soon we are "out of the basket," and defeated again. This intermittent victory is frustrating. But when you understand the spiritual dynamics involved, and you consciously depend on Christ and keep depending on Christ, you will experience more victory than perhaps you have previously ever known. After experiencing this new victory, you may think that you no longer have any tendency to sin. In doing so, you just "stepped out of the basket." The higher you soar, the farther you have to fall. So what is the key? Stay in the basket! Keep depending on Christ. Keep abiding in Christ. For every moment you are depending on Christ, not just some or most, the law of the Spirit counteracts and overcomes the law of sin. It takes only one moment of lack of dependence on Christ to be reminded of the law of sin. But as you abide in Christ, the law of the Spirit frees you from the law of sin. What a remarkable reality!

My home church in Ann Arbor, Michigan, surprised my wife and me by arranging a hot air balloon ride. Truly you step into the basket with one big giant step. When they unclipped the rope, immediately we soared 100 feet into the air and continued upwards. Truly the power was not your own. Also, it was a definite choice to stay in the basket. In fact, if I would have leaned out too far, I would have fallen out. However, to choose to stay in the basket was an easy choice!

The law of sin means that in the *I myself* life, I am able to sin. The law of the Spirit means that in the *not I, but Christ* life, I am able not to sin. In light of this truth, what is the nature of this reality? Understanding God-dependence for Spirit-enabling, what is the nature of the enabling? Is it the Spirit *helping* me to do right? If you mean His strength plus my strength, no. But if you mean His strength through me, yes. Beyond that, is the Spirit enabling my flesh to do right? We might be tempted to answer yes. But the flesh profits nothing (John 6:63). In our flesh dwells no good thing (Romans 7:18). The flesh cannot ever do right. The flesh never gets better. It can only get worse. The reality needed is the Spirit of Christ living the life of Christ through me as the believer in Christ.

This victory is not the Spirit working *to* victory, but *from* victory. Jesus Christ already provided the victory. "It is finished!" (John 19:30). From that platform, the Spirit manifests that victory through us. "But thanks be to God, which giveth us the victory through our Lord Jesus Christ" (I Corinthians 15:57). It does not say "the victories," but "the victory" that has already been won at the cross! This principle of counteraction is not a sinless perfection teaching for we are prone to "get out of the basket." However, when we "stay in the basket," we access the perfection of Jesus Christ.

By way of review, in the first truth we saw that the authority for the Spirit-filled life is the cross. In the second truth we saw that the agent of the Spirit-filled life is the Spirit. In the former, the provision for holiness and service is the finished work of Christ. In the latter, the power for holiness and service is the Spirit. The first reality reveals the work of Christ *for* us. The second reality reveals the work of the Spirit *in* us and *through* us. In the former, we see Christ, our Sanctification. In the latter, we see the Spirit, our Sanctifier.

How then does this become a personal experiential reality in our lives? The third truth reveals the responsibility God has given man. Through divine initiation, the Spirit regularly stirs God's children to take their responsibility.

## THE ACCESS TO THE SPIRIT-FILLED LIFE IS OUR FAITH

Galatians 2:20 adds, *and the life which I now live* [the *not I, but Christ* life] *in the flesh* [here meaning "in the mortal body"] *I live by the faith of the Son of God, who loved me, and gave Himself for me.*" Grammatically we have here an objective genitive, indicating that Christ is not the subject of faith but the object of faith. The issue is our *faith in the Son of God.* Since there is no preposition in the original language, we must derive it from the context. Galatians 2:16 has two cases just like this. In between them is the phrase "even we have believed *in* Jesus Christ," which does include the preposition in the original language. This lets us know the sense of the text. Christ clearly is the object of faith. Man is responsible to choose to depend on Christ.

The object of faith is "the word [*rhema*] of God," according to Romans 10:17. The *rhema* is a specific statement of truth within the *Logos* of God. How then can Galatians 2:20 and other contexts say that the object of faith is *the Son of God?* What is Jesus called in John 1? "The Word." There is a mystery of oneness between the inscribed Word and the incarnate Word. So when you depend on the living words of God, you are depending on the Living Word of God.

This *not I, but Christ* life is accessed through faith. As salvation is a gift received by grace through faith (Ephesians 2:8-9), so likewise the Spirit-filled life is a gift received by grace through faith. Romans 5:2

says, "By whom [Jesus] also we have access by faith into this grace wherein we stand." Although the Spirit moves into us at salvation, the Spirit-filled life of grace is not automatic. It must be accessed by faith. "Being justified by faith" (Romans 5:1) gives us a new standing in grace so that we *have access by faith into this grace wherein we stand* (Romans 5:2). As we choose to depend on the reality of the words of God (faith), we access grace (Spirit-enabling) which is the Spirit-filled life. This is not self-will; it is a cooperating will. The Spirit uses the faculties of our minds and bodies as we depend on His leadership and life. He lives Christ's life through our personalities as we cooperate with Him by faith. This is not receiving something you do not already have as a child of God, as some "second blessing" theologies teach. This is accessing the victory of Christ which was made yours at salvation.

Galatians 2:20 is a *rhema!* Depend on it. *Christ lives in me.* You may ask, "Why, then, do I so often fail?" You must "stay in the basket." Christ actually and literally lives in me and will manifest His personality through mine as I stop trying in the *I myself* life and trust Him for the *not I, but Christ* life. What a difference it would make if we lived in conscious dependence on the life of Christ. When tempted to argue in the home, consciously rest in Christ. He does not argue. When tempted to gripe and complain, depend on Christ. He does not gripe and complain. When prompted to witness, you may think, "I can't." But in reality we are not talking about you but Him—He can! What a difference it would make if Christians allowed Christ to live through them! He does not watch sensual media. He does not choose the wicked site on the Internet. He does not listen to worldly music. He forgives. He is not emotionally unstable. And His life is your life by faith. Colossians 3:4 speaks of "Christ, who is our life." O to always depend on Him!

Let's consider the *rhema* of Galatians 5:16, "Walk in the Spirit, and ye shall not fulfill the lusts of the flesh." When I noticed that verse while in Bible college, I thought, "What a promise! You will *not fulfill the lust of the flesh.*" Then I wondered, "What does it meant to *walk in the Spirit?*" Well, just for a moment let's shorten the question. What does it mean to walk? Walking is reiterated steps. So what is walking in the Spirit? It is reiterated steps in the Spirit. Colossians 2:6 says, "As ye have therefore received Christ Jesus the Lord, so walk ye in Him." How did you *receive* Christ? By grace through faith. How then do you *walk* in Christ? By grace through faith. As you were "born of the Spirit" (John 3:8) by depending on Christ (John 3:16), so you *walk in the Spirit* by depending on Christ.

Perhaps we should note the significance between *receiving* and *walking* in Colossians 2:6. In salvation, you receive Christ. In the Spirit-filled life, you walk in Christ. In other words, in salvation you depend on Christ for what you *receive* (forgiveness of sins, credited righteousness, eternal life); in the Spirit-filled life, you depend on Christ for what you *do*. The former is grace *to* you; the latter is grace *through* you. The former is for a new *standing*; the latter is for a new *walking*. The former is for a new *position*; the latter is for a new *practice*.

In the new standing you receive, there is no movement on your part. It is faith for what you receive. In the walking, there is movement on your part. It is faith for what you do. Therefore in the Spirit-filled life, if you do not tie the dependence to the *step* of the walk, it is not faith but rather acknowledgement. You must take up your bed and walk, as it were, or you will not receive the miraculous enabling to do so. In the Spirit-filled life, the faith must be tied to the step in thought, word, or deed to know the enabling of the Christ-life. In other words, you do not have God-dependence for the step of obedience without taking the step.

For example, consider an *action* step like witnessing. You may say that you believe God can bless witnessing. However, if you do not go up to someone and open your mouth in God-dependence to witness (step of faith), you do not believe; you only acknowledge. Faith is not waiting for a "zap" of power. It is when you trust to obey by declaring the gospel that the Spirit quickens you to actually do what seems impossible. You do not have God-dependence for witnessing without witnessing. You can witness without God-dependence; that is the futility of the flesh. But God-dependence for witnessing goes beyond believing that God can bless witnessing to depending on God to bless as you witness. What a difference faith makes in comparison to witnessing in flesh-dependence. This is the dynamic that Paul, under inspiration, testifies regarding I Corinthians 15:10: "I labored . . . yet not I, but the grace of God which was with me."

Let's consider a *word* step like responding rightly to a provoking statement made by someone. What is the right response? Proverbs 15:1 says, "A soft answer turneth away wrath." Therefore it is not just a matter of praying and waiting for a "zap." You must tie the faith to the step of the soft answer. You might say, "I can't do it!" Isn't that the whole point? For we are no longer talking about the *I myself* life but the *not I, but Christ* life. He can speak the soft answer through you. As you depend on Him to speak the soft answer, you will find that the Spirit of Christ immediately enables you for the soft answer. This is Christ in you! Further, if it is the life of Christ, then He even desires rightly. Victory is not just biting your lip, yet fuming on the inside. Victory is not even having the wrong desire, because you are accessing the life of Christ.

Consider a *thought* step (e.g., pure thinking). When tempted to think wrongly, it is not just praying and waiting for a "zap." The faith must be tied to the step of obedience which, here, is thinking purely. You might say, "I can't do it." That is true, but He can! As you tie the dependence on Christ in you to the step of thinking purely, the Spirit immediately enables you to the victory. This is Christ through you. As you walk in the Spirit, you will not fulfill the lust of the flesh. Walking in the Spirit is allowing, by faith, Christ to live His life through you. He does not fulfill the lust of the flesh.

Walking in the Spirit is simply *trust to obey*. It is God-dependence for Spirit-enabling to obey in holiness and service. Clearly the *walk* makes clear that the *not I, but Christ* life is not a life of passivity, but rather God-dependence for the steps of obedient activity in thought, word, and deed. Colossians 1:29 follows up "Christ in you" in Colossians 1:27 with "Whereunto I also labour, striving according to His working, which worketh in me mightily."

That area of sin that seems impossible, which has defeated you repeatedly and has often brought you to despair, does not need to continue to defeat you. Why? Because the law of the Spirit is able to overcome the law of sin. If you are talking about your life, you are right—it's impossible to win. But if you are talking about Christ's life, "with God nothing shall be impossible" (Luke 1:37). This is the life that wins. Christ can do what is impossible to man.

Daily may we humbly cry, "O Christ, live your life through me. Live Your patience through me, your wisdom, peace, and purity. Live Your words through me. Witness through me." This is not the *I myself* life but the *not I, but Christ* life. The inheritance we have in the bank of heaven is inexhaustible. Appropriate your inheritance. As you trust to obey, the Spirit enables you to actually obey. The need to constantly "look unto Jesus" shows that this is not the same as "second blessing" theology which tends toward the "having arrived" thinking and diminishes man's continual responsibility. Just as we are responsible to "get in the basket" by a choice of faith, we are responsible to "stay in the basket" by further choices of faith.

Notice Galatians 1:15b-16 "by His grace, to reveal His Son in me." Is not this the reality of Galatians 2:20? God desires to reveal Christ in and through us. What a glorious privilege! Why does God desire to do such a marvelous work of union between the human and the divine? The verse continues by saying, "that I might preach Him among the heathen." When I preach, yet *not I, but Christ* preaches through me, the Spirit draws people to the now uplifted Christ. When this revelation of *Christ in and through us* becomes reality, what is the ultimate result? Galatians 1:24 explains, "they glorified **God in me**." God is given the weight, the honor, and the glory that is due Him when He is seen! The glory of God is the result of the Christ-life.

How often do we block the glory of God by walking after the flesh? This is a wretched crime of robbing God of His glory. To block the voice and face of Christ by flesh-dependence is a wicked sin! May we ever depend on Christ so that the Spirit of Christ lives the life of Christ through us. Then God is literally glorified in us.

Who is seen and heard in your home? You or Christ? Would if not make a difference if Christ is revealed? What foolishness to block God's glory to our loved ones. Who is seen and heard in the workplace? You or Christ? What a tragedy if they see only you. When you teach a Sunday school class, who is seen? Who is heard? When you sing in church or play an instrument, who is seen and heard? Are we robbing Christ of His glory by people seeing only us? What a mockery to true worship. When you witness, who really is seen? Who truly is heard? May the lost see and hear the Savior. Anything else is human salesmanship. Although this dimension is invisible, it is marvelously real.

At any given moment, you are either walking in the flesh or walking in the Spirit. There is no mixture. This is not the concept of "two stages," which implies that when you reach the second stage you never return to the first, but rather two conditions, one of which prevails depending on which "walk" you take.

A certain man told me the day after I preached on Galatians 2:20 at his church, that when things were frustrating in his workplace, he kept in the forefront of his mind to "stay in the basket." A few days later, he said he knew a potentially troublesome staff meeting was to take place. So he brought a small basket and placed it in front of him to remind him to "stay in the basket." He testified of victory by the grace of God!

Man is responsible to access this provision of Christ and power of the Spirit by faith. Unhindered sanctification is by faith. Effective service is by faith. O how the disease of unbelief grieves and hinders the Spirit. By faith may we experientially know the words "I am crucified with Christ: nevertheless I live; yet not I, but Christ liveth in me."

My father, who is now with the Lord, incorporated a "section of sermon" into many sermons. In fact, in his last recorded message, which was preached just a few days before his homegoing, he again used this particular section of sermon. Often I heard him, with moistened eyes, quivering lip, and broken voice, say, "When I get to heaven and look on the Lord Jesus for the very first time, and He looks at me, I'm going to recognize that I've seen that look before. When He speaks to me, I will recognize that I've heard that voice before. When He touches me, I will know that I've felt that touch before in the lives of Spirit-filled believers." May we—by faith—allow the Savior to be seen, heard, and felt. Then He will be glorified. This is the reality of the Spirit-filled life.

---

[1]Rosalind Goforth, *Climbing* (Elkhart, Ind.: Bethel Publishing, n.d.), pp. 37-38.

[2]Ibid., pp. 45-46.

[3]Ibid., pp. 171-74.

[4]Ibid., pp. 179-80.

[5]Duncan Campbell, *The Price and Power of Revival* (Vinton, Va.: Christ Life Publications, reprint, n.d.), p. 30.

[6]Ibid., p. 7.

[7]Ibid., p. 8.

CHAPTER EIGHT

# COOPERATION WITH THE HOLY SPIRIT— THE HEAVENLY PARTNER

Endowment: The Promise of the Spirit
Enfeeblement: The Problem of Unbelief
Entitlement: The Provision of Christ
**Enthronement: The Presentation and Practice of Surrender and Faith**
Enablement: The Power of Living
Entrustment: The Purpose of Usefulness

Having seen that the provision of Christ richly provides all that is necessary for victorious living and that this provision is accessed by faith, can we get more specific as to our responsibility? The bottom line is faith—for everything! This is the concept of absolute surrender. We will dwell on this by probing what it means to cooperate with the Holy Spirit, which is the essence of a living surrender.

# II CORINTHIANS 13:14

A.W. Tozer once wrote:

> We who pride ourselves in our orthodoxy . . . have in recent years committed a costly blunder . . . Our blunder (or shall we frankly say our sin?) has been to neglect the doctrine of the Spirit to a point where we virtually deny Him His place in the Godhead. This denial has not been by open doctrinal statement, for we have clung closely enough to the biblical position wherever our creedal pronouncements are concerned. Our formal creed is sound; **the breakdown is in our working creed.** This is not a trifling distinction. A doctrine has practical value only as far as it is prominent in our thoughts and makes a difference in our lives. Truth consists not in correct doctrine, but in correct doctrine plus the inward enlightenment of the Holy Spirit . . . Deity indwelling men! . . . No man has experienced rightly the power of Christian belief until he has known this for himself as a living reality.
>
> In most Christian churches the Spirit is quite entirely overlooked. Whether He is present or absent makes no real difference to anyone. Brief reference is made to Him in the doxology and the benediction. Further than that He might as well not exist . . . Our neglect of the doctrine of the blessed Third Person has had and is having serious consequences. For doctrine is dynamite. It must have emphasis sufficiently sharp to detonate it before its power is released . . . The doctrine of the Spirit is buried dynamite. Its power awaits discovery and use by the Church. The power of the

Spirit will not be given to any mincing assent to pneumatological truth. The Holy Spirit cares not at all whether we write Him into our creeds in the back of our hymnals; He awaits our **emphasis**. [The Holy Spirit] loves us so much that when we insult Him, He . is grieved; when we ignore Him, He is grieved; when we resist Him, He is grieved; and when we doubt Him, He is grieved.[1]

James A. Stewart, evangelist from Scotland, wrote:

Almost all the weakness, both personal and corporate, in the Church of God today may be traced to an incomplete understanding of and recognition to the Holy Spirit. To many saints He is known only as an influence, intermittent at best. They ascribe their new birth to Him, but know little or nothing about His controlling and sanctifying presence and power in their lives. Hence, Christian life to them has become a long weary struggle to attain to the ideal of Christ's example; and very many, sadly recognizing the difference between the ideal and the actual; between Christ's life and theirs, have settled down to the calm of despair. Interpreting the Word of God by their own experience, they have concluded that no higher type of life is possible for them in this world.[2]

Do not these statements from Tozer and Stewart provoke needed consideration among God's people?

Walter Wilson was a medical doctor whom God called to preach. God greatly used him to point people to Christ. Fruitfulness marked his witness. A certain event accelerated his life of usefulness and fruitfulness in harvesting souls. He relates it as follows:

One day the Lord graciously sent across my path a man of God who said to me, "What is the Holy Spirit to you?" I replied that He was one of the persons of the Godhead. The servant of God answered that this was a true statement but did not answer his question, "What is the Holy Spirit *to* you? What does He mean *to* you?" This inquiry produced a deep heart searching and I replied, "He is nothing to me at all. I know who He is, but I have no personal relationship with Him." My friend assured me that my life was barren and my ministry fruitless because of this neglect. I had been treating the Holy Spirit as a servant of mine. I would ask Him to come and help me when I would teach a class. To be more explicit, I really asked the Father to send His Spirit to help me. This left the Spirit as a servant subject to my call and request. He was never more than an agent of the Godhead to serve me whenever I felt His need and asked the Father for His ministry.

The message which this Christian brought to my heart roused within me a great desire to know the Spirit and to serve Him successfully . . . About this time the Lord very graciously sent a devoted minister from Chicago who brought a wonderful message on Romans 12:1. Having finished his address on the subject, he leaned over the pulpit and said, "It is the Holy Spirit to whom you are to give your body. Your body is the temple of the Holy Spirit and you are requested in this passage to give it to Him for His possession. Will you do this tonight?"

I left the service deeply impressed with the thought that no doubt here was the answer to my deep need and the relief from my barren life. Upon arriving home I went to my study, laid myself flat on the carpet with my Bible open at Romans 12:1. Placing my finger on the passage, I said to the Holy Spirit, "Never before have I come to you with myself: I do so now. You may have my body, my lips, my feet, my brain, my hands and all that I am and have. My body is yours for you to live within and do as you please. Just now I make you my Lord and I receive you as my own personal God. I shall see your wonderful working in my life and I know you will make Christ very real to my heart. I thank you for accepting me for you said the gift is 'acceptable.' I thank you for this gracious meeting with yourself tonight."

This is quite an interesting prayer and may provoke some questions. It would be fair to say, based on Walter Wilson's reputation, that he knew that the Holy Spirit already lived within him. He simply was seeing the difference between having the facts (the Spirit's indwelling) and accessing the function (the Spirit's filling). Dr. Wilson continues:

Upon rising the next morning I said to my wife, "This will be a wonderful day. Last evening I received the Holy Spirit into my life as my Lord and gave him my body to use for His glory and for the honor of the Lord Jesus. I know He will do it and He will use me without a doubt." She replied, "If anything unusual happens today, call me on the phone. I will be anxious to know." About eleven o'clock I had the joy of phoning home that the Spirit had spoken through my lips to the hearts of two young women, sisters, who had entered my office on business. Both of them trusted the Saviour. This was the beginning of new days of victory, blessing and fruitfulness which have continued since that time. I ceased to neglect and ignore this gracious Person who had come to live with me. Now He was free to use me in His service for the glory of the Lord Jesus.[3]

When Walter Wilson began to properly relate to the Holy Spirit, his life of barrenness blossomed into fruitfulness. This is the life of absolute surrender. This is the life of "staying in the basket." This began a life of cooperation with the Holy Spirit.

II Corinthians 13:14 is a benediction: "The grace of the Lord Jesus Christ, and the love of God, and the communion of the Holy Spirit, be with you all. Amen." Notice that our text says *the communion of the Holy Spirit be with you all*. This *communion* is not just for preachers. It is not just for "super saints." Truly there is no such category. There is only a great God! This prayer indicates that it is God's will for every believer to commune with the Holy Spirit. If we are not living in communion with the Spirit, then we are living at a substandard, actually disobedient, level.

What does *communion* with the Spirit mean? The word *communion* translates from the Greek word *koinonia*. Defining terms are "participation, sharing in something,"[4] as well as "partnership, fellowship."[5] Personally I love the defining term *partnership*. The closely related word *koinonos* referring to a person means "companion, partner, sharer."[6] It is also translated as "partaker." Therefore, *communion* is a participation in a partnership—obviously with a partner. Simply stated, it is the cooperation of a partnership.

God did not make man a robot. God does not make believers into robots. God chose for man to use the faculties God gave him. In other words, the Spirit of God does not bypass man's faculties, his mind, or his body. Rather, the Spirit uses them. In essence, **the communion of the Holy Spirit is the cooperation of a partnership with the Holy Spirit**. What are the dynamics of cooperating with the Holy Spirit? What is the believer's responsibility? We will seek to answer the first question in this chapter by focusing on the Heavenly Partner, and we will seek to answer the second question in the next chapter by focusing on the human partner. Now, let us investigate three dynamics of cooperating with the Heavenly Partner, the Holy Spirit.

## COOPERATING WITH A SPIRITUAL PERSON

Our text speaks of "communion with the Holy Spirit." The definite article *the* before the name Holy Spirit grammatically emphasizes the person of the Spirit. In this regard, let's ponder four considerations.

# The Deity of the Spirit

What is the Holy Spirit to you? Is He God? When Jesus gives the Great Commission, He tells us to make disciples of all nations. Then He says that we are to baptize them "in the name of the Father, and of the Son, and of the Holy Spirit." Would it not be blasphemy to delete *the Holy Spirit* and add a human's name? The very fact that *the name* of the Godhead includes *the Holy Spirit* indicates that the Spirit is God! Psalm 139:7 asks, "Whither shall I go from Thy Spirit?" There is not a place you and I can hide from the Spirit because He is omnipresent. Only God is omnipresent. Therefore, the Spirit is God. Hebrews 9:14 calls the Spirit "the eternal Spirit." From eternity past to eternity future the Holy Spirit is eternal. Only God is eternal. Therefore, the Spirit is God. He is deity!

What is the Holy Spirit to you? Is He deity? I am afraid we give mental assent to this truth but, in practice, treat Him as less than God. Perhaps this will be further pointed up in the following considerations.

# The Personality of the Spirit

Is the Holy Spirit a person to you, or is He merely an impersonal force? The Spirit of God is a person. He, therefore, is a personality. He is not merely a signpost. Tragically, many treat Him as such. Personality must be cultivated. For example, you may be introduced to a certain person. You may know them by name. But do you really know them? No, it takes time to cultivate personality. If you are saved, then you have been introduced to the Spirit. You may know His name. However, it takes time to cultivate His personality.

God the Spirit is a spirit, and yet He is a person. Although He does not consist of material matter, He is substance. He is a person.

Handley Moule, in his classic work originally entitled *Veni Creator: Thoughts on the Person and Work of the Holy Spirit of Promise*, states:

> For the decisive teaching on the personality of the
> Holy Ghost we go yet deeper into the Scripture taber-
> nacle; we enter its Holiest; we open the pages where

the Lord Jesus himself teaches with his own lips the
secrets of spiritual life. There, as it were under the
Shekinah itself, lies our doctrinal stronghold for this
article of faith (John 14-16). There speaks the Christ
of God in an hour of supreme tenderness, and from
which all ideas of the rhetorical and the merely poeti-
cal are infinitely distant; and he speaks with repetition
and emphasis of this same Holy Spirit, and he speaks of
him as personal.[7]

Throughout the largest instruction in the Scriptures on the Holy
Spirit, Christ repeatedly refers to the Spirit as "Him" and "He." Moule
emphasizes:

> With the Paschal Discourse in our heart and mind,
> we know that it was he, not it, who 'brooded over the
> primeval deep (Gen. 1:2). He not it, 'strove with man',
> or 'ruled in man' of old (Gen. 6:3). He, not it, was in
> Joseph in Egypt (Gen. 41:38) and upon Moses in the
> wilderness (Num. 11:17), and upon judges and kings of
> after-days. He, not it, 'spake by the prophets,' and
> 'moving' those 'holy men of God' (Judg. 6:34; I Sam.
> 10:10). He not it, drew the plan of the ancient Taber-
> nacle and of the first Temple (I Sam. 22:2; 2 Kgs. 2:9,
> 15; 2 Chron. 15:1; Matt. 22:43; Heb. 10:15; I Pet. 1:11;
> 2 Pet. 1:21; Heb. 9:8; I Chron. 28:12). He not it, lifted
> Ezekiel to his feet in the hour of vision (Ezek. 2:2). He,
> not it, came upon the Virgin (Luke 1:35), and
> anointed Her Son at Jordan (Luke 3:22), and led him
> to the desert of temptation (Luke 4:1), and gave utter-
> ances to the saints at Pentecost (Acts 2:4), and caught
> Philip away from the road to Gaza (Acts 8:39), and
> guided Paul through Asia Minor to the nearest port for
> Europe (Acts 16:6, 7). He, not it, effects the new birth
> of regenerate man (John 3:5, 6, 8), and is the breath of
> his new life (Gal. 5:25), and the earnest of his coming
> glory (Rom. 8:11; Eph. 1:13, 14). By him, not it, the
> believer walks (Gal. 5:25), and mortifies the deeds of
> the body (Rom. 8:13), filled not with it, but him (Eph.
> 5:18). He, not it, is the Spirit of faith (2 Cor. 4:13), by
> whom it is 'given unto us to believe on Christ' (Phil.
> 1:29). He, not it, speaks to the Churches (Rev. 2:7, 11,
> 29; 3:6, 13, 22). He, not it, says from heaven that they
> who die in the Lord are blessed, and calls in this life
> (Rev. 14:13) upon the wandering soul of man to come
> to the living water (Rev. 22:17).[8]

If you are a child of God, blood-bought, born of the Spirit, then He, not it, lives in you! This reality ought to make a difference! What is the Holy Spirit to you? Is He truly personality? Or is He just an impersonal force? Do you interact with the Spirit as a real person?

## The Communication of the Spirit

Romans 8:16 states, "The Spirit itself [Himself] beareth witness with our spirit." He *bears witness*. Therefore, He communicates with us. Notice where He speaks to us—in *our spirit*. He communicates with our inner man, not our outer man. Outer man communications, which appeal to our body senses such as audible voices and physical manifestations, often reveal counterfeits of the powers of darkness. The Spirit *bears witness*—He communicates—*with our spirit*.

Is this communication only to be "one-way"? Many practically live as though it is. On the contrary, however, remember the defining terms of *communion*: partnership, fellowship, participation, cooperation. Is this not difficult, actually impossible, without a "two-way" communication? The word *communion* in our text alone authoritatively demands a two-way communication. What kind of marriage partnership would a couple have if only one partner communicated? Certainly you wouldn't have much of a marriage. If we are to truly commune with the Holy Spirit, there must be a two-way communication.

Remember the words of Christ in John 14:16 as He speaks of the Spirit as "another Comforter." Two Greek words translate as *another* in our English Bible. *Allos* means another of the same kind as distinguished from *heteros*, which means another of a different kind.[9] Jesus uses the term *allos*. Therefore, the Spirit is another of the same kind. Furthermore, the word *Comforter* [*Paraklatos*], among several nuances, means "one who appears in another's behalf."[10] So the Spirit is another of the same kind appearing in Christ's behalf.

Did the disciples communicate with Jesus? Certainly they did. Since the Spirit is another of the some kind appearing in Christ's behalf, should we not communicate with Him as the disciples did with Jesus? The issue is communication. When a husband and wife communicate with each other, not all of it would be considered asking or "praying." It is simply the communication of a partnership. So it is with the Spirit.

Having emphasized the need to communicate with the Spirit, let me also point out the scriptural balance regarding praying. Generally speaking, the tenor of Scripture, especially if you consider the Lord's prayer, indicates that you pray to the Father, on the merits of the Son, through the ministry of the Holy Spirit. Yet this does not deny the possibility of ever addressing the Son or the Spirit. Is it wrong to ever address Christ in prayer? Let's consider when He walked on earth. Did people at the time of Christ ever pray to Jesus? Peter cried out as he began to sink in the Sea of Galilee, "Lord, save me" (Matthew 14:30). Others prayed to Christ to have mercy on them and heal them. Was it wrong for people to pray to Jesus? Even though there is no explicit Old Testament precedent for doing so Jesus never rebuked them, for He is God! The oneness of the Godhead must not be forgotten. The disciples communicated with, and even prayed, to Jesus Christ. In fact, some of the prayers recorded in Acts begin with "Lord" instead of "Father."

Is it wrong to ever address the Spirit? Consider the exhortation from Christ in Matthew 9:38, "Pray ye therefore the Lord of the harvest, that He will send forth labourers into His harvest" (cf. Luke 10:2). Who is *the Lord of the harvest*? The Book of Acts, which is the book of the harvest, answers this question. Who descended in mighty power on the Day of Pentecost so that 3,000 souls were harvested? We are explicitly told it was the Spirit. Who spoke to Philip in Acts 8 to join himself to the chariot of the Ethiopian eunuch, leading to his being harvested? We are told explicitly that it was the Spirit. In Acts 10, when the delegation came from Cornelius to Peter, who told Peter to "go with them, doubting nothing," which led to Cornelius' salvation and the harvesting of the Gentiles? We are told explicitly that it was the Spirit. Who spoke to the church at Antioch in Acts 13 saying, "Separate Me Barnabus and Saul for the work whereunto I have called them"? That *work* was the first missionary journey, a journey of mass harvests. Again, we are told explicitly that it was the Holy Spirit. Who was it in Acts 16 that forbade Paul and Silas to, at that time, go further into Asia in order to get them into Macedonia for more harvesting? Once more, we are told explicitly that it was the Spirit of God. So who is *the Lord of the harvest*? I believe the answer clearly is *the Spirit*. And Jesus said, "Pray ye therefore the Lord of the harvest, that He will send forth labourers into His harvest."

Handley Moule beautifully cautions and yet admonishes:

> So, while watchfully and reverently seeking to remember the laws of Scripture proportion, and that according to it the believer's relation to the Spirit is *not so much* that of direct adoration as of a reliance which wholly implies it, let us trustfully and thankfully worship him, and ask blessing of him, as our spirits shall be moved to such action under his grace. Let us ever and again recollect, with deliberate contemplation and faith, what by his Word we know of him, and of his presence in us and his work for us, and then let us not only "pray *in* the Holy Ghost" (Jude 20) but also *to* him . . . [emphasis Moule's][11]

I am not saying we should get out of balance and never address the Father or even the Son. I am saying we should get back into balance and stop neglecting the Spirit. Again, the issue is communication, not necessarily prayer. Actually, there is more indication from the New Testament for believers at the present time regarding communicating with the Holy Spirit than there is in the Old Testament for believers at the time of Christ to communicate with Christ. If you reject any communication to the Holy Spirit, then you expose the fact that you do not apprehend fully the reality of "Christ in you" (Colossians 1:27) and the Christ-life or Spirit-filled life. If you reject any communication to the Spirit, you are not treating Him as a real person. Personal presence carries with it the privileges of communication.

Interestingly, the hymnal includes prayers to the Holy Spirit. "Spirit of God, Descend upon My Heart," "Breathe on Me, Breath of God," "Spirit of the Living God, Fall Fresh on Me" are a few examples. Evidently this was considered acceptable in bygone days.

Years ago, an evangelist friend of mine heard Walter Wilson preach. Wilson was quite elderly at the time. According to my friend, Wilson began, in essence, saying, "How many of you have spoken to the Holy Spirit today?" You can imagine the response. He continued, "Now if you're saved, the Holy Spirit lives in you. If He lives in you, He's always with you. Now to have someone always with you, and you never speak to them—That's not very nice!" This little anecdote helps put the picture into proper perspective. What is the Holy Spirit to you? Is He one with whom you may communicate?

## The Dispensation of the Spirit

When Jesus was exalted to the right hand of the Father and sent the Spirit, He launched the age of the Spirit. Moule refers to the Puritan writer, John Owen, in this regard and specifies some divine tests of living orthodoxy:

> The theme is one of altogether special importance for the believing church of these latter days. In John Owen's *Pneumatologia*, his deep, massive and most spiritual "Discourse Concerning the Holy Spirit" (1674) occurs a remarkable passage (bk. 1, ch. 1), in which he traces through the ages and dispensations a certain progress of divine tests of living orthodoxy, related to each of the three persons in succession. Before the first advent the great testing truth was "the oneness of God's nature and his monarchy over all," with special

respect to the person of the Father. At the first advent
the great question was whether a church orthodox on
the first point would now receive the divine Son,
incarnate, sacrificed and glorified, according to the
promise. And when the working of this test had gathered out the church of Christian believers, and built it
on the foundation of the truth of the person and work
of the Lord Jesus Christ, then the Holy Spirit came in
a new prominence and specialty before that church as
a touchstone of true faith.[12]

Interestingly, Satan's attacks on God's people correspond to the person of the Godhead in prominence. During the age of the Father (the
Old Testament), Satan's attack on God's people focused on tripping
them up regarding the oneness of God. Notably, idolatry ensnared the
people of God repeatedly. During the age of the Son when Christ
walked this earth at the first advent, Satan's attack on God's people
focused on the person of Christ. This became the test of living orthodoxy. Sadly, "He came unto His own, and His own received Him not"
(John 1:11). When Christ ascended and sent His Spirit, beginning the
age of the Spirit, Satan's attack on God's people shifted to the Holy
Spirit. This introduced a new test of "living" orthodoxy. It is no accident that today there is much confusion regarding the Holy Spirit. The
Charismatic excess has caused many to embrace counterfeits of the
Spirit. Yet many today have overreacted to this problem. For if Satan
can deceive God's people into either excess regarding the Spirit or simply ignoring the Spirit—their source of power—he has successfully crip-
pled the church from moving forward. It should not surprise us that doctrinal disagreement among even conservative believers does not primarily surround the Father or the Son, but rather the Spirit. Satan seeks to
keep us powerless through a wrong relationship to the Spirit.

John Owen concludes by saying, "Wherefore the duty of the church
now immediately respects the Spirit of God, who acts towards it in the
name of the Father and of the Son; and with respect unto him it is that
the church in its present state is capable of an apostasy from God . . .
The sin of despising his person and rejecting his work now is of the same
nature with idolatry of old, and the Jews' rejection of the person of the
Son."[13] II Corinthians 3 states, " . . . for the letter killeth, but the Spirit
giveth life." Dead orthodoxy is the mark of an apostasy from the Spirit.
Historically the condition of "no fire" tends to pressure believers to
either embrace "strange fire" (e.g., compromise as seen today in the
contemporary-style church permeating evangelicalism and, to some
degree, parts of fundamentalism) or to seek God for "Spirit-fire."

Is it legitimate then to honor the Spirit? Let us consider the
implications of Scripture. Who revealed the Father? The Son. In

John 14:9 Jesus said, "He that hath seen Me hath seen the Father." The Son revealed the Father. Who reveals the Son? The Spirit. In John 16:14 Jesus said, "He [the Holy Spirit] shall glorify Me: for He shall receive of Mine, and shall shew it unto you." The Spirit clearly *shall shew* or reveal Christ, the Son. Christ explicitly teaches that the Spirit reveals the Son.

Remember what Jesus taught in John 5:23: "That all men should honour the Son, even as they honour the Father. He that honoureth not the Son honoureth not the Father which hath sent Him." Why? Because the Son revealed the Father. So when Jehovah's Witnesses claim to honor Jehovah (the Father), and yet deny the deity of Christ, we know that their claim is not true. In order to honor the Father, you must honor the Son because the Son revealed the Father. Who, then, must you honor in order to honor the Son? The Spirit. Yet some think you cannot glorify the Spirit. But this is a gross deception, for although Jesus said, "He [the Spirit] shall glorify Me," He never said that we should not glorify the Spirit. If you think you cannot glorify the Spirit, then you do not believe in the deity of the Spirit. Honoring the Spirit does not negate the proper understanding of the order of the Godhead. Also, the persons of the Godhead are not jealous of each other.

A. W. Tozer points out in his helpful book *How to Be Filled with the Holy Spirit*: "The historic church has said that He is God. Let me quote from the Nicene Creed: 'I believe in the Holy Ghost, the Lord and Giver of life, Which proceedeth from the Father and the Son, and with the Father and the Son together is worshipped and glorified.' That is what the Church believed about the Holy Ghost 1,600 years ago . . . Now let's look at the Athanasian Creed. Thirteen hundred years old it is. Notice what it says about the Holy Spirit: 'Such as the Father is, such is the Son, and such is the Holy Ghost.'"[14]

If you cannot glorify the Spirit, then He is less than God. However II Corinthians 3:17 says, "Now the Lord is that Spirit." Notice inspiration here calls the Spirit *Lord*. Therefore He must be treated as Lord. Yet some today think that if you honor the Spirit, you are breaking the first commandment. This replaces the Trinity with a duality, and you no longer have the God of the Bible! If you slight the Spirit and the Spirit reveals the Son, then you have slighted the Son, which means you have also slighted the Father because the Son reveals the Father.

Handley Moule states:

> The question perhaps arises from the thoughts just suggested, whether acts of direct adoration to the Holy Spirit are prescribed to us in the Scriptures. It is certainly remarkable that we have very little in their pages which bears explicitly on the question, a fact which however falls very naturally in with what we

have already seen of the general comparative reticence
of the author of the Book about his own nature and
glory. And, again, it is a fact in harmony with what we
have seen of the character of his work for the Christian; a work pre-eminently subjective, so profoundly so
as to occasion such a statement as that of Paul that the
Spirit intercedes for the saints with groanings that cannot be uttered (Rom. 8:26), words whose context at
least suggests that the intercession has its action in the
region of the inner man, and breathes itself or groans
itself forth through the regenerate man, and breathes
itself or groans itself forth through the regenerate
human spirit. If it is the Holy Spirit's special function
not only to speak to and deal with, but also to speak
and work through, the man he renews and sanctifies,
we can just so far understand that he the less presents
himself for our articulate adoration. But meanwhile
the sacred rightfulness of our worship of the Holy
Spirit is as surely established as anything can be that
rests on large and immediate inferences from the
Scriptures. If he is divine, and if he is personal, how
can we help the attitude of adoration when, leaving for
the moment the thought of his work in us, we isolate
in our view the thought of him the Worker? Scripture
practically prescribes to us such an attitude when it
gives us our Lord's own account, in his baptismal for-
mula, of the eternal *name* as his disciples were to know
it—'The name of the Father, and of the Son, and of
the Holy Ghost'; and when in the Acts and Epistles
the Holy Ghost is set before us as not only doing his
work in the inmost being of the individual but presiding in sacred majesty over the community; and when
in the Revelation he, in the mystical sevenfoldness of
his operation (Acts 5:3; Acts 13:2; Acts 15:28; I Cor.
12:11-13), Seven yet One, appears in that solemn pre-
lude as the concurrent Giver, with the Father and the
Son, of grace and peace; above all when in the Paschal
Discourse (Rev. 1:4; John 14:16) the adorable and
adored Lord Jesus presents him to our faith as co-ordi-
nate with himself in glory and grace, "another Comforter."[15]

Some consider this personal interaction with the Spirit scary and
even "spooky." But that is another deceptive lie of Satan. For what is the

Spirit like? He is like Jesus because He is the Spirit of Jesus. As Jesus was moved with compassion when He saw the multitudes, so is the Spirit.

On a personal note, let me give a testimony in this regard. There was a time in my life when I felt as though I did not properly "know" the Son. Please don't misunderstand me. I knew Christ in salvation. Yet I did not sense a deep experiential knowledge of the Son. I would read of men like Jonathan Edwards going into the woods and gazing on Christ for two hours, and I would ask myself, "What in the world are they talking about?" But when I began to properly relate to and depend on the Spirit, thus "honor" the Spirit, soon I experienced a greater reality of knowing Christ—because the Spirit reveals the Son.

Philip said to Christ, "Lord, shew us the Father, and it sufficeth us" (John 14:8). Jesus answered, "Have I been so long time with you, and yet hast thou not known Me, Philip? He that hath seen Me hath seen the Father" (John 14:9). Perhaps when we, in essence, say to the Spirit, "Show us the Son," He responds with, "Have I been so long time with you, and yet hast thou not known Me?" Remember He is the Spirit of Christ.

What is the Holy Spirit to you? Is He a person with whom you fellowship? Is He God and glorified as such? Is He a person with whom you communicate and interact? Do you relate to the Holy Spirit as a spiritual Person?

The first dynamic in this *communion* with the Holy Spirit is recognizing that we are cooperating with a spiritual Person.

## COOPERATING WITH A SENIOR PARTNER

In this partnership of the human and divine, the Spirit is the Senior Partner to lead the partnership. Therefore, we must surrender to, which is to depend on, the Spirit's leadership. Our will must be brought into complete submission to His will. We must yield to His control. Hence, the Spirit-filled life equates to the Spirit-controlled life.

He is in charge whether we recognize His leadership or not. But in order to fully benefit from His leadership, we must follow it. The Holy Spirit does not, however, violate our human will. When we hold back even one aspect of our lives to our control, we are acting like we are in charge. In other words, lack of surrender reveals our pride in acting like we are the senior partner.

What is the Holy Spirit to you? Is He the senior partner in your partnership? When you got saved, He moved into your spirit. Yet that does not mean that He automatically possesses all of you. We must yield to Him. How many would show a guest into the guestroom and lock him inside? Yet many do this, in essence, to the Holy Spirit! Does the Spirit have free reign to the house of your life? Does He possess your family room, the kitchen, the basement, or even the attic? If we hold back the key to even one closet of our lives, we are usurping His rightful position as the senior partner.

In light of this, many (to switch analogies) say things such as, "Okay, I will just let the Holy Spirit take over the steering wheel of my life." But as my father often pointed out, the Holy Spirit will not do that. If He were "behind the wheel," you would have to do His will. On the contrary, the Christian life is not robotic. God holds man responsible to use his will. My father further emphasized that the Spirit will, in essence, say, "I'll stay in the passenger seat. You stay behind the wheel. Just do everything I say. Go when I say, 'Go.' Turn right when I say, 'Turn right.' Stop when I say, 'Stop!'" In other words, we must witness when the Spirit says, "Witness." We must look another direction when the Spirit says, "Don't look over there." We must remain quiet when the Spirit says, "Hold your tongue." And as we yield to His commands, we are thus yielding to the control, or leadership, of the Spirit. This is cooperation with the Spirit as Senior Partner. What is the Holy Spirit to you? Are you yielding to Him as senior partner?

## COOPERATING WITH A SUPERNATURAL POWER

We have emphasized already His personality. Yet He is the Person of power—the almighty power of God! In this partnership of the human and the divine, the Spirit is the Supernatural Power to enable the partnership. Therefore, we must surrender to, which is to depend on, the Spirit's enablement.

We will return to this thought in a moment. However, first consider the nature of "surrender" and "faith." Faith for everything is absolute surrender. True surrender is dependence (for when you abandon all to Him you are depending only on Him). Also, true dependence is surrender (for when you depend only on Him you are surrendering all to Him). Therefore, surrender and faith are distinguishable in their emphasis but at oneness in their essence. If you separate surrender entirely from faith, you no longer have true surrender, nor do you have true dependence.

Let's return to our flow of thought. Surrender/dependence must be to the Spirit's will (Senior Partner) and way (Supernatural Power). You cannot truly surrender to His will without also surrendering to His way. It is not "His will, my way," or it is not His will. The Spirit-controlled life is not "I surrender to whatever God desires, and I'll do it!" For you cannot do it. If you attempt to yield to His control in your power, then you really have not yielded to His control.

By way of personal testimony, I grew up in a pastor's home. Memories of my father's preaching include a classic series on Romans 12:1-2.

During my teen years, more than once I saw the need to surrender all, and I "attempted" absolute surrender. However, somehow down deep I knew something was missing but couldn't put my finger on it. I had no sense that my offering was accepted. Also, my life remained unchanged. During Bible college years, more "attempts" were made. Even in the early years of full-time ministry, I made a few more "attempts" of absolute surrender.

It was not until I finally realized the futility of flesh-dependence that the truth at hand "clicked." I came to understand that not only was I to surrender to the Spirit's leadership but also to His enablement. It was not until then that I had any sense that the gift was accepted by God. Dependence on the Spirit's leadership and enablement accesses the reality of "I live; yet not I, but Christ lives in me" (Galatians 2:20) When it is *not I, but Christ*, God accepts Himself! This is what makes the gift "holy" and "acceptable unto God." Our worthiness resides only in Christ. Isn't it amazing that God has provided everything for which He is asking! When this became a living reality to me by faith, my life began to be transformed by the Spirit.

True surrender is exchanging your leadership for the Spirit's leadership **and** your power for the Spirit's power. Therefore, true surrender is exchanging your all for His ALL. It is in this context of the absolute surrender of *the believer* to Christ that Hudson Taylor wrote, "Unless the LORD JESUS is LORD OF ALL, He is not LORD at all" [emphasis Taylor's]. The context was not "Lordship Salvation" but the believer's surrender to the Lordship of Christ. The believer must not hold back one key to one room in his life. This is also the original background of the phrase "Let go and let God" (i.e., Let go of self-dependence, and let God lead and empower). This differs from the usage of that phrase by many today. The idea is not passive irresponsibility, but active cooperation. It is not the Spirit instead of you, but the Spirit through you.

We are to surrender to, which is to depend on, the Spirit as both Lord to lead and Life to enable, as both President to give the orders and as Power to carry out the very orders He gives us! What an amazing plan of God! The Spirit is both Director to guide and Dynamic to follow His guidance. He is both Emperor and Empowerment. The Spirit is both the Presiding Officer and the Energizing Agent. We are simply to surrender to, which is to depend on, the Spirit as both Senior Partner to lead us and Supernatural Power to enable us to follow His leadership. What is the Holy Spirit to you? Do you relate to Him as a Spiritual Person? Do you yield to Him in everything as the Senior Partner? Do you depend on Him as the Supernatural Power to do His will?

The Holy Spirit is a Spiritual Person, the Senior Partner, and Supernatural Power. May we cooperate with the blessed third Person of the Godhead. This is *communion with the Holy Spirit.* What is the Holy Spirit to you?

---

[1] A. W. Tozer, *Tozer on the Holy Spirit*, comp. Marilynne E. Foster (Camp Hill, Penn.: Christian Publications, Inc., 2000), pp. 2-3.

[2] James A. Stewart, *Heaven's Throne Gift* (Asheville, N.C.: Revival Literature, reprint, n.d.) pp. vii-viii.

[3] Walter Wilson, *Ye Know Him* (Grand Rapids: Zondervan, 1939), pp. 10-11.

[4] William F. Arndt and F. Wilbur Gingrich, *A Greek-English Lexicon of the New Testament*, 2d ed. (Chicago: University of Chicago Press, 1979), p. 439.

[5] Wigram-Green, *The New Englishman's Greek Concordance and Lexicon* (Peabody, Mass: Hendrickson Publishers, Inc., 1982), p. 489.

[6] Arndt and Gingrich, p. 439.

[7] Handley G. C. Moule, *The Holy Spirit* (Geanies Aouse, Fearn, Ross-shire, Great Britian: Christian Focus Publications, 1890, reprint 1999), pp. 10-11.

[8] Ibid., pp. 12-13.

[9] Richard C. Trench, *Synonyms of the New Testament* (Grand Rapids: Wm. B Eerdmans Publishing Company, London 1880, reprint 1983), p. 357.

[10] Arndt and Gingrich, p. 618.

[11] Moule, pp. 17-18.

[12] Ibid., pp. 7-8.

[13] Ibid., p. 8.

[14] A. W. Tozer, *How to Be Filled with the Holy Spirit* (Camp Hill, Penn.: Christian Publications, n.d.), pp. 13-14.

[15] Moule., pp. 16-17.

CHAPTER NINE

# COOPERATION
# WITH THE HOLY SPIRIT—
# THE HUMAN PARTNER

Endowment: The Promise of the Spirit
Enfeeblement: The Problem of Unbelief
Entitlement: The Provision of Christ
**Enthronement: The Presentation and Practice of Surrender and Faith**
Enablement: The Power of Living
Entrustment: The Purpose of Usefulness

Having allowed the question "What is the Holy Spirit to you?" to search us, let us now consider our needed response to the Heavenly Partner. The impact of real cooperative living with the Holy Spirit is monumental. O for eyes to see, ears to hear, and a heart to receive scriptural truth on this vital subject!

# II CORINTHIANS 13:14

II Corinthians 13:14 states "the communion of the Holy Spirit, be with **you**." Every child of God has the privilege of living in partnership with the Holy Spirit. This is the biblical norm. Anything less is subnormal. *Communion* is the intelligent cooperation between two persons. The Spirit longs to bring the victory of Christ to every child of God. He is ready and able. Any absence of power reveals a lack of cooperation on the part of the child of God. **The communion of the Holy Spirit is the cooperation of a partnership with the Holy Spirit.** In the last chapter we focused our attention on the Heavenly Partner. But what is the believer's responsibility? The New Testament records five commands to believers with the Holy Spirit as the direct object. These five commands outline the believer's responsibility in this partnership with the Spirit.

Of the five commands, one is event-oriented (the aorist tense); the other four are process-oriented (the present tense). Of the four "continuous" commands, one is a command of allowance (the passive voice);the other three are commands of action (the active voice). Of the three active commands, one regards the Spirit's power (absence of the definite article), and two regard the Spirit's person (presence of the definite article). The grammar which may seem to some to be technical, actually provides a practical way to outline the five commands.

## THE COMMAND OF RECEPTION

John 20:22 states, "He breathed on them, and saith unto them, **Receive ye the Holy Spirit**." The command *Receive* is in the aorist tense, which speaks of the fact of an action. Generally it is event-oriented. The background of this command in John 20 is resurrection day. "Then the same day at evening, being the first day of the week, when the doors were shut where the disciples were assembled for fear of the Jews, came Jesus and stood in their midst" (John 20:19). After Jesus calms them twice with the words "Peace be unto you," He gives the first articulation of the Great Commission "as My Father hath sent Me, even so send I you" (John 20:21). Then we read, "And when He had said this, He breathed on them, and saith unto them, Receive ye the Holy Spirit" (John 20:22). On only one other occasion do we read in Scripture of God breathing on man. Is this not of great significance?

Genesis 2:7 records, "And the LORD God formed man of the dust of the ground, and breathed into his nostrils the breath of life; and man became a living soul." I believe we have a parallel between the two passages. In Genesis 2:7 God breathed, and man became a living soul. In John 20:22 Christ breathed, and man became a living spirit. The spirit, formerly dead to God and alive to sin, was now alive to God and dead to sin. I believe the disciples were indwelt by the Spirit when Christ *breathed on them*. Something important had to occur.

These two references record the only two times that God directly breathed on man. The first occurrence was highly significant—physical life! The second occurrence must also have significance—spiritual life! When Christ breathed on the disciples, they were indwelt by the Spirit. However, He then commands them to *receive* the Holy Spirit. This may seem puzzling at first. The solution to the enigma lies in noting that, in the original language, the definite article *the* is absent before the name of the Holy Spirit. The emphasis, therefore, is on the power of the Spirit as opposed to the person of the Spirit. In other words, when Christ *breathed on them*, they received the person of the Spirit (the indwelling Spirit). However, Christ then commands them to receive functionally (power) what they had just received factually (person). What about the present age? Regardless of what one believes regarding John 20:22, the Epistles clarify.

## Factual Reception of the Spirit

Galatians 3:2 asks, "Received ye the Spirit by the works of the law, or by the hearing of faith?" The answer, of course, is *by . . . faith*. Several grammatical facts may be helpful. *Received* is an aorist tense, active voice, indicative mood verb. The aorist tense indicates the fact of an action. The active voice indicates that man is responsible for this reception (by faith). The indicative mood indicates the mood of reality. Also, the definite article *the* is present before *Spirit*, thus emphasizing the person of the Spirit (as opposed to the power of the Spirit). Therefore, the factual reception of the Spirit occurs at the moment of salvation. The moment you believe in Christ, you receive the indwelling of the Spirit. This is positional truth.

# Functional Reception of the Spirit

Galatians 3:13-14 state, "Christ hath redeemed us." Why? "**That** the blessing of Abraham might come on the Gentiles through Jesus Christ [According to verse 8, this is justification by faith]; **that** we might receive the promise of the Spirit through faith." Notice there are two purposes indicated by *that* occuring twice. Also, several grammatical facts may provide some practical help. *Receive* is here an aorist tense, active voice, subjunctive mood verb. Again, the aorist tense indicates the fact of an action. Again, the active voice indicates man is responsible for this reception (by faith). But here the subjunctive mood indicates the mood of probable reality (as opposed to the indicative mood of reality). *Might receive* shows this aspect.

Two clear distinctives must be noted between the reception of Galatians 3:2 and the reception of Galatians 3:14. The first distinction is the use of the indicative mood (reality) in Galatians 3:2 and the subjunctive mood (probable reality) in Galatians 3:14. This simply indicates that the second reception is not automatic. It, too, occurs according to Galatians 3:14 *through faith*. Man is, therefore, responsible. The second distinction is that the reception of Galatians 3:2 refers to the person of *the Spirit* [definite article preceding the name *Spirit*], whereas the reception of Galatians 3:14 refers to receiving *the promise of the Spirit*.

*The promise of the Spirit* emphasizes the power of the Spirit. We know this from studying *the promise of the Spirit* in chapter three. In Luke 24:49 Jesus says, "I send the promise . . . be endued with power from on high." In Acts 1:4-5 Jesus describes "the promise" as "ye shall be baptized with the Holy Spirit [no definite article in the original language, therefore, the power of the Spirit].

Therefore, the first reception (Galatians 3:2) is receiving the indwelling of the Spirit (person), and the second reception (Galatians 3:14) is receiving the filling of the Spirit (power). As the factual reception occurs at salvation, so the functional reception occurs at surrender. As in the moment you believe in Christ, you factually receive the indwelling of the Spirit, so in the moment you surrender all to, which is to depend on, the Spirit, you functionally receive the filling of the Spirit. As the first reception emphasizes positional truth, so the second reception emphasizes practical truth.

To further clarify these two receptions, let me say that the functional reception of surrender can occur with the factual reception at salvation if enough scriptural background is in place (e.g., the Apostle Paul). But for many it is subsequent to salvation. How many have gotten saved, but later have come to a fork in the road of their life where they surrendered all? Many have this testimony.

Galatians 4:4 and 6 indicate the need to "receive" God's gifts. Galatians 4:4 says, "God sent forth His Son." This is God's great gift to the world. John 3:16 explains, "For God so loved the **world**, that He **gave** His only begotten Son." Yet clearly each individual person must receive this gift in order to benefit from it. How do you receive the gift of the *Son*? John 1:12 answers, "But as many as **received** Him, to them gave He power to become the sons of God, even to them that **believe** on His name." The way you receive the gift of the Son is by believing (depending) on the Son.

Galatians 4:6 says, "And because ye are sons, God hath sent forth the Spirit of His Son into your hearts." This is God's great gift to the church. *God hath sent ... the Spirit ... into your hearts.* Yet clearly each individual believer must receive this gift in order to fully benefit from it. So how do you receive the gift of the *Spirit*? As seen already in John 1:12, the way you receive is by believing (depending) in this case on the Spirit.

You can be rightly related to the Son without being rightly related to the Spirit. To be rightly related to the Spirit, you must surrender to, which is to depend on, the Spirit for everything. This life of surrender must have a beginning. You receive/believe on the Spirit. This is simply the "presentation" of Romans 12:1, "I beseech you . . . brethren . . . that ye present your bodies a living sacrifice." The term *present* is in the aorist tense. The emphasis is the fact of an action. It is event-oriented. Used with the infinitive, the idea is to *present* on a definite occasion. Therefore, the presentation is not a process. However, it should begin a process. For *living* is in the present tense, which emphasizes continuous action. Therefore, the presentation/reception is simply the entrance into a new practice/relationship. This presentation and living sacrifice is to be "unto God." Although we are not told which person of the Godhead is referred to here, which person of the Godhead lives in the believer? The Spirit. The question is: Who has the "hands-on" possession of your body?

In modern society it is possible to purchase a product, to have the title deed in hand, and yet not have the product delivered until a later time. Likewise, Jesus Christ purchased you through His work of redemption. When you trust Him as your Savior, He holds the title deed of your life. He owns you. You "are not your own" for you "are bought with a price" (I Corinthians 6:19-20). The Romans 12:1 presentation is simply delivering to Christ what He already owns, for full possession. It is a matter of "hands-on" possession.

Should it not fill us with awe that the Christ who already owns us does not subjugate us by force, but rather beseeches us to recognize His lordship by presenting all to Him? He is Lord whether you recognize it or not, but in order to benefit fully from it, you must recognize it.

Perhaps you might wonder, if "your body is the temple of the Holy Spirit" at salvation, why does Romans 12:1 beseech you to present your body? Because the Spirit who lives in your spirit at salvation yearns to possess all of you at surrender. When you were saved, you received as much of the Holy Spirit as you are going to receive (He is one Person), but He does not necessarily possess all of you. This is in contradistinction to "second blessing" theology, which receives something that you did not already have. At salvation you possess in fact all that you are going to possess. The question we are dealing with relates to the function of what you already possess in fact. When you surrender all to Him as Lord and Life, He then possesses all of you, and you experience Him as Leader and Enabler. For some, this is immediately dramatic; for others, this is increasingly dramatic. The fact that Romans 12:1 articulates both a presentation/reception and a practice/relationship indicates that this is not a "second work of grace" or "second blessing" mentality with a "having arrived" concept. Rather, it is a second work of grace, and a third, and a fourth, and so on. In other words, the life of surrender and faith is a continual responsibility. But it continually accesses the Spirit of grace.

When you are saved, you receive the Person of the Spirit. When you surrender to and, thus, depend on the Person, you receive the power (or promise) of the Spirit. Have you presented your body to the Holy Spirit to possess all of you, and, thus, received Him as Lord and Life? In other words, have you *received* the Spirit? Simply put, have you definitely transferred your dependence to the Spirit as Senior Partner to lead you, and Supernatural Power to enable you?

C. L. Culpepper of the Shantung Revival, several years prior to the revival, was confronted by a sister missionary named Marie Monsen. She asked him, "Have you been filled with the Holy Spirit?" Culpepper stammered out "something less than a definite reply." Then, recognizing his uncertainty, "she carefully related a personal experience 15 years earlier when she had prayed for and received the promise of the Holy Spirit as recorded in Galatians 3:14" based on the worthiness of Christ.[1] Culpepper then began to search the Scriptures for the reality of this truth. Then, with understanding, by faith he entered into the Spirit-filled life. This and more led to a mighty outpouring of the Spirit which lasted for fifteen years.[2]

## THE COMMANDS OF RELATIONSHIP

Having studied the one event-oriented command, now let us turn our attention to the four process-oriented commands. These are all present tense commands indicating linear, or continuous, action. Of these four "continuous" commands, one is a command of allowance (the passive voice), and the other three are commands of action (the active voice).

# The Command of Allowance

Ephesians 5:18 commands, "And be not drunk with wine, wherein is excess [debauchery]; but **be filled with the Spirit.**"

## Present

The present tense indicates continuous action: *keep on being filled with the Spirit.*

## Plural

The plural indicates that the command is for every believer, not just preachers and so forth.

## Pilotage

The term *filled* denotes control. The same word was used when Peter confronted Ananias in Acts 5:3, "Why hath Satan filled thine heart to lie to the Holy Spirit?" Ephesians 5:18 contrasts yielding to the controlling influence of spirits (alcohol) negatively, to yielding to the controlling influence of the Spirit positively. Just as it is wicked to be under the influence of alcohol, it is also wicked to not be under the influence of the Holy Spirit. Just as drunkenness is a serious offense in the Christian church, so walking in the flesh is a serious matter!

## Power

The definite article *the* is absent before the name of the Spirit, therefore emphasizing the power of the Spirit.

## Passive

With the active voice of a verb, you initiate the action; but with the passive voice, you allow the action to be done to you. The use of the passive voice in Ephesians 5:18 shocks many, but it highlights the concept of the Spirit-filled life. The agent of the Spirit-filled life is not you but the Spirit.

So the command here is literally *keep on allowing yourself to be filled with the leadership and power of the Spirit.* This does not imply passivity, or it would not be commanded. God holds the believer responsible. When we do not allow ourselves to be filled with the Spirit, we are being disobedient to this command. The scriptural terminology seems to indicate being "filled" for a specific need (e.g., Acts 4:31), as well as being "full" as a condition (e.g., Acts 11:24).

The question is this: How do you "allow" such leadership and enablement? The answer is through obeying the three active commands.

# The Commands of Action

All three of these commands use the active voice, indicating that you must initiate the action (to allow the passive part—God's part—to take place). Of the three active commands, one regards the Spirit's power and two regard the Spirit's person.

## The Command Regarding the Spirit's Power

Galatians 5:16 exhorts, "**Walk in the Spirit**, and ye shall not fulfil the lust of the flesh." The absence of the definite article *the* in the original language emphasizes the Spirit's power or operation (as opposed to His Person). What does it mean to *walk in the Spirit*? As we have noted in previous chapters, what is walking? Walking is reiterated steps. So, walking in the Spirit is reiterated steps in the Spirit. Colossians 2:6 teaches, "As you have therefore received Christ Jesus the Lord [How do you receive Christ? By faith.], so walk ye in Him [How do you walk? By faith.]. II Corinthians 5:7 plainly says, "For we walk by faith." Steps of faith provide the walk of faith. The Spirit-filled life is one step at a time. Do not let Satan defeat you by focusing on the past and fearing that you will repeat the same mistakes, or by focusing on the future and fearing you will miss step again. This will get you off the position of faith. Rather, focus on the present step. Simply trust the promise for each step and the Spirit will enable.

Galatians 3:5 says, "He therefore that ministereth [lit., is supplying] to you the Spirit, and worketh [*energeo*/energizes] miracles [*dunamis*] among you, doeth He it by the works of the law, or by the hearing of faith?" Clearly, steps of faith access the supply of the Spirit for miraculous living! A life that is not on the miraculous plane of holy living and powerful service is substandard to cooperative living with the Holy Spirit. A life that is not supernatural is superficial. A life that is not miraculous is mundane.

Remember from earlier chapters that the dependence must be tied to the steps of obedience, or it is not dependence. The steps are generally thought-steps, word-steps, or action-steps. Without the movement of the step of faith, it is not faith. *Walk in the Spirit* pictures the life that, step by step depends on the Spirit for holiness and service.

## The Commands Regarding the Spirit's Person

Two more active voice commands remain. Ephesians 4:30 says "And **grieve not the Holy Spirit of God**, whereby ye are sealed unto the day of redemption." The presence of the definite article *the* emphasizes the Spirit's person. He is a Person who can be grieved. The word *grieve* is translated "sorrow" in John 16:6. The Spirit is a Person who feels sorrow. The present tense command with the negative *not* indicates the cessation of an action already in progress. Literally it means: *Stop grieving the Spirit.*

The context is a series of commands to do right. Therefore, the implication of *stop grieving the Spirit* is "Deal with your sin!" The emphasis of this command is confession. I John 1:9 states, "If we confess [admit; agree with God] our sins [plural, therefore, be specific], He is faithful and just to forgive us our sins, and to cleanse us from all unrighteousness." Proverbs 28:13 warns and exhorts, "He that covereth his sins shall not prosper: but whoso confesseth and forsaketh them shall have mercy." Friend, are you willing to deal with your sin and stop grieving the Spirit? Ask Him to search your heart. You may be surprised, for without His searchlight, "the heart is deceitful above all things, and desperately wicked: who can know it?" (Jeremiah 17:9) Perhaps the following categories may aid in the searching of your heart:

First, have you confessed all known sin? Is there any sin you have not been willing for the Spirit's searchlight to expose? Have you forgiven where you need to forgive? Everyone? Will you confess your sin and stop grieving the Spirit?

Second, have you surrendered every doubtful thing? If something is questionable and you continue in it, are you not giving the Devil the benefit of the doubt and, thus, grieving the Spirit? If something is doubtful, will you banish it, "for whatsoever is not of faith is sin" (Romans 14:23)?

Third, is there anyone that you need to be reconciled to? Jesus said in Matthew 5:23-24, "Therefore if thou bring thy gift to the altar [certainly the *living sacrifice* of absolute surrender applies], and there rememberest that thy brother hath ought against thee [implying that you did something to provoke him]; Leave there the gift before the altar, and go thy way; first be reconciled to thy brother, and then come and offer thy gift." Generally the principle of private sin demands private confession. But here we see that personal sin (wronging a brother and he is aware of it) demands personal confession. On the same basis, public sin demands public confession. Even if another wrongs you initially, have you wronged them back? Have you spoken an unkind word or criticized them to others? Have you spoken negatively about them to those who are not a solution to the problem? Is there bitterness or resentment toward another person? Friend, is there anyone to whom you need to be reconciled? Will you make that visit or phone call, or write that letter to deal with your sin, and stop grieving the Spirit? Many times I have been convicted by the Spirit to make things right with another. But what joy comes when you trust the Spirit's enablement to deal with sin.

Fourth, does restitution need application in any account? Have you restored anything wrongfully taken? Many are convicted in revivals to restore even small things from years earlier.

While crossing a busy street one day, C. H. Spurgeon stopped in the middle of the road. He tipped his hat downward for a moment, and then continued making his way across. Someone who knew him saw him do this and scolded him for stopping in the middle of the street because of the danger of possibly being hit (perhaps by a horse and buggy!). Spurgeon replied that a cloud had come between him and God, and he had to stop at once to deal with it! May we, too, be sensitive to not grieve the Holy Spirit.

In this regard, consider the names of the Spirit in Scripture:

He is the Spirit of wisdom (Isaiah 11:2; Ephesians 1:17). When we rely on man's thoughts and reasonings, we grieve the Spirit.

He is the Spirit of understanding (Isaiah 11:2). When we depend on our intellect alone and do not look to the Spirit to illumine the Word, thus making the Scripture merely dry facts and not the living realities that relate to those facts, we are grieving the Spirit.

He is the Spirit of counsel (Isaiah 11:2). When we look to man's counsel and psychology without looking to God, we grieve the Spirit.

He is the Spirit of might (Isaiah 11:2). When we "trust in chariots, and . . . in horses," we grieve the Spirit.

He is the Spirit of knowledge (Isaiah 11:2). When we do not look to the Spirit to teach us and are content to be ignorant of the knowledge of God, we grieve the Spirit.

He is the Spirit of the fear of the Lord (Isaiah 11:2). When we fear man, man's pressure and man's power, we are ensnared and grieve the Spirit.

He is the Spirit of judgment (lit., justice, Isaiah 28:6). When we deal unfairly with others making false judgments, we grieve the Spirit.

He is the Spirit of grace (Zechariah 12:10; Hebrews 10:29). Grace is the undeserved favor of supernatural enablement. When we content ourselves with our natural ability instead of looking to God for Spirit-enabling, we grieve the Spirit.

He is the Spirit of supplication (Zechariah 12:10). When we are prayerless or merely ritualistic in our praying, we grieve the Spirit.

He is the Spirit of truth (John 14:17; 15:26; 16:13). When we embrace deceptions and "doctrines of demons," not looking to the Spirit to reveal the Scriptures as the plumb line of truth, we grieve the Spirit.

He is the Spirit of holiness (Romans 1:4). When we love the world, the things that are in the world and the lifestyles of worldliness, we grieve the Spirit.

He is the Spirit of revelation (Ephesians 1:17). When we do not seek Him to reveal to us "the deep things of God," we grieve the Spirit.

He is the Spirit of power (II Timothy 1:7). When we continue ineffectively in service for God, sickly and anemic, we grieve the Spirit.

He is the Spirit of love (II Timothy 1:7). When we are selfish rather than selfless, when we do not do right to others regardless, when we do not possess *agape* love, we grieve the Spirit.

He is the Spirit of a sound mind (II Timothy 1:7). When we are emotionally unstable, we grieve the Spirit.

He is the Spirit of glory (I Peter 4:14). When we glorify man or veil the glory of Christ within because of walking in the flesh, we grieve the Spirit.

He is the Spirit of life (Revelation 11:11). When we have "a name that [we live], and art dead," we grieve the Spirit.

O may we stop grieving the Spirit!

The second active voice command is I Thessalonians 5:19: **"Quench not the Spirit."** Again, the presence of the definite article *the* emphasizes the Spirit's person. Also, the present tense command with the negative *not* indicates the cessation of an action already in progress. Literally, *stop quenching the Spirit.*

The focus here is to always say "yes" to the Spirit. Once you know it is His voice, obey. Consider how many more people we would witness to if we would stop quenching the Spirit. Charlie Kittrell, a pastor in Indianapolis, prays every morning that the Spirit will guide him regarding to whom he should give tracts or a verbal witness. Then he looks to the Spirit to guide him throughout the day. Consequently, he passes out an incredible amount of tracts and regularly leads people to Christ! He tells of one occasion when the Spirit convinced him that a certain relative in Pennsylvania was ready to get saved. So Charlie Kittrell and his wife packed their car and, in obedience to the Spirit, left for Pennsylvania. They did not contact this relative ahead of time to tell her they were coming. When they arrived, within the first day this relative asked Pastor Kittrell if he would explain the meaning of John chapter three to her. Before they left town, this relative came to Christ!

How we need to cooperate with the Spirit and stop quenching the Spirit!

Simply put, the three active commands teach us to depend on the Spirit to deal with sin and to obey in all things. Walking in the Spirit (steps of dependence) enables us to stop grieving the Spirit (by dealing with sin) and to stop quenching the Spirit (by always saying "yes"). Again, the bottom line is dependence. This "allows" us to be filled with the Spirit.

To summarize the believers responsibility from all five commands, there is an initial surrender/dependence and there is a continual surrender/dependence. The former is a presentation; the latter is a practice. The former is a reception; the latter is a relationship. The former is an entrance into the Spirit-filled life; the latter is the pathway of the Spirit-filled life.

## Conclusion

When the believer cooperates with the Holy Spirit in living reality, then he can begin to understand passages like Acts 15:28, "For it seemed good to the Holy Spirit, and to us." What a blessed partnership! My friend, is the reality of God supreme in your daily experience? Just as an unsaved man does not truly believe in Jesus until he depends on Jesus, a saved man does not truly believe in the Holy Spirit until he is depending on the Holy Spirit. Many fundamentalists are as guilty regarding the Holy Spirit as Roman Catholics are guilty regarding Christ. The Roman Catholics know *about* Jesus. Much of what they know is correct—not all, but much. But they do not depend on Him as a living, personal Savior because they are depending on themselves. Fundamentalists know *about* the Holy Spirit. Much of what we know is correct—not all, but much. But many are not depending on Him as a living personal Sanctifier because they are depending on themselves. Just as salvation is not a religion, but a relationship with a person—Jesus Christ, likewise sanctification is not a religion, but a relationship with a person—the Holy Spirit.

To overreact to the Charismatic error regarding the Spirit is to reveal an incomplete grasp regarding the truths of the Spirit. For example, when Mormons or Jehovah's Witnesses pervert the gospel, we do not overreact the other way because we have a firm grip on the gospel. If we have overreacted to the excesses of Charismatics regarding the Spirit, then it reveals that we do not have a solid grip on the truths of the Spirit. True, it is wrong to interpret the Scriptures by one's experience as some Charismatics may do. However, it is also wrong to interpret the Scriptures by one's lack of experience.

Jesus said in John 4:24, "They that worship [God] must worship Him in spirit and in truth." Consider the twofold dimension of true worship. One without the other is incorrect. Subjective experience without objective truth is not orthodoxy. An example of this is the "strange fire" of the Charismatic excess. On the other side of the issue, objective truth without subjective experience is dead orthodoxy. Fundamental churches with "no fire" sadly exemplify this extreme. The balance of objective truth with subjective experience is living orthodoxy. This is the biblical reality of "Spirit-fire."

Paul's "declaring . . . the testimony of God [Word of God] . . . was not with enticing words of man's wisdom, but in demonstration of the Spirit and of power: That [their] faith should not stand in the wisdom of men, but in the power of God" (I Corinthians 2:1, 4-5). Notice Paul did not say, ". . . but in the Word of God" but rather *but in the power of God.* This does not de-emphasize the Word of God since we know already he was *declaring . . . the testimony of God.* This simply emphasizes that the Word of God demands *the demonstration of the Spirit and of power* to be truly effective. Do we not desperately need the partnership of the Spirit?

G. Gampbell Morgan wrote in a book originally published in 1900: "During the last quarter of the century, men in all sections of the Christian Church have spoken and written upon this great theme of the ministry and work of the Holy Spirit. Dr. Scofield, of Northfield, says: *More books, booklets, and tracts upon that subject have issued from the press during the last twenty years than in all the time since the invention of printing.* The truth thus proclaimed has resulted in new life within the churches; and everywhere eager souls are enquiring after fuller, more definite, more systematic knowledge of this great ministry of the Spirit. The ministries that are forceful in the accomplishment of definite results in the interests of the kingdom of God to-day, are the ministries of men who are putting the whole burden of their work upon the Holy Spirit of God . . . Wherever the Spirit of God is being enthroned in preaching and in all Christian work, and having His rightful place as the Administrator of the things of Jesus Christ, apostolic results are seen to follow."[3]

Are we willing to thus cooperate with the Holy Spirit? "Absolute surrender" perhaps states this truth in a nutshell. Are we willing for this? We must be willing to move from "controlled carnality," where we have a sense of control, to dependence on the Spirit for leadership and enablement, where He is in control.

In early 1859 the tightrope walker from France named Blondin left Barnum's circus and entered a partnership with Harry Colcord. Colcord acted as the "clerk and agent" while Blondin acted as the stuntman. In hopes of making a fortune, they arranged for a tightrope to be stretched across the Niagara Falls. "The final length of the rope pathway stretched 1,100 feet across the wild torrent of the Niagara River which was 190 feet below . . . Installed . . . the heavy strand sagged about 20 feet in the middle of the span. Since the gorge is normally windy, the rope moved sluggishly sideways and up and down." With a massive crowd watching with fright and anticipation, Blondin made his first walk on June 30, 1859.

"A quarter of the way out, Blondin stopped, yawned, and stretched before lying down on the rope and placing the 38-foot balancing pole across his chest. He even appeared to snooze for a few minutes. Neatly arising, not using his hands, Blondin casually ambled out to midpoint, pausing on the swaying strand to unroll a coil of thin lead-tipped rope.

"He patiently dangled the rope 180 feet down to a waiting boat, where a small bottle was attached. The daredevil reeled the rope back, sat down, and took a drink. Resuming his journey toward Canada, Blondin abruptly performed a backflip somersault, raising the tempos of many hearts throughout the crowd. Then he ran lightly up the mooring as the applause from both banks momentarily suppressed the roar of Niagara Falls." He was good at it! He continued throughout the summer performing crowd-pleasing acts.

"On July 4, Blondin crossed in a heavy sack of blankets blindly feeling his way. On his return, he walked backward. He bicycled. Once he came out pushing a wheelbarrow bearing a small stove. In midair, Blondin fired the stove and prepared, cooked, and ate an omelet. At least once, he stood on his head on the rope." Not only was he good, perhaps he was crazy!

Yet in order to keep the crowds coming, Blondin thought of an incredible stunt. "In early August, Blondin told Colcord, 'Harry, here's a stunt that will complete our fortunes! I'll find a man and carry him over.'" They put out the word for volunteers, yet strangely no one volunteered! "Then Blondin proposed, 'Harry, you're a small man like myself. I can carry you. Be a good fellow and come along.' Harry blushed and stammered—he couldn't say yes or no. But at a meeting of the star and his agent with the press, Blondin cheerfully announced that he would carry his friend, Harry Colcord" across.

"On August 17, after landing on the Canadian side, Blondin realized that Colcord was in a state of terror, hardly responding to him, staring into the gorge where the roiling water sped by at 42 miles per hour. So Blondin firmly took hold and led his companion out to the brink beside the rope as about 100,000 people called encouragement. In a daze, Harry M. Colcord, apprentice daredevil, mounted Blondin's back, wrapped his arms around Blondin's neck, and placed his feet into harnessed stirrups. It was a load! Colcord weighed a little less than Blondin—136 pounds. The balancing pole added about 40 more pounds. As Blondin walked out, Colcord tightened his embrace. As Blondin barely grunted to release his grip, Harry, by supreme will, obeyed. Harry remembered the moment:

'Out over that horrible gulf I heard the roar of the water below and the hum which ran through the crowd. As we cleared the brink the hum ceased—the strain had spread to them.

'Blondin walked on steadily, pausing for one brief moment at each point where the guy ropes joined the main cable. The line was a trifle steadier at these points . . . Blondin halted at the last resting point before the middle span and yelled above the roar of water and wind, "Harry, you are no longer Colcord; you are Blondin. Until I clear this place be a part of me—mind, body, and soul. If I sway, sway with me. Do not attempt to do any balancing yourself.""[4] And Harry Colcord—cooperated, and they made it across!

Notice the analogy: Compare "Harry, you are no longer Colcord; you are Blondin" with "not I, but Christ." Compare "Be a part of me—mind, body, and soul" with absolute surrender—the initial surrender/dependence. Also, compare "If I sway, sway with me. Do not do any balancing yourself" with continual surrender/dependence.

What a difference it makes when we cooperate with the Spirit. Ritualistic prayer meetings become real. Faith is increased for souls and for revival. The greatest prayer meetings we have ever known have been when we openly depended on the Holy Spirit to guide the prayer time. O the blessing when time is lost because of the keen awareness of the presence of God.

What is the Holy Spirit to you? What does the Spirit mean to you? Will you unashamedly receive Him by a definite choice to depend on Him for everything, thus presenting your all to Him? Will you continue a relationship of dependence on Him as a living offering in practice? As you daily depend on Him and, thus, walk in the Spirit, as you deal with sin and, thus, grieve not the Spirit, as you obey His voice, and, thus, quench not the Spirit, you are allowing yourself to be filled with the Spirit. The commands and promises of Scripture reveal that you can be filled with the Spirit and know it. If you will deal with all known sin and depend on the Spirit for a clean heart, you can say by faith, "I have a clean heart. I have trusted the Lord for it. He has done it regardless of how I feel." This act of consecration opens the way for a life of consecration. This is the blessed communion with the Spirit of Jesus Christ. This is the partnership revealed in "I live; yet not I, but Christ liveth in me" (Galatians 2:20), "I labored: . . . yet not I, but the grace of God which was with me" (I Corinthians 15:10), and "I also labor, striving according to His working, which worketh in me mightily" (Colossians 1:29). What an amazing possibility! The communion of the Holy Spirit is the cooperation of a partnership with the Holy Spirit.

---

[1] C. L. Culpepper, *The Shantung Revival* (Atlanta: Home Mission Board, 1971, reprint 1993), p. 8.

[2] Ibid., pp. 12-14.

[3] G. Campbell Morgan, *The Spirit of God* (Grand Rapids: Baker Book House, reprint 1983), pp. 14-15.

[4] K. C. Tessendorf, "White Knuckles Over Niagara," *Highlights for Children*, September 1998, pp. 28-30.

CHAPTER TEN

# TRUE BREAD FROM HEAVEN

Endowment: The Promise of the Spirit
Enfeeblement: The Problem of Unbelief
Entitlement: The Provision of Christ
Enthronement: The Presentation and Practice of Surrender and Faith
**Enablement: The Power of Living**
Entrustment: The Purpose of Usefulness

When we actually admit in contrite confession our unbelief and, rising in faith, focus on our grand provision in Christ; when we then present our bodies to the Spirit of Christ and depend daily on Him to make us living sacrifices, what is the constant result? This brings us to the Spirit-filled life in practical living. At this point, we will go beyond the broad concepts and meditate on the bite-sized pieces of the Spirit-filled life of feeding on Christ. Will you look to the Spirit of truth for illumination of truth?

# JOHN 6:56

One time I overheard my wife speaking on the telephone with her mother, and they were talking about "feeding the starter." I did not know we had a pet to feed! Later I discovered it has something to do with baking fresh sourdough bread. Though I do not understand how all of that works, I soon learned that when the compelling scent of fresh-baking bread wafted under my nose, it was time to make my way into the kitchen. I would gauge it so that I just "happened" to be at the kitchen table when the oven door would open and out came the loaves of fresh-ly baked bread! Mary Lynn would melt butter on the tops of the loaves, letting it drizzle down the sides. Then she would slice that fresh bread, and we would devour a half a loaf or sometimes a whole loaf at once!

There's nothing like freshly baked bread. I like all sorts of breads. I like the grain breads, oat bread, wheat bread, and rye bread (especially when it's thinly sliced with melted butter and fresh strawberry jam!). Ital-ian bread with the chewy dough on the inside and French bread with a crunchy crust on the outside are quite delicious. I certainly enjoy Irish brown bread and Greek pita bread. We cannot forget the delicious Mexi-can tortillas. Then there is a type of bread from India, which you tear off piece by piece and dip it into delicious sauces. It's very nice! It is interest-ing that people around the world are familiar with bread. Are you hungry?

After feeding the 5,000 with barley loaves and fishes, Jesus gives the discourse on "true bread from heaven" (John 6:32). The analogy to bread is extremely helpful as it is a common reality in nearly everyone's life. Certainly as a figure for food, it is a reality in everybody's life.

## SETTING THE TABLE

In order to set the table, I want to begin by noting six principles in John 6 regarding *true bread from heaven*.

First, the Bread of God is life-giving. John 6:33 says, "For **the bread of God** is He which cometh down from heaven, and **giveth life** unto the world." This Bread gives life!

Second, Jesus is the Bread of Life. John 6:35 says, "And Jesus said unto them, **I am the bread of life.**" So He is the One who came down from heaven to give life to the world.

Third, we eat this bread by believing on Christ. John 6:35 says, "And Jesus said unto them, I am the bread of life: he that cometh to Me shall never hunger [therefore the one who comes *eats*]; and he that believeth on Me shall never thirst [therefore *believing* correlates to *eating* and *drinking* Christ]."

In John 6:47 Jesus says, "He that believeth on Me hath everlasting life." What is the condition for receiving everlasting life? Believing on Christ. In John 6:54 Jesus says, "Whoso eateth My flesh, and drinketh My blood, hath eternal life." Here what is the condition for receiving everlasting life? Eating Christ's flesh and drinking His blood. Although this may seem repulsive, do you see the parallel? In verse 47 the condition for having everlasting life is believing on Christ. Yet in verse 54 the condition for having eternal life is eating Christ's flesh and drinking His blood. Therefore, **believing** corresponds to **eating and drinking Christ.** Eating and drinking Christ simply pictures the act of faith. Remember, to believe on Christ is to trust or depend on Christ. We eat the Bread of Life by depending on Christ. So eating True Bread is parallel to depending on Christ. This is vitally significant to understanding this passage.

Fourth, we believe on Christ by depending on His words. John 6:63 says, "It is the Spirit that quickeneth [gives life]; the flesh profiteth nothing: the words [plural of *rhema*] that I speak unto you, they are spirit [i.e., spiritual, demanding the work of the Spirit], and they are life." Jesus is called "the Word" in John 1. There is a mystery of oneness between the incarnate Word [Christ, the *Logos*] and the inscribed Word [the Scripture, the *Logos*]. John 1:4 says, "In Him [the Word] was life." John 6:63 says, "the words . . . are life." There is also a mystery of oneness between the Word [the *Logos* as the whole Scripture] and the words [the *rhemas* as the specific parts which make up the whole]. Jesus is the Word, which is the Words, which is life. We depend on the living Word [Christ the *Logos*] by depending on the living words [the *rhemas* of Scripture]. The *rhema* is the foundation of faith in Romans 10:17: "So then faith cometh by hearing, and hearing by the word [*rhema*] of God." Yet Christ is the foundation of faith in John 6:47, 54, 56, and so on. No wonder John 6 gives a parallel between *the Bread of Life* (John 6:35, 48) and *the words [of] life* (John 6:63). Therefore, we believe on Christ [feed on Christ] by depending on His words. Feeding on Christ, the True Bread, simply is one bite at a time.

Fifth, this begins with salvation. John 6:47 says, "He that believeth on Me hath everlasting life." When a person comes to understand and agree that he has sinned against a holy God and, therefore, falls short of His standard of perfection, that he deserves the just judgment of hell, that

Christ died for his sins and rose again, and then he transfers his dependence from himself and whatever he was trusting in to only Jesus Christ to save him from sin and hell, Christ gives him everlasting life. Since this everlasting life is forever, it cannot ever be lost. "O taste and see that the Lord is good." Have you truly eaten this first meal of salvation?

Sixth, this continues with the Spirit-filled life. John 6:56 says, "He that eateth My flesh, and drinketh My blood, dwelleth in Me, and I in him." The word *dwelleth* is the word translated *abideth* in John 15. *Abide* is a word dealing with the Spirit-filled life, not salvation itself. So here the passage goes beyond salvation to the abundant Christian life.

## THE MAIN MEAL

Having set the table, let us now focus on the main meal. In John 6:56 Jesus declares, "He that eateth [is eating] My flesh, and drinketh [is drinking] My blood, dwelleth [is abiding] in Me, and I in him." As physical food is necessary for physical growth, so spiritual food is necessary for spiritual growth. As we feed on the True Bread, we abide in Christ, and He abides in us. This verse teaches us that **spiritual growth occurs only through the twofold nature of abiding**. What is the twofold nature of abiding? John 6:56 reveals by analogy two factors which comprise the twofold nature of abiding.

## Bread Is Necessary

The first factor is that bread or food is necessary. Although we enjoy food, we must eat. If we did not eat, we would die. Food is staple. A staple is a chief commodity and absolutely necessary. In other words, we depend on it. Why do we depend on food? What does food do for us?

## Bread Is Nourishing

The second factor is that bread or food is nourishing. It strengthens and sustains us so that we can be productive. We could say it enables us physically.

In summary, bread is necessary; we depend on it. Because bread is nourishing, it enables us. Now let's see the spiritual truth behind the picture that Christ is painting. True Bread is necessary; we depend on Him. Because True Bread is nourishing, He enables us.

A youth pastor once approached me after I had preached several nights on the Spirit-filled life and asked, "Is it possible that I am stumbling over the simplicity of the Spirit-filled life like a lost person stumbles over the simplicity of salvation?" I answered, "That's exactly right!" God-dependence accesses Spirit-enabling. This is the case in both salvation and the Spirit-filled life.

Herein lies the twofold nature of abiding. First, as bread is staple physically, and we depend on it, so the Bread of Life is staple spiritually, and we depend on Him. Secondly, as bread is sustaining physically, and it strengthens us, so the Bread of Life is sustaining spiritually, and He enables us.

Man's responsibility is God-dependence. This is how we abide in Christ. God's promise is Spirit-enabling. This is how Christ abides in us. John 6:56 unfolds the twofold nature of abiding: "He that eateth My flesh, and drinketh My blood [This is our believing on Christ], dwelleth [is abiding] in Me, and I [am abiding] in him." We abide in Christ by depending on Him, and He abides in us by enabling us. Christ here defines the word *abiding*.

The one who is eating and is drinking Christ is abiding in Christ, and Christ is abiding in him. In other words, since eating and drinking Christ corresponds to believing on Christ, as already seen, the one who is believing on Christ is abiding in Christ, and Christ is abiding in him. This is what verse 56 plainly says. For years I wondered what it meant to *abide*. Many explanations I heard differed. However, John 6 provides the key to spiritually understanding the word *abide*. This key unlocks the *abide* passages such as John 15 and I John 2-4.

## ANALOGIES

To add more understanding to this feeding on *true bread from heaven* and, therefore, the twofold nature of abiding, let's open the window of analogy to allow more light to shine on this table of Bread. Christ gives us the analogy of feeding on bread (food), of which we are well experienced, to help us understand how to feed on Him. Consider the following lessons by way of analogy.

First, physically when we eat (depend) on bread, we are abiding in the bread (*He who is eating . . . is abiding*). Likewise, spiritually when we feed (depend) on Christ, we are abiding in Christ (*He who is eating My flesh . . . is abiding in Me*). The way we abide in Christ is by believing. May we never forget this staple truth.

Second, when the bread sustains us physically, it is abiding in us (*He who is eating . . . is abiding . . . and* [the bread is abiding] *in him*). Likewise when Christ enables us spiritually, He is abiding in us (*He who is eating My flesh . . . is abiding in Me, and I in him*). The way Christ abides in us is through enabling. Again, may we never forget this sustaining truth.

Third, when you physically eat bread, it fills you, it lives in you, in a sense it becomes you through your physical look. The food you eat sustains every cell in your body. So there is truth to the cliché "You are what you eat." However, it is all through your physical look. Likewise, when you spiritually eat True Bread by depending on Christ, He lives in you and even through you, and yet it is through your spirit, soul, and body.

Fourth, eating is necessary for physical growth and productivity. Likewise, eating True Bread by depending on Christ is necessary for spiritual growth and productivity. Herein lies a great truth with many ramifications. A baby may be born physically, but if the child does not eat, he will die. Therefore, although a child is born, growth is not automatic. The child must eat in order to grow. Likewise, one may be born again, but if he does not eat, he will not grow. Being born again does not mean one will automatically grow. He must eat in order to grow spiritually. Many are deceived into thinking spiritual growth will somehow automatically occur. Spiritual growth occurs only through the appropriation of faith. Just as it is vitally necessary to eat food for physical growth and productivity, it is vitally and absolutely necessary to feed (depend) on Christ for spiritual growth and productivity.

Why is it that you can have two Christians in the same church, for the same number of years, under the same pastor, hearing the same preaching, eating at the same table, and having access to the same food—yet the one has grown into a mature, useful Christian while the other is still a babe in Christ? The answer is that one has fed on Christ; the other has not. One has depended on the words of life (faith), and the other has depended on the flesh (unbelief). Obviously, you must be born in order to grow. But growth is not automatic, physically or spiritually. It only comes as you feed. Spiritual growth occurs only through the daily choices to depend on the reality of the words of God.

Feeding on the Bread of Life is vital for spiritual life and living. You can even be at the table, but that does not mean that you are eating. Most parents know what it is like to have a child who comes to the table but decides that he does not want to eat. A good parent has means of helping the child to change his way of thinking! Our heavenly Father also has ways of helping us change our way of thinking. Now certainly it is helpful to be at the table—to read the Word of God and to hear the preaching of the Word. But that does not mean that you are eating. Physically speaking, food does not somehow come off the plate and ooze into your pores! You must eat to benefit from the food. Likewise, spiritually speaking, spiritual food does not somehow ooze into your pores while you are in church. You must eat True Bread by making choices of faith in order to benefit from this heavenly manna. Spiritual growth is not automatic or inevitable. Spiritual growth occurs only through the twofold nature of abiding.

I remember the husband of a lady in my father's church who got saved. For two years he did not grow much. Then he finally started feeding on the Word and grew very rapidly. In fact, though his wife had prayed for his salvation and later for his spiritual growth, when he finally advanced spiritually, he passed her up. Soon she was thinking he was going too far!

Fifth, we eat bread (food) one meal at a time. In other words, we are not constantly eating at the table. You eat a meal and go forward in the strength of the meal until the next meal. Both the eating and the going in the strength of the food are acts of dependence. Likewise, we depend on Christ one conscious feeding at a time. Then He, as the Bread of Life, enables us to live in accordance to the words on which we are depending. The reality is that both the conscious feeding and the living in the strength of that food are acts of dependence. The former is the conscious act of faith as you choose to depend on the words of life. The latter is the quiet transaction of faith as you go forward in the confidence that the "food" will sustain. You are depending on the Bread of Life for both. Just as when you eat physically, you go forward in quiet confidence that the food is strengthening you without even thinking about it, so spiritually it is the same principle.

Let me illustrate. I was with a dear pastor friend in a church just two blocks outside of Queens, New York City. The pastor had grown up in Queens and is a true native of New York City with its own accent and ways. While visiting new contacts with the pastor and a teen from his church, we visited a lady from Haiti. She graciously invited us in and led us into the living room, offering us a seat on a large L-shaped sofa. She sat on the farthest end. The pastor sat just past the joint of the "L" as it turned perpendicular. Then the teen sat down next to him. Since there was a coffee table and I did not want to climb over their legs, I sat down next to the teen at the end of the sofa. We had no sooner sat down when the preacher briskly said in the typical New York manner, "Well, this is Evangelist John Van Gelderen, and he's going to tell you how to get saved. All right, Brother John, go ahead!" This was the quickest version of phase one in witnessing that I had ever seen! The lady showed no outward sign of excitement either. Well, I knew I at least needed to get closer to where the lady was seated. So I said to the lady, "Do you mind if I move to your part of the sofa?" As I was climbing over the legs of the teen and the pastor, I had just enough time to "eat." Are you with me? I had just enough time for a conscious transaction of faith.

Digressing from this story for just a moment, isn't it true in the physical realm that there are certain foods that you like so much, you eat them over and over? In fact, many who frequent the same restaurant order the same meal every time! The same is true spiritually. Some meals you will eat over and over again. One such meal for me is Psalm 55:22: "Cast thy burden upon the Lord, and He shall sustain thee." This applies to many situations.

Now, back to our story. I did not pray publicly, but as I crossed over their legs I exercised faith based on Psalm 55:22. It went something like this in my own heart, "Lord, HELP!" But once I sat down and began declaring the gospel, I could no longer think about my exercising faith. I had to now go forward in the confidence that the "food" was doing what it said it would do.

Although this dear lady did not show much expression, she did follow the gospel and answer my questions. The Spirit was convincing even though, on the surface, it was not obvious. When confronted with depending on Christ to save her from sin and hell, she said yes and was gloriously saved!

From this witnessing situation we see an example of this analogy regarding eating one meal at a time. You must look to the Spirit of Christ to enable you to declare the gospel. However, once you consciously cast your dependence on God, you must stop thinking about that and now focus on communicating the gospel, knowing that the Spirit is enabling you. While you are witnessing, you may not be thinking of faith in God. You are thinking about what you are saying. But based on your choice of God-dependence, you can go forward in the confidence of His enablement.

Sixth, closely akin to this last analogy is that fact that you must eat repeatedly both physically and spiritually. Often we eat a meal and feel so full that we say, "I'm so full that I'm not going to eat for a week!" Yet a few hours later we say, "Hey, what's cookin'?" Likewise, just because you trusted God today for a given need does not mean you will never need to trust Him again. Rather you eat a meal and go forward in the strength of that meal, but when the sustenance wanes, you come back for more nourishment.

Seventh, as you physically eat bread, it automatically begins sustaining you. The eating is not automatic. Yet, whether you consciously think about it or not, once you have eaten, the food starts sustaining you. Likewise, as you eat (depend) on Christ spiritually, He begins to enable you. Notice in John 6:56, Jesus promises "He that eateth My flesh, and drinketh My blood, dwelleth [is abiding] in Me, **and I in him.**" It is not "and I will sometime later abide in him." It is *and I in him.* So when you depend on Christ for the enabling to obey in holiness of life or power in service, He will enable you by His Spirit to obey. Why? Because it says so!

Eighth, the physical sustenance from food is for productivity. It is not so you can sit down and do nothing. Likewise, the spiritual enabling from the Bread of Life is for spiritual productivity (obedience in holiness to be what you ought to be and obedience in service to do what you ought to do). So the eating or dependence is for the enabling to obey in God's cause. The Spirit-filled life is not passivity. It is trust to obey, one bite at a time. Any concept of the Spirit-filled life that does not lead to practical holiness and powerful service is not the Spirit-filled life! Any concept of the Spirit-filled life that cuts corners and makes small compromises in the name of "resting" is missing the point of trusting to obey.

Ninth, physically you develop an appetite for what you eat. It amazes me how this works. You can ask a child about a certain food, "Do you like such and such?" He replies, "No, that's awful." So you ask, "Have you ever tried it?" And he says, "No, I never have!" Yet when he does, he may begin to find he likes it.

It amazes me how the palate differs around the United States. The Midwest is known as "meat-and-potatoes" country. If you go down South, they add some cornbread and freshly baked rolls with butter and jam, along with green beans (fatback included), black-eyed peas, and a myriad of vegetables. They also serve big pieces of fried chicken and plenty of ham. Amazingly, it's all in one meal! If you go West, they add a Mexican flare to their cuisine.

If you go overseas, the appetites vary greatly. In some countries, the eyeball of a fish is the valued part! Americans cringe at the thought. Yet one time a Chinese man in Singapore showed shock that Americans like cheese. If you stop and think about it, Chinese food does not use cheese. He said to me, in disgust, "Cheese is mold!" Well, it is—but we like it! Why? Because you develop an appetite for what you eat.

The same is true spiritually—you develop an appetite for what you eat. Therefore, if you do not have a hunger for the things of God, it is because you are eating at another table. Sadly, many Christians feed off the junk food of the world, the table of Hollywood with its sensuality that feeds the flesh, the table of humanism, the table of materialism, and so forth. These dry husks of the world dull one's spiritual appetite ever so subtly; they do not nourish. Rather, they are harmful to your spiritual health. However, those deceived by the delicacies of the Evil One may go through the motions of coming to the table; yet they do not feed because they are eating at another table.

A teen girl said to me, "Church is boring." I said, "Do you want to know why? It is because you are feeding at another table." When you are hungry, the food does not have to be fancy to be good. To the hungry soul, even plain food is good! Appetites must be fed. Your appetites reveal at which table you are feeding. Do you have an appetite for God and His Word? When you depend on God for His enablement in various areas of the Christian life, and experience victory over your tongue, victory over bitterness, victory in witnessing, and so forth—there is nothing boring about it! You develop an appetite for what you eat. At which table are you eating?

Tenth, eating is enjoyable. One man said, "In fact, it's the highlight of the day!" Spiritually, when you feed on True Bread and experience the enablement for victory over sin and power in service, there is great joy in the Lord. It's exciting as the life of the Bread of Life enables you to do what man cannot do.

In review, the twofold nature of abiding is simply God-dependence for Spirit-enabling. Man's responsibility is to abide in Christ (God-dependence). God's promise is to abide in us (Spirit-enabling). Bread is necessary—we depend on it. Bread is nourishing—it enables us. Spiritual growth occurs only through the twofold nature of abiding. We eat True Bread one bite at a time, one *rhema* at a time, one promise at a time.

## APPLICATION

The menu of Scripture offers a variety of foods for daily needs. However, let's limit some final application to the word *abide*. This is the key in discipleship. John 8:31 says, "Then said Jesus to those Jews which believed on Him. If ye continue in My word, then are ye My disciples indeed." God's plan is for believers to become disciples (learners). While a believer is a disciple in the sense of being a learner regarding the event of salvation, discipleship is a process of learning. However, discipleship is not automatic; it is conditional. Christ said to those who *believed on Him, If . . . then are ye My disciples indeed* [in truth or substance]. They were already disciples in the broad sense of being saved. Christ here speaks of being disciples in substance. What is the condition for discipleship? *If ye continue in My word.* The word *continue* is the same word translated *abide* in John 15. Christ teaches us that if we abide in His Word (dependence on His Word), then we are true disciples learning from Him. If there is God-dependence, what is God's promise? Spirit-enabling. John 8:32 promises, "And ye shall know the truth, and the truth shall make you free." The freedom is not just the right to obey in discipleship but the power (enabling) to obey in discipleship. This is freedom indeed.

For example, Jesus commands in John 15:4, "Abide in Me, and I in you." Notice we cannot obey the second part of this command, but thankfully His part of *and I in you* is automatic when the conditional part is fulfilled by our abiding (depending) on Him. Then He promises in John 15:5, "He that abideth in Me [God-dependence], and I in him [Spirit-enabling], the same bringeth forth much fruit: for without Me ye can do nothing." Here is a promise, a meal, words of life. Eat them! We cannot bear fruit on our own, but He can and will through us as we depend on Him (abiding in Christ) for the enabling (His abiding in us) to bear fruit. As you open your mouth in God-dependence to declare the gospel, He enables you and does the convincing work in the hearer so that through His power you bear fruit.

When you abide in Christ, He abides in you. When He abides in you, it's *not I, but Christ*. When it is *not I, but Christ*, He bears much fruit. That is what it plainly says. So if we are not bearing much fruit, what's wrong? We are not abiding.

I have seen several brothers in Christ embrace the promise of the harvest, whether here in Scripture or elsewhere, who have been radically changed into fruit-bearing Christians. They were faithful in witnessing before. The "motions" did not change. But their dependence changed, and so did their results. This is simply the power of the Spirit which glorifies God.

Concerning answers to prayer, John 15:7 says, "If ye abide in Me [dependence on His words] and My words abide in you [enablement for the purpose of those words], ye shall ask what ye will, and it shall be done unto you." What a promise! What words of life! Eat that bread. This is why George Mueller would search the Scripture for a promise to plead before God so that he could have confidence that God would answer. For when you abide in Christ, He abides in you. When He abides in you, it is *not I, but Christ.* When it's *not I, but Christ,* He prays according to God's will, and God answers! Is this not true praying in the Spirit? I have observed several who have stepped into the Spirit-filled life soon comment that they were seeing definite answers to prayer.

I John uses the term *abide* repeatedly in chapters 2-4 tying the promise for victory to abiding in Christ (the Spirit-filled life). For example, I John 3:6 says, "Whosoever abideth in Him [God-dependence for Spirit-enabling] sinneth not." Why? Because abiding in Christ accesses by faith "Christ in you" Who does not sin. Does this not shed light on the "seed" of God that "cannot sin" in I John 3:9? What a power for victory! What wonderful words of life! What a meal. Eat the Bread of Life for true life and living in Christ. This truth is what transformed Rosalind Goforth, Handley Moule, J. Elder Cumming, and a host of others. Victory over sin, or the "evidences" in I John, is primarily connected to abiding, and, therefore, secondarily to salvation. Consequently, lack of "evidence" may mean one of two possibilities: no genuine salvation or lack of abiding. Perhaps the real need for many professing Christians today is not to get "saved again" (which is impossible), but rather to start living the Spirit-filled life of abiding in Christ.

Spiritual growth occurs only through the twofold nature of abiding. At what table are you eating? The world, media, man's philosophy? You develop an appetite for what you regularly eat. From which table do you feed? Some come to the right table of God's Word but are deceitfully full from feeding at the table of the world. Reading the Word of God and hearing the preached Word is like reading the menu. Meditation and even memorization is like ordering a particular meal or putting groceries in the cabinets. But choices of faith constitute real feeding. The table of the Word—the Bread of Life—is the table of the King's diet. How foolish to be content with a prisoner's portion! How foolish to feed on the husks of the world! Is this not an insult to Christ, the True Bread? May we ever apply the twofold nature of abiding for spiritual growth by feeding on the True Bread from heaven! *O taste and see that the Lord is good!*

CHAPTER ELEVEN

# MANIFESTING THE CHRIST-LIFE IN SPIRIT-EMPOWERED WITNESSING

Endowment: The Promise of the Spirit
Enfeeblement: The Problem of Unbelief
Entitlement: The Provision of Christ
Enthronement: The Presentation and Practice of Surrender and Faith
Enablement: The Power of Living
**Entrustment: The Purpose of Usefulness**

If you dwell on inflow and never get to outflow, you will eventually end up with a "Dead Sea." Many are those who revel in inflow truth only to find that their newfound joy fades. What is the problem? The Spirit-filled life is not for selfish purposes. Rather the purpose is usefulness. Outflow without inflow is emptiness produced by flesh-dependence. Inflow without outflow becomes stagnant. What we need is an even inflow and outflow so that the channel is full of the Holy Spirit. Will you ask the Lord of the Harvest to enable you to see "outreach" in the light of the radiance of the Spirit-filled life?

# II CORINTHIANS 2-4

The story is told that as D. L. Moody once witnessed to a man on a street in Chicago, the man abruptly exclaimed, "Why don't you mind your own business!" To which D. L. Moody replied, "This is my business!" When you think of men used of God to effectively point people to Christ, certainly names like D. L. Moody, R. A. Torrey, Jonathan Goforth, Walter Wilson, and others come to mind. Did you ever consider why these men were so effective in seeing souls saved? They were made out of the same clay we are. Why were they so fruitful?

R. A. Torrey wrote a little book entitled *Why God Used D. L. Moody.* One of several reasons listed was Moody's dependence on the Holy Spirit. The significance of this must not be overlooked.

Jonathon Goforth, who literally saw thousands of Chinese come to Christ through his ministry, once said toward the end of his earthly pilgrimage, "Oh how I covet, more than a miser does his gold, twenty more years of this soul-saving work." Is this the expression of one who simply went through the motions of mere duty? Is there not a delight in his words? What made "soul-saving work" so delightful? Rosalind, his wife, wrote that when Jonathan preached to the saints "his soul was ever eager to tell out to others the message of 'the fulness of the Christ-life through the Holy Spirit's indwelling.'" Therein lies the secret. Jonathan Goforth knew the importance of fullness of power through the Holy Spirit.

In both cases cited, there is a clear connection between a real dependence on the Spirit's power and effectiveness in leading souls to Jesus Christ. In this light, we may ask: How is the Spirit-filled life powerfully manifested to the saving of lost souls? How is the life of Christ in us to be manifested through us so that others around us are impacted by Christ's life? In a glorious section of Scripture from II Corinthians 2:14-4:18, which teaches the ministry of the Holy Spirit, we read "in the sight of God speak we in Christ" (2:17). "We use great plainness of speech" (3:12), "we preach not ourselves, but Christ Jesus the Lord" (4:5), and "we also believe, and therefore speak" (4:13). Notice the emphasis on speaking or communicating. Remembering that these phrases occur in the context of God-dependence for Spirit-enabling, we learn a great truth: **To fully manifest the Christ-life, you must declare Christ in God-dependence.** This is true in declaring Christ for both salvation and the Sprit-filled life for holiness and service. Great impact demands communication of truth. Is this really the case? The question many ask is, "Can't we just live the life and, even though we don't verbally witness of Christ, still manifest the Christ-life?" The answer is only to a very limited degree. Manifesting the Christ-life occurs primarily through declaring Christ in God-dependence, which accesses the Spirit's enablement.

The bottom line is that to fully manifest the Christ-life, you must declare Christ in God-dependence. How can we effectively implement this bottom line truth? We must understand and apply three scriptural lessons to do so.

## PICTURES WHICH ILLUSTRATE THIS TRUTH

Our text paints four pictures that beautifully illustrate this bottom-line truth. In order to guide this part of our study, let's note the four concepts in our bottom line. The first concept is to *manifest*. The idea of this is to reveal. The second concept is the *Christ-life*, or we could say the Spirit-filled life. The third concept is *declaration*. To fully manifest the Christ-life, you must declare, or proclaim, Christ. The emphasis is communication of truth. The fourth concept is God-dependence. The declaration must be in *God-dependence* (faith) to access Spirit-enabling (grace).

## The Fragrance of Christ (II Corinthians 2:14-17)

This passage begins with an exclamation of praise: "Now thanks be unto God, which always causeth us to triumph in Christ." What an amazing victory promise to access by faith! Then the verse continues with "and maketh manifest the savour of His knowledge by us in every place." Notice our first concept: *manifest*. What is being manifested? The word *savour* means fragrance. Verse 15 clearly states it as the "savour of Christ." Verse 16 uses the term two more times. Here the passage emphasizes the *fragrance of Christ*, which pictures the Christ-life being manifested. How is the *fragrance of Christ* to be made *manifest* as the passage says *by us in every place*? Verse 17 explains, "For we are not as many, which corrupt [peddle] the word of God: but as of sincerity, but as of God, in the sight of God speak we in Christ." We *speak*, or communicate, *in Christ*, which reveals God-dependence. This passage clearly unfolds the four concepts in our bottom-line truth.

# The Glory of Christ (II Corinthians 3:1-18)

Verse three uses the terminology "manifestly declared." However, the picture of the Christ-life switches from the fragrance of Christ to "the glory of the Lord" (v. 18). In fact, the chapter is permeated with this imagery using the term *glory* or *glorious* fourteen times. How is the *glory of the Lord* to be *manifested?* Although there are many lessons being taught throughout this passage, it is significant that after using the terms *glory* or *glorious* eleven times from verses seven through eleven, verse twelve says, "Seeing then that we have such hope, we use great plainness [boldness] of speech." Again we see declaration. Also verses four through six emphatically demonstrate the God-dependence: "And such trust have we through Christ to God-ward: Not that we are sufficient of ourselves to think any thing as of ourselves; but our sufficiency is of God; Who also hath made us able ministers."

# The Light of Christ (II Corinthians 4:1-7)

In verse two we see again the word *manifestation.* However, now the picture of the Christ-life switches to "the light . . . of Christ" (v. 4). The word *light* is used once in verse four and twice in verse six. The same is true of the word *shine,* referring to the *light.* How is the *light* powerfully *manifested* to others? Sandwiched between verses four and six with the emphasis on *light* and *shine,* we read, "For we preach not ourselves, but Christ Jesus the Lord." The emphasis is *we preach ... Christ!* The God-dependence is seen in verse six as it states, "For God." It is God who does the supernatural work.

# The Life of Christ (II Corinthians 4:8-18)

Verse ten and eleven state, "That the life also of Jesus might be made manifest." Verse ten says "in our body," and verse eleven says "in our mortal flesh." *Manifest* occurs twice, but here the picture switches from fragrance, glory, and light to *the life also of Jesus.* By the way, notice the amazing possibility *that the life also of Jesus might be made manifest in our body.* The actual *life of Jesus* can be *made manifest in our body!* Is this not amazing? Verse twelve also mentions "life." So how is the *life of Jesus* going to be *made manifest* through us? Verse thirteen says, "We also believe, and therefore speak." Clearly we must *speak* in God-dependence.

Why would God allow the fragrance, glory, light, and life of Jesus to be manifested through a vessel of clay? II Corinthians 4:7 answers, "But we have this treasure in earthen vessels, that the excellency of the power may be of God, and not of us." However, we must declare Christ in God-dependence for the Christ-life to be powerfully manifested through us in order to impact others.

Remember the woman who brought the alabaster box filled with sweet-smelling perfume to Jesus. The indication is that there was no "lid." Rather, she had to break the alabaster box in order for the fragrance to be shed abroad. What is it that breaks the alabaster box of our lives so that *the fragrance of Christ* can be shed abroad to others? It is when we *speak ... in Christ.* Truly, it involves "breaking." As receiving the gospel humbles the sinner, so giving the gospel humbles the saint.

If you are saved, then the glory of the Lord lives within your body. What is it that unveils His glory so that it radiates manifestly to others? It is *when we use great plainness [boldness] of speech.* Truly if you are born again, then Jesus, the light of the world, lives within you. What takes the bushel away so that *the light ... of Christ* in you can be manifested through you? It is when *we preach ... Christ Jesus the Lord.* If you are blood-bought, then *the life ... of Jesus* lives within the tomb of your body. What is it that rolls the stone away so that *the life ... of Jesus* in you can be manifested through you? It is when *we ... believe, and therefore speak.* The Scripture boldly states *we also believe, and therefore speak.* So if we do not speak and declare Christ, what does it imply? We do not believe! It is not enough to "say" you believe that God blesses the gospel and that God blesses witnessing. You really do not believe until you depend on God to bless the gospel as you witness. You do not have God-dependence for witnessing without witnessing. You can witness without God-dependence. This is the futility of flesh-dependence. But you do not have God-dependence for witnessing without tying the dependence to the step of witnessing. To fully manifest the Christ-life, you must declare Christ in God-dependence.

Obviously, we should live, by God's grace, godly lives and not hypocritical lives. But witnessing for Christ is not just a lifestyle; it is a message that must be communicated. If the Spirit-filled life never brings you into service for Christ, you do not have the Spirit-filled life.

## PRINCIPLES WHICH UNDERGIRD THIS TRUTH

Two simple principles understood and applied allow the Spirit to make the spoken message powerful.

## The Proclaimer's Confidence

First, the Spirit of Christ, accessed by faith, is the proclaimer's confidence. Man's way is to think that we must feel confident when witnessing for Christ. But God's ways differ greatly from man's ways. God wants us to recognize that we are weak, whether we feel weak or not, so that we look to Him in faith for His strength. In this light, Ephesians 3:12 provides an exceeding great and precious promise: "In whom [Christ] we have boldness and access with confidence by . . . faith." Notice it does not say "in whom we will have boldness" but *in whom we have boldness*. This is a present reality for every child of God! You might wonder, "Then why am I so timid in witnessing?" The promise stands, but the *access* is by *faith*. Unbelief enfeebles us; faith emboldens us with a supernatural boldness. The dynamic involved here has nothing to do with human tactics and personality. It has everything to do with supernatural *boldness* accessed by *faith*.

## The Prospect's Convincer

Second, the Spirit of Christ, accessed by faith, is the prospect's convincer. Our job is not to convince; our job is to declare in dependence on the Spirit to convince. Remember the promise that Jesus made in John 16:7-8. He said, "I will send Him [the Comforter] unto you. And . . . He will reprove [convince] the world of sin, and of righteousness, and of judgment."

Let me digress from our thought here for a moment to emphasize the precision of Christ's words. He does not say, "I will send the Holy Spirit to the world, and He will convince the world." He said, "*I will send* the Holy Spirit to *you* and He will convince *the world*." Do you see the significance of Christ's wording? The Spirit convinces *the world* through *you* and me as yielded believers. God has chosen to "limit" Himself to yielded, believing saints in order for the Spirit to convince the world. The message must be communicated. Every child of God has much more responsibility than most realize. Although the Spirit prepares hearts apart from human instrumentation, the message must be communicated. The message, whether printed or spoken, comes through the channel of a disciple of Christ.

Herein we are faced with the need to be a clean and ready channel. If you hang on to sin, the Spirit must stop convincing *the world* of sin and go back to convincing *you* of sin. What a hindrance to the evangelization of a hell-bound world! Throughout this book, we have emphasized *the Spirit-filled life for holiness and service*. Holiness precedes service. Holiness is not an end in itself; it is a means to an end. Holiness is the pruning of the branch in order that it may bear more fruit (John 15). Holiness is the cleansing of the channel so that the Spirit might flow with rivers of living water (John 7). To hang on to one bitterness, one grudge, one worldly television program, one worldly musical recording, one compromising article of clothing, and so forth—though it may seem ever so small—is to hang on to the one dirty rag choking the usefulness of the channel of your life. As we must depend on the Spirit for holiness, we must be holy to be used in Spirit-empowered service.

Returning to our thought, Jesus promises that the Holy Spirit will convince the world of sin, righteousness, and judgment. Imagine if this were not true. What if you took the supernatural convincement of the Spirit out of the equation of witnessing? Would it make any sense for us to speak to a total stranger and, in essence, say to him that he is a dirty rotten sinner, headed to hell, and that Christ is the only way to escape, and for him to listen? Without the Spirit, it would be ludicrous for anyone to be positively impacted. But with the Spirit's convincement, the message makes all the sense in the world!

The Spirit is the great Convincer. Once while I was witnessing to a Chinese student at the University of Michigan, he asked, "In my country of China, we don't have Bibles, we don't believe in the Bible, we don't believe in God; how do you know that's true?" Holding my Bible up in my hand, I replied, "Sir, all I have to do is tell you what the Bible says, and I can depend on the Holy Spirit of God to convince you that it is true—and down deep in your heart, you know it." As he humbly hung his head, he responded, "You're right." Here was a man who one moment before was saying words of skepticism and the next moment was saying, "You're right." That is the Spirit of God doing what man cannot do.

One summer my wife, Mary Lynn, and I were waiting to board a ferryboat going from Wales to Ireland. A young English mother quite frazzled from trying to keep tabs on her toddler (or should I say terror!) and infant and all their paraphernalia stood behind us in the line. When a voice on the speaker system announced for us to move through the causeway onto the ferryboat, this mother, somewhat panicked, asked my wife to hold her infant so that she could get everything else. I immediately sensed this was a divine appointment. Later after settling down, I began to witness to her. She quickly said, "I just believe that you live and then you die, and then it's all over." That is annihilationism. I asked, "May I show you what the Bible says anyway?" She agreed. As I began to declare Christ, within about five minutes, her countenance changed, and she said, "I've been thinking about this a lot lately. I'm so glad we're having this conversation!" That is God convincing during the moments of declaration. Within another thirty or forty minutes, she bowed her head, admitting to God that she was a sinner who deserved hell, and cast her dependence on Christ to save her!

One time a lady made a big point of telling me she did not believe in hell. To think of herself being thrown in a fiery place was not acceptable. However, within about fifteen minutes of declaration, she admitted she was headed to hell and, in another fifteen minutes or so, preciously trusted Christ!

May we always depend on the Spirit as "our" confidence and "their" convincer!

## PATHWAYS WHICH APPLY THIS TRUTH

Practically speaking, how do we apply the truth of declaring Christ in God-dependence to allow the Christ-life to be manifested through us? Two simple, yet biblical, pathways are found in the pattern of Christ Himself.

## Creating Opportunities

In John 4, we read that Jesus "must needs go through Samaria." Why? Because He was creating an opportunity. It was not an obvious opportunity. Jews normally did not go through Samaria; they went around it. It was "a bad section of town." But Jesus went through it because He was creating an opportunity for "the woman at the well" and many others in Samaria.

One might reason, "Well, Jesus could do that because He is God. He knew there was someone ready." Isn't He still God? Doesn't He still know? Does He not live in you if you're saved? Beyond that, has He not given us the promise of the harvest? Listen to the words of Christ in the same context later in John 4 as He challenges His disciples to see with eyes of faith: "Lift up your eyes, and look on the fields; for they are white already to harvest." He dies not say they will be—*they are!* In Matthew 9:37, Jesus promises, "The harvest truly is plenteous." He does not say it will be—it *is!*

Yet God's people "bad-mouth" the harvest. For example, in New England some people say, "This is cold, formal New England. It's hard to see people saved here." Yet in the South, the Bible belt as it is often called, people say, "Everyone down here says they're saved, and it's obvious they don't understand. It's hard to see people saved here." In the Rocky Mountains of the West, people say, "Out here, hardly anyone even goes to church. This is pagan territory. It's hard to see people saved here." In California people say, "This is California! People are free thinkers and have independent spirits. It's hard to see people saved here." Overseas people say, "In this country, a certain religion has dominated for the last number of centuries. The effects are suffocating. It's hard to see people saved here." Need I continue? If we are honest, probably all of us have made such a statement at some time. What we are saying is, "The harvest is bad." Yet Jesus said, "The harvest truly is great" (Luke 10:2) and "The harvest truly is plenteous" (Matthew 9:37), "but the laborers are few." Therein lies the real problem: true Spirit-filled laborers are few.

Think of it—*the fields ... are white already to harvest*; not will be, they *are*; *the harvest truly is plenteous*; not will be, but it *is*! That means within the sphere of your life and mine, there are people right now ready to be saved. Jesus said it! It is not a matter of our trying to get God to work; God is working. It is a matter of our looking to Him to guide us to where He is working. God is preparing Corneliuses all around us. But as with Cornelius, he could not get saved without the message of the gospel and, therefore, a messenger. There had to be a man—a saved man, a Spirit-filled man—for Cornelius to get the message in convicting power. However, God is constantly preparing the harvest.

This truth, spiritually apprehended, changes everything. Have you ever knocked on a door and when no one responds, you think to yourself, "Am I ever glad no one is home"? Instead, now you can knock on a door and, with anticipation, think, "I wonder if this is going to be my divine appointment." The facts (the promise of the harvest) accessed by faith (dependence on the reality of the promise) produce expectation. Somewhere there is a divine appointment where you will see the hand of God either in a soul's salvation or in a key step toward his salvation. If it is not "this one," then fine, keep going until you intersect with God's promise.

If you are thinking, "Within the sphere of my life, I can't think of one person who shows any sign of being 'ready,'" do you know what the problem is? Is it because you have not declared Christ in God-dependence to find out where God is working? If everyone hurried to us to hear the truth, this would not be a matter of faith. It would be sight. *The fields are white*. Jesus said so. Therefore, as you depend on the reality of these words by declaring Christ, you will find out that someone has been thinking of life after death recently or some such indication. God is preparing the harvest. Even when the situation is not obvious on the surface, we must depend on the promise by creating opportunities.

Once while flying to a meeting, I was seated on the plane next to a lady who was a realtor. Upon bringing up the gospel, she laughed and basically said, "You don't believe that, do you?" I said yes and asked if I could show her from the Bible how she could know that her sins were forgiven and how she could receive eternal life. Still laughing, she agreed. For the first part of the gospel declaration, she still laughed skeptically, especially when I brought up the subject of hell. This was not an "obvious" prospect. Yet she did not ask me to stop. It was not a matter of my obnoxiously pushing ahead in the flesh. Finally, her countenance changed. The Spirit had been working all along. Soon she prayed to receive Christ! The promise is true. May we depend on it by creating opportunities.

How can we create opportunities? Let's consider the old-fashioned method of door-to-door. Some say it's passé and does not work. Yet personally I've seen God use it all over the United States and in other countries. It's not that it doesn't work—it's that we don't. What if they put buzzer-lock systems on the apartments in your area? Go buzzer-to-buzzer! My brother-in-law, Gary Hirth, who pastors in Michigan, says he likes it better. You get through the "no's" quicker, and when someone buzzes you in, you're usually in for a good visit. He has seen people saved through "buzzer-to-buzzer" witnessing. A ministry to mothers with new babies is an effective witnessing tool. When I was an assistant pastor to my father in the Chicago area, we had, among several avenues for outreach, a "new birth" evangelism. Our ladies would call to set up appointments with mothers of new babies. They would bring a gift for the mother and infant, seeking to declare Christ in that visit. Within the space of three years, many ladies professed Christ, and five family units were assimilated into our church through that one ministry alone. Of course, there is the avenue of new move-ins, new married couples, and so forth.

I learned from Pastor Charlie Kittrell of Indianapolis, who gives out more tracts than anyone else I know, to pray for the Spirit's leading in passing out tracts. God does lead with precision, and I've never had so many people thank me for giving them tracts!

Once I heard a preacher challenge people to carry their Bible with them wherever they go. He emphasized that it must look like a Bible. Then he related amazing experiences of God using it to open doors. Since then I have sought to do this. The "opened doors" on airplanes and restaurants have been exciting. Usually I carry a little black Bible which clearly says in solid letters on the binding "Holy Bible." Once while speaking with a store employee regarding a product, he saw my Bible and asked, "Is that a little black Bible?" Then he went on to say that he had just bought a Bible on a computer disc—an open door! May we constantly apply the pathway of creating opportunities.

## Seizing Opportunities

This second pathway is illustrated by Christ in John 3 with Nicodemus. Here is a man who comes to Christ and starts talking about religion! Jesus seized the opportunity, and, I believe, as a result we will see Nicodemus in heaven. Have you ever wondered, "Why does so-and-so always get the good ones?" Is it not because he is looking? I have found that faithfulness in creating opportunities helps us to be conscious of seizing opportunities. I am convinced that every child of God has some "Nicodemus appointments," but some are blinded through unbelief to see them. I'm also convinced that if you pray for Nicodemus opportunities and look for them, God will intersect your path with the prepared heart.

Once my wife and I were flying from Detroit to Atlanta. A winter storm was soon to close the airport. As we boarded the plane, they announced that it was a full flight. Seeing the seat to my left still open, I prayed that if someone was ready to receive Christ, that God would place that person there. It was a few minutes before a young man sat in that seat. We struck up a conversation as they were de-icing the plane. I asked, "Do you live in Detroit or Atlanta?" He said, "I'm moving to Atlanta." He then poured out his story. "I grew up in Grand Rapids, but my life is a mess. I've gotten in all sorts of trouble and have had problems with drugs." He went on to say, "Some of my relatives live in Atlanta, so I'm moving there in order to get a new start." What a divine appointment! I then said, "If you seek a new start in Atlanta without God, you are going to find that the problems of Grand Rapids are going to find you right there in Atlanta. You need the Lord." As he hung his head, he said, "You're right." Within thirty or forty minutes, he was trusting Christ!

What about the person who enters a Bible-believing church and yet no one has invited him—humanly speaking? Is he not a Nicodemus? It is not accidental. Would it not be tragic for him to come and leave without anyone taking the opportunity to declare Christ to him?

Occasionally someone "out of the blue" will approach me in conversation. I am not even speaking of a transaction with a cashier. I mean "out of the blue." For me, I have previously thought it strange since I do not have an out-going personality. Occasionally, I have given them a gospel tract. Sometimes after they walked away, I wondered to myself, "Was I supposed to witness to that person?" How dull can we sometimes get! When an unsaved person out the blue starts speaking with a saved person, it is God at work. With God there are no "accidents." When God showed me the truth of this chapter—speaking Christ in God-dependence—it was those types of scenarios that came to mind. Quite frankly it was devastating, for every missed opportunity from God represents blood on my hands (Ezekiel 3). After a heart-searching time with the Lord, I determined that when someone "out of the blue" spoke to me, I would take it from the Lord to speak to that person, to give them a tract, and go as far as the occasion allowed.

The next day coming out of Sacramento, California, my wife and I pulled our pickup truck into a service station to get some diesel fuel. Diesel is a dirty fuel, so my uncle gave me a pair of rubber gloves to wear in order to protect my clothes. So I had my rubber gloves on while putting diesel into my truck. A man fueling his jeep on the other side of the pump exclaimed, "That is a great idea!" I was not sure what he was taking about. He said, "The gloves—that is a great idea." So we began to talk about rubber gloves. The Spirit's voice got louder, reminding me to *speak*. So I handed the man a gospel tract and said, "May I give you something to read? This will tell you how you can know for sure that your sins are forgiven and how you can have eternal life." He took the tract and said with amazement, "Really?" He even began to read the tract. Then he asked some questions. For about five minutes I had the privilege of declaring Christ before he got into his jeep and drove away. That was a divine appointment.

A few days later, while my wife and I were walking through a store, another lady customer coming the other way in our direction holding purchases in both hands started talking with us like we were old-time friends. As I was pondering, "Who is this lady?" the Spirit's voice got louder reminding me to *speak*. I actually had to catch up to the lady as she had already passed us up. I said, "Ma'am, may I give you something to read? This will tell you how you can know that your sins are forgiven and how to have eternal life." She stopped and, with deep gratitude, said as she took the tract, "Oh, thank you. Yes, I will read it." Again, that was the hand of God.

A few days after that, I was in a Chinese restaurant. While I was going through the buffet line, a Chinese teenage girl wiping the counter looked up and said in English, "Hello." By this time I knew—speak. Taking a Chinese tract from my pocket and putting it before her, I asked, "Can you read this?" She could not respond—in English, that is. So I assumed she could read it. Then I said, "You can have that"—not that she could understand that! Later while I was eating, a middle-aged Chinese lady worker came up to me, holding that tract in her hand. In very broken English, she tried to ask if I had given that tract to the girl. I responded that I had. Then she looked at me with searching eyes. O how many times have I seen those searching eyes. In very broken English, she asked, "Can I . . . ahhh . . . Can I . . ." Realizing that she was wanting to keep the tract, I said, "Yes, ma'am. You can have that." Pulling it to herself as though she had a treasure, she exclaimed with deep gratitude, "Oh, thank you," and quickly slipped away. That was the hand of God! Many times since then God has brought people across my path who have initiated conversations.

May we constantly apply for the pathway of seizing opportunities.

## Conclusion

The next passage in II Corinthians says, "For we must all appear before the judgment seat of Christ" (5:10). According to I Corinthians 3, the "building" of our lives as believers will be put to the test of fire to see of what sort it is. That which we did in the flesh—the wood, hay, and stubble—will be incinerated. That which we did in the Spirit by allowing Christ to live through us—the gold, silver, and precious stones—will pass the test. Do you realize that the word *appear* is the same word translated as *manifest* in our four pictures. The impact is this: At the judgment seat of Christ, it will be made *manifest* how much we allowed Christ to be *manifested*! The next verse says, "Knowing therefore the terror of the Lord, we persuade men." We *speak*!

To fully manifest the Christ-life, we must declare Christ in God-dependence. O may we speak out the glorious gospel of Jesus Christ!

# PART III

## PUBLIC REVIVAL:
## THE OUTPOURING
## OF THE SPIRIT

# CHAPTER TWELVE

# THE AGE OF PENTECOST

As the indwelling of the Spirit is the necessary plat-form of truth for the filling of the Spirit, so the filling of the Spirit is the necessary platform of truth for the outpouring of the Spirit. When a believer confesses his lack of power and unbelief, and then steps by faith into the Spirit-filled life, continuing to, moment by moment, look unto the all-sufficient Savior, he experiences personal revival! This is true restoration to life—Christ's life! Is this possible in a corporate setting? Will you again ask the Spirit of truth to "guide you into all truth" on this ever-needed subject in the Christian church today?

# ACTS 2:1, 33

On audiotape I heard Duncan Campbell relate the following story. He once went to preach a ten-day meeting on the Isle of Skye in a small village church. The young pastor had a good heritage and training. Yet he could not seem to see the church grow. During the special meetings, seven people attended the Sunday morning service. Five attended Sunday night. By Friday they had averaged seven. On Saturday the young pastor requested Duncan Campbell to join him on Monday for a day of prayer and fasting. Campbell, well experienced in the spiritual realities involved, agreed. Also, he called John Smith on the Isle of Lewis, who was one of the "praying men" during the Lewis Awakening of 1949-53, to gather together the men who knew how to pray. Campbell specified he did not want anyone else—just those who knew how to pray. He asked them to also fast and pray on that coming Monday, asking God to supernaturally intervene in the meeting on Skye.

After praying and fasting all day that Monday, Duncan Campbell and the young pastor broke their fast in late afternoon to get a little sustenance before the evening service. In typical Scottish style, they had a cup of tea. While drinking their tea, there was a knock at the door. A well-known merchant had come to offer his car to drive the preachers to the church house. The young pastor knew who the merchant was. He was not a saved man, nor was he a God-fearing man. He had never attended that village church before. As the two preachers rode with him, he asked with anticipation, "What is happening at the church tonight? Already there is a busload of people from another village. There are so many cars in the parking lot, I doubt if we will find a spot to park. Would you please tell me what is happening at the church?"

What had happened? Was this mere coincidence? Is this explainable simply by human reasoning? Why would those who were, up to that point, indifferent now suddenly come flocking to church on a Monday evening? Is this natural or supernatural? Is there such a thing as a divine magnetism?

Duncan Campbell then preached in an atmosphere charged by the presence of Almighty God. The moving of God over the next few days literally built the church overnight. Also, the converts lasted. It was a true work of God.

How do you explain this? Does God still manifest His presence? Is this what is meant by the "outpouring of the Spirit"? Is the outpouring of the Spirit still for today?

The outpouring of the Spirit—past, present, or future? Some argue that it was in the past, never to be repeated. In essence, they are saying that the Day of Pentecost was a one-time-only event. Others admit that there is also a future outpouring pertaining to Israel. Both of these positions deny or doubt the possibility that the outpouring of the Spirit is for today. This skepticism undermines faith for revival. Misconceptions, perhaps as a reaction to the excesses of the Charismatic movement, have woven their way into the fabric of the mindsets of many of God's people. As a result, some write off the Old Testament as irrelevant to today as if there is no legitimate application. Furthermore, some scoff at the testimony of revival history as if it contradicts Scripture.

While acknowledging the past and future aspects of the outpouring of the Spirit, we affirm that God still pours out His Spirit in this present age. The Day of Pentecost launched the Age of Pentecost. In essence, the Day of Pentecost was a prototype, a specimen day, a foretaste of God's plan throughout the age of grace, which is the age of the Holy Spirit. This is not to say the Spirit is "sent" from the throne repeatedly, but rather that we live in the age of the Spirit. He has not been sent back. Therefore, new pentecosts are possible because we live in the Age of Pentecost.

By "outpouring of the Spirit," we refer to the broad historical usage of this concept, that of the manifestation of the Spirit in revival. It is God's presence, because of the sent Spirit, being manifested. It is "God coming down," which is defined in Isaiah 64:1-3 as "at Thy presence." It is "God causing His face to shine on His people," which manifests His favorable presence as in Psalm 80:3, 7, 19 and Daniel 9:17. This is the goal of the "seek My face" concept in II Chronicles 7:14. By "outpouring of the Spirit," we mean the powerful, spiritual manifestation of the presence of God that leads believers to a restoration of spiritual life and unbelievers to a reception of eternal life. This is revival! This can occur individually or corporately. But it is the same dynamic. On an individual basis we may call this personal revival. Corporately we may distinguish between what we might call a localized revival or what someone has termed "revival with a little 'r'", and what might be called a regional revival, or "revival with a big 'R'." But all of it is revival.

While it is true that good men disagree on this matter of "the outpouring of the Spirit," it is also true that the position one takes on this issue affects his faith in regard to the present-day work of God.

Therefore, we believe the present controversy regarding the outpouring of the Spirit is important. The truth involved affects each generation of believers and its responsibility to fulfill the Great Commission. Therefore, theological hurdles must be overcome by the Spirit of truth in conjunction with the Word of truth.

Acts 2:1 says "And when the day of Pentecost was fully come." Then verse 33 states that the exalted Jesus "having received of the Father the promise of the Holy Spirit, He hath shed forth [lit., poured out] this, which ye now see and hear." The Spirit was sent. He has not been sent back. Christ launched a new era—the Age of Pentecost. This is the age of the poured-out Spirit. **The outpouring of the Spirit is for today.** How does the Scripture address this issue? Because of the present confusion on this subject, we will seek thoroughness at the risk of tediousness by surveying the Old Testament usage of the concept, studying the New Testament usage, and also noting the historical usage based on past understanding of what the Scripture teaches.

## OLD TESTAMENT USAGE

In citing Old Testament passages, we must grapple with whether or not it is fair to apply these passages to today. Often the emphasis is on the nation of Israel. Does this mean we can receive no real practical application today? Thankfully New Testament passages like I Corinthians 10 and Hebrews 3-4 teach us how to deal with such passages. Both New Testament passages cited refer to Old Testament passages which are clearly dealing with Israel as a nation. Yet these New Testament passages apply the Old Testament passages to individual believers. Therefore, the Scripture provides an inspired hermaneutic (which is simply a principle of interpretation)—the way God dealt with Israel as a nation in the Old Testament is the way He deals with individual believers now. My father often emphasized this New Testament precedent.

Some Old Testament passages are primarily millennial. While this should be recognized, it should also be recognized that many Old Testament prophecies have an ultimate final and full fulfillment, yet have earlier foretastes or repetitive fulfillments. Also, while we must seek for the literal interpretation, we must also allow the Spirit to speak to our hearts His applications. Otherwise, much of the Old Testament would not have any import to us today. Spirit-led application never leaves the boundaries of the vein of truth involved. Although the exact interpretation may be past or future, the Spirit's application to the present is legitimate application.

Several words are used for the concept "pour out." The terms are used often literally as in the "shedding" of blood or the "pouring out" of oil. They are also used figuratively as in "pouring out" wrath or indignation. This figurative sense means that God's indignation is manifested. This figurative sense of manifestation is the use of the term when applied to the Spirit being "poured out." God's presence is manifested.

## Explicit Passages

Isaiah 32:15—"Until the Spirit be poured upon us from on high, and the wilderness be a fruitful field, and the fruitful field be counted for a forest." The effects of this outpouring according to verses 16 and 17 are "justice," "righteousness," and "peace." Notice *the Spirit* is poured out *from on high* with the radical result that *the wilderness* will become *a fruitful field*. The implication is that as water brings life and fruitfulness, so does the manifestation of the Spirit spiritually.

Isaiah 44:3-5—"For I will pour water upon him that is thirsty, and floods upon the dry ground: I will pour My Spirit upon thy seed, and My blessing upon thine offspring: And they shall spring up as among the grass, as willows by the water courses. One shall say, I am the LORD'S; and another shall call himself by the name of Jacob; and another shall subscribe with his hand unto the LORD, and surname himself by the name of Israel." Notice this promise first applies to one intercessor (*him that is thirsty*), then to backslidden saints (*the dry ground* [Note: "the desert" is described as "My people" in 43:20]), and then to the lost (*thy seed, and . . . thine offspring . . . One shall say, I am the LORD'S*). The promise of Isaiah 44:3 became the foundation for intercession preceding and during the Lewis Revival of 1949-1953 in the Outer Hebrides islands of Scotland. This fact is emphasized repeatedly in all the accounts of the Lewis Awakening. Were these folk misled into thinking this verse was for them or did God's Spirit convince them that they could claim the promise? I believe the inspired Author guided them into the truth necessary for the occasion.

Ezekiel 39:29—"Neither will I hide My face any more from them: for I have poured out My Spirit upon the house of Israel, saith the Lord GOD." Notice that God equates, *I have poured out My Spirit upon the house of Israel* with *Neither will I hide My face any more from them*. In other words, the issue is the manifestation of God's presence. This is divine favor.

Joel 2:28-29—"And it shall come to pass afterward, that I will pour out My Spirit upon all flesh; and your sons and your daughters shall prophesy, your old men shall dream dreams, your young men shall see visions: And also upon the servants and upon the handmaids in those days will I pour out My Spirit." In studying the preceding verses leading up to this passage, the indication is that the literal fulfillment of this prophecy is yet a future event pertaining to Israel. The key words which clarify this are *And it shall come to pass afterward*. Amazingly, this passage is cited by Peter on the Day of Pentecost as a foretaste of fulfillment. We will investigate this further later.

Zechariah 12:10—"And I will pour upon the house of David, and upon the inhabitants of Jerusalem, the Spirit of grace and of supplications." Remember that *grace* refers to the undeserved favor of divine enablement. This is the power for holiness and service. *The Spirit of grace* restores God's people to life in the Spirit. This is the essence of revival impact among believers.

## Implicit Passages

Proverbs 1:23—"Turn you at my reproof: behold, I will pour out my spirit unto you, I will make known my words unto you." In this section of Proverbs "wisdom" is personified (1:20). Wisdom is speaking in verse 23. Remember, however, that I Corinthians 1:30 states that "Christ Jesus . . . is made unto us wisdom."

Isaiah 45:8—"Drop down, ye heavens, from above, and let the skies pour down righteousness: let the earth open, and let them bring forth salvation, and let righteousness spring up together; I the LORD have created it." What a beautiful picture of revival!

Malachi 3:10-12—"Bring ye all the tithes into the storehouse, that there may be meat in Mine house, and prove Me now herewith, saith the LORD of hosts, if I will not open you the windows of heaven, and pour you out a blessing, that there shall not be room enough to receive it. And I will rebuke the devourer for your sakes, and he shall not destroy the fruits of your ground; neither shall your vine cast her fruit before the time in the field, saith the LORD of hosts. And all nations shall call you blessed: for ye shall be a delightsome land, saith the LORD of hosts." Notice here the outpouring is conditioned on good stewardship, which is an expression of dependence on God. This passage incorporates the revival imagery of "opened windows" of God's blessing.

These passages all use the terminology of "pouring out" with the Spirit being implied or inferred as the Agent. Other passages use the same type of imagery without the terminology of "pouring out." For example, Isaiah 43:19-21, Ezekiel 34:26, Hosea 10:12, and Zechariah 10:1 all use the imagery of "rain," which correlates with the outpouring picture. Again, the imagery pictures God manifesting His presence and blessing.

Many other terms and imageries referring to revival occur throughout the Old Testament. The purpose here is to peruse those passages dealing with the terminology or imagery of the outpouring of the Spirit. It is a fact worth noting that many revivals of the past two millenniums have had as their foundation for faith an Old Testament promise. This cannot be overlooked. Were the saints of the past misled simpletons who coincidentally experienced the outpouring of the Spirit in revival? We believe honesty says no. Rather the Spirit of truth guided them to the truth that could be stood upon in faithful intercession for that occasion.

# NEW TESTAMENT USAGE

## Overview

To begin our study of New Testament usage, we will focus on the Greek words used explicitly for the outpouring of the Spirit. One word is used for the God-ward side—God pouring out. Three words are used for the event—the pouring out. One word is used for the man-ward side—the receiving.

### God-ward Side (God pouring out)

The term *ekcheo* is the key word for the outpouring of the Spirit concept. The term is used of the wine bottles bursting and the contents being *spilled*, of blood being *shed*, and of the vials of Revelation being *poured out*. The term occurs five times directly referring to God pouring out His Spirit. To attempt to keep matters clear, I will just give the key phrases involved with the translation of *ekcheo* italicized. For those interested, I will also list the verb tense, voice, and mood in brackets.

1. Acts 2:17: "I *will pour out* of My Spirit" [future, active, indicative]
2. Acts 2:18: "I *will pour out* in those days of My Spirit" [future, active, indicative]
3. Acts 2:33: "He *hath shed forth* this" [aorist, active, indicative]
4. Acts 10:45: "on the Gentiles also *was poured out* the gift of the Holy Spirit" [perfect, passive, indicative]
5. Titus 3:6: "which He *shed* on us abundantly" [aorist, active, indicative]

Notice that the outpouring of the Spirit occurred explicitly on the Day of Pentecost (Acts 2:17, 18, 33) and approximately eleven years later in Acts 10:45. Clearly the outpouring of the Spirit occurred beyond the Day of Pentecost. Also, the term is used explicitly as occurring to every believer factually at their salvation (Titus 3:5-6).

### The Event (the pouring out)

The terms *epipipto, erchomai,* and *eperchomai* are all used for the event of the outpouring. All five passages occur with the preposition *epi-*, emphasizing the pouring out *upon* the object.

1. Acts 1:8: "power, *after that* the Holy Spirit *is come upon* you" [*eperchomai*: aorist, active, participle]
2. Acts 8:16: "as yet He was *fallen upon* none of them" [*epipipto*: perfect, active, participle]
3. Acts 10:44: "the Holy Spirit *fell on* all them which heard the word" [*epipipto*: aorist, active, indicative]
4. Acts 11:15: "the Holy Spirit *fell on* them, as on us at the beginning" [*epipipto*: aorist, active, indicative]
5. Acts 19:6: "the Holy Spirit *came* on them" [*erchomai*: aorist, active, indicative]

Notice Acts 1:8 promises the event. Then Acts 8, Acts 10-11, and Acts 19 record the event as explicitly occurring on three different occasions. It is highly significant that Acts 10 uses *ekcheo* (the God-ward side) and *epipipto* (the event) synonymously in the same context. Also, Peter said in Acts 11:15 *the Holy Spirit fell on them, as on us at the beginning.* Acts 10, referred to by Peter in Acts 11, was therefore a *repeat of* Acts 2. By explicit statement the outpouring of the Spirit was repeated in Acts 10. We should also note that Acts 2 dealt with Jews, Acts 8 with half-Jews (the Samaritans), and Acts 10 with Gentiles. One might be tempted then to argue that since the outpouring occurred to the three groups, it was all over. Yet the event occurs again in Acts 19. Acts 19 may be argued various ways, but nonetheless it is a "problem" passage. The fact is this outpouring occurred approximately seventeen years after Acts 10 and twenty-eight years after Acts 2. Acts directly records repeated outpourings, beautifully illustrating the manifestation of the sent Spirit.

## Man-ward Side (the receiving)

The term *lambano* means primarily to take or to receive. It has many contexts. Eleven passages relate explicitly to receiving the Spirit or the power of the Spirit.

1. John 20:22: "*Receive* ye the Holy Spirit" [aorist, active, imperative]
2. Acts 1:8: "But ye *shall receive* power, after that the Holy Spirit is come upon you" [future, middle deponent, indicative]
3. Acts 2:38: "and ye *shall receive* the gift of the Holy Spirit" [future, middle deponent, indicative]
4. Acts 8:15: "that they *might receive* the Holy Spirit" [aorist, active, subjunctive]

5. Acts 8:17: "and they *received* the Holy Spirit" [imperfect, active, indicative]
6. Acts 10:47: "which *have received* the Holy Spirit" [aorist, active, indicative]
7. Acts 19:2: "*Have* ye *received* the Holy Spirit since ye believed?" [aorist, active, indicative]
8. Romans 8:15: "but ye *have received* the Spirit of adoption" [aorist, active, indicative]
9. I Corinthians 2:12: "Now we *have received* . . . the Spirit" [aorist, active, indicative]
10. Galatians 3:2: "*Received* ye the Spirit" [aorist, active, indicative]
11. Galatians 3:14: "that we *might receive* the promise of the Spirit" [aorist, active, subjunctive]

Of the historical passages, Acts 2, 8, 10, and 19 all use this term referring to man receiving the outpouring of the Spirit. Again it is highly significant to note that Acts 10 uses synonymously in the same context *ekcheo* (the God-ward side), *epipipto* (the event), and *lambano* (the man-ward side). Acts 19 uses *lambano* (the man-ward side) and *erchomai* (the event). Also, the prophetical passage of Acts 1:8 uses *lambano* (the man-ward side) and *eperchomai* (the event).

We should also note that the term for receiving the Spirit or the power of the Spirit is used several times in the epistles. The distinction must be made, however, between receiving the person of the Spirit factually at salvation (Galatians 3:2) and the promise or power of the Spirit functionally after justification (Galatians 3:14—note the use of the subjunctive *might*.)

In Acts 11, when Peter is relating the events of Acts 10, he says in Acts 11:15-17, "And as I began to speak, the Holy Spirit fell on them, as on us at the beginning. Then remembered I the word of the Lord, how that He said, John indeed baptized with water; but ye shall be baptized with the Holy Spirit. Forasmuch then as God gave them the like gift as He did unto us, who believed on the Lord Jesus Christ; what was I, that I could withstand God?" Notice it appears that Peter uses the term *baptized* as an umbrella word describing the event. Acts 11:16 refers to Acts 1:4-5. Acts 2, their personal fulfillment, uses terms like "filled" (Acts 2:4), "poured out" (Acts 2:17-18), and "repent . . . and . . . receive the gift" (Acts 2:38) all in reference to the Spirit. I believe this indicates that the "baptism with the Spirit" may well be an umbrella term including many aspects such as the indwelling, the filling, and the outpouring of the Spirit. Factually this occurs at salvation, but functionally the empowering aspects must be accessed by faith as we saw demonstrated in chapters three and four. Peter connects the baptism with the Holy Spirit to believing (11:16-17).

The Book of Acts overflows with the demonstration of the out-poured Spirit. Though we have so far noted the explicit passages, there are many implicit passages. We see 3,000 saved in the explicit passage of Acts 2. Yet we see the number 5,000 by Acts 4, and "multitudes" in Acts 5. In Acts 9 we read of two entire towns turning to the Lord! In Acts 10 we see the explicit outpouring on the Gentiles with Cornelius. Yet by Acts 11 we read that "a great number believed." Acts 13 records nearly an entire city coming to hear the Word of God and that many believed. "A great multitude believed" in Acts 14. Acts 17 records that "a great multitude" believed. After reading the explicit passage in early Acts 19 we also read "all they which dwelt in Asia heard the word of the Lord Jesus." This is simply a few peaks in a mountain range of revival blessing. Acts 2-28 records pentecostal power for a fifty-year period!

# Key Passages

### Acts 2:16-18

Acts 2:16-18: "But this is that which was spoken by the prophet Joel; And it shall come to pass in the last days, saith God, I will pour out of My Spirit upon all flesh: and your sons and your daughters shall prophesy, and your young men shall see visions, and your old men shall dream dreams: And on My servants and on My handmaidens I will pour out in those days of My Spirit; and they shall prophesy."

Notice Peter did not say, "This is the fulfillment of that which was spoken by the prophet Joel." referring to the exact fulfillment. Rather, he said *this is that*, indicating "This is in the principle of that which was spoken by the prophet Joel." Inspiration-wording takes great care to be accurate as we see demonstrated in the prophecies fulfilled by Christ's first advent listed in the Gospels up to the point of fulfillment and not beyond to Christ's second advent (e.g., Luke 4:18-19; cf. Isaiah 61:1-2).

We noted earlier that Joel 2:28 used wording which, in its context, places the promise into a future fulfillment for the nation of Israel. "And it shall come to pass afterward, that I will pour out My Spirit upon all flesh." Notice the wording difference in Acts 2:17: *And it shall come to pass in the last days, saith God, I will pour out of My Spirit upon all flesh.* The phrase *in the last days, saith God* is not in Joel. There are no textual variants. The wording was changed under inspiration. Acts 2:17, there-fore, takes what will be a future literal fulfillment for Israel and applies it as a series of repetitive foretastes during the period called *the last days*.

Some understandably argue that Acts 2:17-18 cannot be for today because verses 19-20 say, "And I will shew wonders in heaven above, and signs in the earth beneath; blood, and fire, and vapour of smoke: The sun shall be turned into darkness, and the moon into blood, before that great and notable day of the Lord come." However, these statements seem to be connected to *before that great and notable day of the Lord*. Also, the next verse concludes the quotation from Joel 2 with "And it shall come to pass, that whosoever shall call on the name of the Lord shall be saved." Would not all agree that this applies to the entire period known as *the last days*? We know this is true from Romans 10:13. As with other prophecies there is a future, literal, and complete fulfillment as well as a series of repetitive foretastes leading up to the final fulfillment.

*The last days*, according to Peter, began on the Day of Pentecost. Yet we are still in the period known as *the last days*. II Timothy 3:1 states "in the last days perilous times shall come." Some argue that Peter's words refer just to the Day of Pentecost. Yet the wording is *the last days*, not "the last day" or "a day in the last days."

Also, *saith God* is in the present tense, generally indicating continuous action. This, in combination with the future *I will pour out*, is interesting. By itself, this argument would not stand, for there are passages which combine the present and future, and they do not indicate that the future is continuous. However, in the light of the period *the last days*, it does seem to lean toward "God is saying, I will pour out of My Spirit."

The future tense indicates time of action (chronological), not type of action (e.g., punctilear versus linear). But again, when put with the phrase *in the last days*, the emphasis seems to be "I will be pouring out My Spirit during this period of the last days."

Regardless of the potential grammatical supplements of *saith God* and *I will pour out*, the phrase *in the last days, saith God* is in contrast to Joel 2:28, making the Day of Pentecost a prototype, a foretaste of coming fulfillment which is to be repeated throughout the period known as *the last days* which we are still in. The outpouring of the Spirit is for today because we are still in *the last days*. Remember, God "is able to do exceeding abundantly above all that we ask or think" (Ephesians 3:20). Therefore, the works of God are increasing, not diminishing.

Think of it—according to Acts 2:17 God has already scheduled revival! It appears His intent is for *all flesh* in every generation during *the last days* to know the outpouring of His Spirit. That is to say God means for those who live in *the last days* to know the manifestation of His presence. "The Lord of the harvest" has been sent to take out a harvest, to call out a people for the name of the Lord Jesus Christ who died for the sins of the world. The power for reaching our Jerusalem, Judea, Samaria, and the uttermost part of the earth is the power of the sent Spirit of the glorified, triumphant Christ. He has not been sent back. The Day of Pentecost launched the Age of Pentecost. The day of the sent Spirit launched the age of the Spirit. This is the age of revival power; the power of the manifested presence of the Spirit. This is revival power to the ends of the earth! Why, then, do we not see regular (seasonal) outpourings of the Spirit? Because the promise must be accessed by faith. Unbelief causes much blood to be on the hands of God's people during the period of promise *the last days*.

### Titus 3:5-7

Titus 3:5-7: "Not by works of righteousness which we have done, but according to His mercy He saved us, by the washing of regeneration, and renewing of the Holy Spirit; Which He shed on us abundantly through Jesus Christ our Saviour; That being justified by His grace, we should be made heirs according to the hope of eternal life."

This passage indicates the outpouring of the Spirit is a part of the believer's grand inheritance in Christ. Notice the Holy Spirit is *shed* [*ekcheo*—poured out] *on us*. It is connected to our *being justified* [aorist, passive, participle]. But the full benefits of this heirship arc in the subjunctive mood *we should be made heirs* [aorist, passive, subjunctive]. The subjunctive mood expresses what might or should happen, but it indicates it has not yet been experienced. It is possible to have the facts without the function. Our salvation gives us access rights to all that is in Christ, including the mighty outpouring of His Spirit. However, we must access our inheritance by faith.

Obviously not every child of God accesses his full inheritance in Christ. For example, many miss out on the filling of the Spirit. This is the problem with carnal Christians. By not experiencing the Spirit-filled life, they may be skeptical that it is even possible. But just because they have not experienced it does not mean it is not possible. Likewise, just because some have not experienced the outpouring of the Spirit does not mean it is not possible. John R. Rice said, "Men do not believe in the power of Pentecost simply because they do not themselves have the power of Pentecost."

## HISTORICAL USAGE

The Church of Jesus Christ has freely used the terminology and imagery of the "outpouring of the Spirit," referring to revival. This can be documented from the last several centuries. The general sense of the usage referred to the powerful, spiritual manifestation of the presence of God, which leads believers to a restoration of the Spirit-filled life for holiness and service, and leads unbelievers to a convincement of sin, righteousness, and judgment for salvation.

For example, going back to the time period of the First Great Awakening, Jonathan Edwards said, "The work of God is carried on with greater speed and swiftness, and there are often instances of sudden conversions at such a time. So it was in the apostles' days, when there was a time of the most extraordinary pouring out of the Spirit that ever was! How quick and sudden were conversions in those days . . . So it is in some degree whenever there is an extraordinary pouring out of the Spirit of God; more or less so, in proportion to the greatness of that effusion."[1] "These words convey the doctrinal understanding of revival that prevailed among the evangelical leaders of the eighteenth century. Edwards' phraseology was common to them all. Whitefield saw the great change that began in America in the winter of 1739-40 'as an earnest of future and more plentiful effusions of God's Spirit in these parts'. Samuel Blair wrote of the same change: 'It was in the spring of 1740 when the God of salvation was pleased to visit us with the blessed effusions of the Spirit of God.' For these men the words 'effusion', 'baptism', and 'outpouring of the Spirit' were synonymous in meaning with 'revival of religion'."[2] From the same time period, Samuel Davies preached on "The Happy Effects of the Pouring Out of the Spirit" from Isaiah 32:13-19, and argued that "the outpouring of the Holy Spirit is the great and only remedy for a ruined country."[3]

In the 1859 revival in Wales, a young man wrote, "We had all heard our fathers speak of the great effects which they in their youth had seen accompanying the preaching of the word, and the influences which the outpouring of the Spirit was wont to have on the minds of the people assembled for worship; but we had never seen the like ourselves, at least in the measure which our fathers were accustomed to say they had seen; and, therefore, a kind of scepticism concerning its reality frequently passed us. But now this scepticism was to be taken away for ever."[4] This testimony is enlightening. Much skepticism today regarding revival is based on experience, not the lack of biblical foundation. We must be fair. Just as it is wrong to base one's beliefs on experience apart from biblical foundation, it is also wrong to base one's doubts on experience when there is a biblical foundation.

A preacher wrote of the condition of Wales in 1902 before the mighty 1904 Welsh Awakening, "The principal need of my country and dear nation at present is still spiritual revivals through a special outpouring of the Holy Spirit."[5]

Regarding the 1905 Sialkot Convention where John (Praying) Hyde was a channel of God's blessing, one wrote, "He entered the hall with great joy, and as he came before the people, after having obeyed God, he spoke three words in Urdu and three in English, repeating them three times : 'Ai Asmani Bak,' 'O Heavenly Father.' What followed who can describe? It was as if a great ocean came sweeping into that assembly, and 'suddenly there came a sound from Heaven as of a rushing mighty wind, and it filled all the house where they were sitting.' Hearts were bowed before that Divine presence as the trees of the wood before a mighty tempest. It was the ocean of God's love being outpoured through one man's obedience. Hearts were broken before it. There were confessions of sins with tears that were soon changed to joy and then shouts of rejoicing."[6] Notice that "Divine presence" describes "God's love being outpoured."

In the 1907 revival which swept Korea, a Mr. Adams describes a meeting where "the Holy Spirit came like a flood on the seventh day and revived them."[7]

In William Schubert's biography of John Sung, recounting the great revival in China in the 1930s, we read on one occasion: "Just then the Holy Spirit fell on everybody."[8]

A biographer of Duncan Campbell, in relating the Lewis Awakening of December 1949 through 1953, speaks of "vivid outpourings of the Spirit."[9] Campbell himself speaks of intercessors who "cried for an outpouring of the Spirit."[10]

Speaking of the beginning of the 1921 revival with Douglas Brown in East Anglia, England, an eyewitness pastor recounts: "We had been praying for 'showers' that night, and He gave us a 'cloud-burst.'"[11]

Dr. Martyn Lloyd-Jones sums up the use of the terminology and imagery of the outpouring of the Spirit, equating it with the manifestation of God's presence:

> The essence of a revival is that the Holy Spirit comes down upon a number of people together, upon a whole church, upon a number of churches, districts, or perhaps a whole country. This is what is meant by revival. It is, if you like, a visitation of the Holy Spirit, or another term that has often been used is this—an outpouring of the Holy Spirit. And the terms are interesting because you see what the people are conscious of is that it is as if something has suddenly come down upon them. The Spirit of God has descended into their midst, God has come down and is amongst them. A baptism, an outpouring, a visitation. And the effect of that is that they immediately become aware of his presence and of his power in a manner that they have never known before. I am talking about Christian people, about church members gathered together as they have done so many times before. Suddenly they are aware of his presence, they are aware of the majesty and the awe of God. The Holy Spirit literally seems to be presiding over the meeting and taking charge of it, and manifesting his power and guiding them, and leading them, and directing them. That is the essence of revival.[12]

## Conclusion

Sadly, since the Charismatic movement of the 1960s went to such excesses with good terms that relate to the Holy Spirit, many have unwittingly overreacted in the other direction. It has only been since the 1960s that some have rejected the terminology "the outpouring of the Spirit" in regard to revival. Personally, I do not believe we should give away biblical imagery and terminology to those who misuse it. Rather, let us—by God's grace—take it back and use it in the biblical sense.

Today some argue that we cannot base a doctrine on the Book of Acts, and yet the Epistles do not contradict the Book of Acts. Stewart Custer, in his commentary on Acts, describes Acts as "the historical background necessary to understand the teachings of the Epistles that will follow."[13] The Epistles must not be read in the dim light of one's substandard experience, but rather in the bright light of the standard of the Book of Acts. In this light, Jonathan Goforth, who experienced true revival, connects phraseology from the Epistles to the Book of Acts:

> But though we speak of the manifestations at Pentecost as being abnormal, yet we maintain that Pentecost was normal Christianity. The results, when the Holy Spirit assumed control in Christ's stead, were according to Divine plan. Each one was strengthened with might by His Spirit in the inner man. Christ then did dwell in their hearts by faith, and they were rooted and grounded in love. They were filled unto all the fulness of God, and God did work in and through them above all they had asked or thought, even unto the "exceeding abundantly." Anything short of that would have defrauded their Lord of His Calvary merits. The purpose of the Holy Spirit was to glorify the Lord Jesus Christ every day from the crowning to the coming. It is unthinkable that He should grow weary in well-doing. My conviction is that the Divine power, so manifest in the Church at Pentecost, was nothing more or less than what should be in evidence in the Church today. Normal Christianity, as planned by our Lord, was not supposed to begin in the Spirit and continue in the flesh. In the building of His temple it never was by might nor by power, but always by His Spirit.
>
> The Lord Himself met and foiled Satan after first being filled with the Spirit. And no child of God has ever been victorious over the adversary, unless empowered from the same source. Our Lord did not permit His chosen followers to witness a word in His name until endued with power from on high. It is true that before that day they were the "born-again" children of

the Father and had the witness of the Spirit. But they were not the Lord's efficient co-workers and never could be until Spirit-filled. This Divine empowering is for us as for them. We, too, may do the works which our Lord did, yea and the greater works. The Scriptures convey no other meaning to me than that the Lord Jesus planned that the Holy Spirit should continue among us in as mighty manifestation as at Pentecost. One should be able to chase a thousand and two put ten thousand to flight—as of old. Time has not changed the fact that "Jesus Christ is the same yesterday, today and for ever."[14]

The outpouring of the Spirit is for today. A. W. Tozer boldly declares:

God desires to advance His work among men by frequent outpourings of the Spirit upon His people as they need them and are prepared to receive them. . . . The Bible . . . encourages us to expect "showers of blessing" and "floods upon the dry ground." It was impossible for the outpouring which came at Pentecost to affect persons who were not present or congregations not yet in existence. The Bible does not sponsor [the] chilling doctrine of once-for-all blessing. It is obvious that the spiritual benefits of Pentecost must be prolonged beyond the lifetimes of the persons who were the first to receive them. . . . In brief, the teaching of the New Testament is that the outpouring of Pentecost was the historic beginning of an era which was to be characterized by a continuous outpouring of the Holy Spirit.[15]

Pentecost did not come and go—Pentecost came and stayed. Chronologically the day may be found in the historic calendar; dynamically it remains with us in all its fullness of power. Today is the day of Pentecost. With the blessed Holy Spirit there is no Yesterday or Tomorrow—there is only the everlasting Now. And since He is altogether God, enjoying all the attributes of the Godhead, there is with Him no Elsewhere; His bound is Nowhere. It is impossible to leave His presence, though it is possible to have Him withdraw the manifestation of that presence. Our insensibility to the presence of the Spirit is one of the greatest losses that our unbelief and preoccupation have cost us. We have made Him a tenet of our creed, we have enclosed Him in a religious word, but we have known Him little in personal experience.[16]

May our hearts beat like C. H. Spurgeon's when he wrote:

> It is the work of the Holy Spirit that I wish to especially direct to your attention, and I may as well mention the reason why I do. It is this: in the United States of America there has been a great awakening [1858]. Two hundred and fifty thousand people profess to have been regenerated. . . . Now, this great work in America has been manifestly caused by the outpouring of the Spirit. . . . To have a similar effect produced in this land, the one thing we must seek is the outpouring of the Holy Spirit. I thought that perhaps my writing about the work of the Holy Spirit might fulfill the text, 'Them that honor me I will honor' (I Sam. 2:30). My sincere desire is to honor the Holy Spirit, and if He will be pleased to honor His church in return, unto Him be the glory forever.[17]
>
> Whatever the Holy Spirit was at the first, He is now. . . . Whatever He then did, He is able to do still, for His power is by no means diminished. . . . If at the commencement of the Gospel, we behold the Holy Spirit working great signs and wonders, may we not expect a continuance—if anything, an increased display—of His power as the ages roll on? . . .
>
> It ought not to be forgotten that Pentecost was the feast of first fruits. . . . If, then, at the commencement of the gospel harvest we see so plainly the power of the Holy Spirit, may we not most properly expect infinitely more as the harvest advances?
>
> My object is not to talk of the descent of the Holy Spirit as a piece of history but to view it as a fact bearing upon us at this hour. . . . The gift of the Comforter was not temporary, and the display of His power was not to be seen just once and no more.[18]

This position is important because it affects the possibility of faith. There is no faith for revival where doubt undermines the scriptural promises. Without faith, prayer for revival is wishful thinking. In order to truly intercede for the outpouring of the Spirit you must, by the Spirit, come to a convinced confidence. Is the outpouring of the Spirit for today? I believe the Scriptures clearly indicate it is. May God's people look to the Spirit to convince them of the scriptural foundation, and then plead the promises in faith. May God then be glorified once again through the mighty outpouring of His Spirit! The outpouring of the Spirit is for today. When embraced by faith, this greatly impacts one's view of God's power. May we seek God's face to once again come down and manifest His presence that His glory may be revealed to this generation. Then we may say as they did during the 1904 Welsh Awakening, "A sense of the Lord's presence was everywhere."[19]

---

[1]Jonathan Edwards, The Works of Jonathan Edwards (London, 1834; Edinburgh: Banner of Truth, 1974) 1 : 539.

[2]Iain Murray, Revival and Revivalism (Edinburgh: Banner of Truth, 1994), p. 20.

[3]Ibid., p. 21.

[4]Thomas Phillips, The Welsh Revival (Edinburgh: Banner of Truth, reprint 1998), p. 12.

[5]Eifion Evans, The Welsh Revival of 1904 (Bridgend, Wales: The Evangelical Press of Wales, reprint 1997), p. 47.

[6]E. G. Carré, ed., Praying Hyde (Asheville, N.C.: Revival Literature, n.d.), pp. 19-20.

[7]Jonathan Goforth, When the Spirit's Fire Swept Korea (Elkhart, Ind.: Bethel Publishing, reprint 1984), p. 13.

[8]William E. Schubert, I Remember John Sung (Singapore: Far Eastern Bible College Press, 1976), p. 34.

[9]Andrew A. Woolsey, Channel of Revival: A Biography of Duncan Campbell (Edinburgh: The Faith Mission, reprint 1982), p. 134.

[10]Duncan Campbell, The Lewis Awakening in Heritage of Revival by Colin N. Peckham (Edinburgh: The Faith Mission, 1986), p. 173.

[11]Stanley C. Griffin, A Forgotten Revival (Bromley, Kent, England: Day One Publications, 1992), p. 22.

[12]D. Martyn Lloyd-Jones, Revival (Wheaton: Crossway Books, reprint 1992), p. 100.

[13]Stewart Custer, Witness to Christ: A Commentary on Acts (Greenville, S.C.: Bob Jones University Press, 2000), p. xix.

[14]Jonathan Goforth, By My Spirit (Elkhart, Ind.: Bethel Publishing, reprint 1983), pp. 10-11.

[15]A.W. Tozer, Tozer on the Holy Spirit, comp. by Marilynne E. Foster (Camp Hill, Penn.: Christian Publications, Inc., 2000), March 22.

[16]Foster, March 14.

[17]C. H. Spurgeon, Power for You (New Kensington, Penn.: Whitaker House, reprint 1996), pp. 10-11.

[18]Ibid., pp. 87-89.

[19]James A. Stewart, Invasion of Wales by the Spirit (Asheville, N.C.: Revival Literature, 1963), p. 43.

CHAPTER THIRTEEN

# FROM GREATER WORDS TO GREATER WORKS

How do you come to faith regarding revival for today? Every revival has had, either known or unknown, an intercessor or intercessors to reach and receive the mercies of God for others. How can you become an intercessor? Will you not ask the Great Convincer to convince you of this necessary responsibility in revival?

# JOHN 14:12

Lewis, an island in the Outer Hebrides Islands off the northwest coast of Scotland, has been rightly called "the land of revivals." "Since 1828, when the whole island was shaken out of the slumber of superstition and formalism through the preaching of Rev. Alexander Maclead, Lewis had experienced repeated visitations of the Spirit of God."[1] Is this not the biblical plan of "seasons of refreshing from the presence of the Lord"?

However, the late 1940s saw again a low ebb of spiritual life. It was time for the tide of revival to come in again. The last awakening there took place in 1939. "Gradually in many praying hearts, concern deepened into a conviction that God's time to favor them with a further outpouring of His Spirit had come. Prayer was intensified and faith encouraged. Expectation grew that something would happen."[2] Among the intercessors were two elderly women in the village of Barvas by the names of Peggy and Christine Smith. "They were eighty-four and eighty-two respectively. Peggy was blind and her sister almost bent double with arthritis. Unable to attend public worship, their humble cottage became a sanctuary where they met with God. To them came the promise: 'I will pour water upon him that is thirsty and floods upon the dry ground,' which they pleaded day and night in prayer."[3] They contacted their pastor of the village church in Barvas, James Murray MacKay, and told him that revival was coming. They asked him to call the leading men of the church together "for special times of waiting upon God" asking God to do what He had promised He would do.[4]

The men met weekly while Peggy and Christine met "before the peat fires three nights a week pleading one promise, 'I will pour water on him that is thirsty, and floods on the dry ground.' A promise made, as they declared, by a covenant-keeping God who must ever be true to His covenant engagements. So they waited and the months passed and nothing happened"[5] until the praying men of Barvas, while interceding "in a barn, experienced a foretaste of coming blessing. As they waited upon God a young deacon rose and read part of the twenty-fourth Psalm: "'Who shall ascend into the hill of the Lord? Or who shall stand in His holy place? He that hath clean hands and a pure heart; who hath not lifted up his soul unto vanity, nor sworn deceitfully. He shall receive the blessing from the Lord.' Turning to the others he said, 'Brethren, it seems to me just so much humbug to be waiting and praying as we are, if we ourselves are not rightly related to God.' Then lifting his hands toward heaven he cried: 'Oh God, are *my* hands clean? Is *my* heart pure?'

"He got no further, but fell prostrate to the floor. An awareness of God filled the barn and a stream of supernatural power was let loose in their lives. They had moved into a new sphere of God-realisation, believing implicitly in the promise of revival."[6]

There in the presence of God "hearts were searched and vows renewed, and, in the words of one who was present, they gave to their lives the propulsion of a sacred vow, and with Hezekiah of old, found it in their hearts to 'make a covenant with the Lord God of Israel.'"[7] "So they entered into a solemn covenant that they would not rest or cease from prayer until He made 'Jerusalem' a praise on the Island."[8]

Finally the intercessors with their pastor sensed that it was time to plan a mission, or meeting, for that coming winter. Pastor MacKay, while attending a convention on the mainland, received a recommendation to invite Duncan Campbell for this winter mission. How he rejoiced to discover upon arriving home that God had laid it on the heart of Peggy Smith to encourage the pastor to invite Duncan Campbell! When Duncan Campbell received the first two invitations, he declined because of a schedule conflict where he already had been ministering on the Isle of Skye. Yet he sensed "something different about the appeal from Barvas and was inclined to accept it. . . . When Mr. MacKay told [Peggy] that a second appeal to Duncan had produced no further response and that he was unable to come, she replied: 'That is what man says; God has said otherwise! Write again! He will be here within a fortnight!'"[9]

Amazingly, by the time the third invitation came to Duncan Campbell, the plans for the conflicting meeting had fallen through! Within that fortnight of two weeks, Campbell was headed to Lewis by way of ferryboat. "His first contact with the men of Barvas convinced him that he was in the company of those who were living on a high spiritual plane. As he walked down the village road next day his sensitive spirit quickly discerned that God was at work; he realised that revival had already come; it would be his privilege to share in it." On the second night of preaching, "The service closed in a tense silence and the building emptied. As he came down from the pulpit a young deacon raised his hand and moving it in a circle above his head whispered: 'Mr.

Campbell God is hovering over. He is going to break through. I can hear already the rumbling of heaven's chariot-wheels.'

"Just then the door opened and an elder beckoned: 'Come and see what's happening!' The entire congregation was lingering outside, reluctant to disperse; others had joined them, drawn from their homes by an irresistible power they had not experienced before. There were looks of deep distress on many faces.

"Suddenly a cry pierced the silence; a young man had remained in the church, burdened to the point of agony for his fellow-men, was pouring out his desire in prayer . . . the congregation swept back into the church. The awful presence of God brought a wave of conviction of sin that caused even mature Christians to feel their sinfulness, bringing groans of distress and prayers of repentance from the unconverted. Strong men were bowed under the weight of sin and cries for mercy were mingled with shouts of joy from others who had passed into life. A mother was standing with her arms around her son, tears of joy streaming down her face, thanking God for his salvation. 'Oh, praise the Lord, you've come at last!' Prayers of years were answered."[10]

When Pastor MacKay went to tell Peggy and Christine about it the next day, they already knew. They told him "how they had been battling in prayer the previous night reminding God again of His promise. 'We struggled through the hours of the night refusing to take denial. Had He not promised and would He not fulfil. Our God is a covenant-keeping God and He must be true to His covenant engagements. Did He fail us? Never! Before the morning light broke we saw the enemy retreating, and our wonderful Lamb taking the field.' On being asked what supported their faith in prayer, Peggy replied: 'We had a consciousness of God that created a confidence in our souls which refused to accept defeat."[11] Duncan Campbell came for what he thought would be a ten-day meeting. But because of the outpouring of the Spirit, he stayed for nearly three years! What an amazing moving of the Spirit of the living God! In fact, my wife and I visited the Isle of Lewis to study this revival. While there, God graciously allowed us to meet four people converted in this revival. Truly the glow of God is still on their faces!

I love stories like this. But quite honestly this story raises a lot of questions. How did Peggy and Christine Smith know that they could stand on the promise of Isaiah 44:3? It does say, "For I will pour water on him that is thirsty, and floods up on the dry ground: I will pour My Spirit upon thy seed, and My blessing upon thine offspring." But it does not say from December 1949 to 1953 on the Isle of Lewis. How did they know that they could claim it for that occasion? How could they have such confidence that they told their pastor that revival was coming? This kind of confidence is far beyond wishful thinking. How could they and the praying men pray for months pleading the promise? The best I can figure, based on the various accounts, the intercession continued approximately eighteen months. If they had not been convinced, they never would have lasted eighteen months. How did they know it was time to schedule a mission? How did they know Duncan Campbell was the instrument of God's choosing to declare truth for that occasion? How did they know the secret of the Lord?

Now we come to our subject of "From Greater Words to Greater Works." Our text is the words of Jesus Christ in John 14:12, "Verily, verily, I say unto you, He that believeth on Me, the works that I do shall he do also; and greater works than these shall he do; because I go unto My Father." What a promise! But what are the *greater works*? Notice Christ explicitly ties the *greater works* to *because I go unto My Father*. In verse 16 He further explains, "And I will pray the Father, and He shall give you another Comforter." The *greater works* are directly related to the sent Spirit. Therefore, they are spiritual works. They are movings of the Spirit as we read about in the Book of Acts from the Day of Pentecost and onwards.

The *works*, or "regular works," could well refer to the Spirit-filled life, which is to be the norm. Yet it is miraculous. This was epitomized by Christ Himself. The *greater works* seem to refer to the outpouring of the Spirit. Some think that *greater works* is simply quantitative because the Spirit is sent to multiple believers. But Jesus said, "*Greater works ... shall he do.*" The *greater works* are promised to an individual, not a group. The *greater works* are explained by Christ to be related to the powerful ministry of the Spirit during the age of the Holy Spirit. We are still in this spiritual age.

The promise in our text is conditional. That condition is our believing on Christ. The verb *believeth* is in the present tense, indicating "is believing." Therefore, **Jesus promises greater works to those who keep depending on Him.** What then is involved in going from greater words to greater works? From John 14 and 16 notice five principles interacting as that which brings us from greater words to greater works.

## FIRST PRINCIPLE:

# The words of God provide the foundation for the works of God.

Remember that Romans 10:17 teaches, "So then faith cometh by hearing, and hearing by the word of God," or the *rhema* of God. Faith comes by a convincement of some specific truth of God. Faith is depending on the reality of the words of God even though it is not yet seen. The words provide the basis for the works which those words promise.

In this light, John 14:10 adds further understanding. Jesus says to Philip, "Believest thou not that I am in the Father, and the Father in me? [This is the perfect illustration of the reality of you in Christ and Christ in you.] The words [plural of *rhema*] that I speak unto you I speak not of [from] Myself: but the Father that dwelleth in Me, He doeth the works." In the flow of Christ's wording, we think Christ is going to say, "He speaks the words." But instead Christ says, "*He doeth the works*"! Do you see it? From God's vantage point, there is a mystery of oneness between the *words* of God and the *works* of God. Therefore, when you come to the convincement of the words of God, you now have the foundation for the works of God. Perhaps this is why Peggy and Christine Smith were confident that revival (the works of God) was coming—they were convinced of the words of Isaiah 44:3.

## SECOND PRINCIPLE:

## Dependence on the words of God accesses the works of God.

The words of God are in the Scriptures. Many are the "exceeding great and precious promises." What connects the words of God to the works of God reflected in those words? Faith is the access. Jesus says in John 14:12, "*He that believeth in Me.*" This believing is of necessity in conjunction with the Word of God, the foundation of faith. Jesus is "the Word" (John 1:1). There is a mystery of oneness between the incarnate Word (Christ) and the inscribed Word (the Scriptures). When you depend on the living words of God, you are depending on the living Word of God. So Jesus says that he who believes on Me (by depending on My words), *the works that I do shall he do also, and greater works*. Clearly, faith is the necessary link between the words of God and the works of God. The access is faith. To access the mighty works of God, you must depend on the words of God for those works.

## THIRD PRINCIPLE:

## The Holy Spirit must convince you of the words of God in order for you to depend on them.

Jesus explains in John 16:13, "Howbeit when He, the Spirit of truth, is come, He will guide you into all of truth." Jesus declares in John 17:17, "Thy word is truth." How do we know what *rhema* of truth we can stand on for a given occasion? *The Spirit of truth . . . will guide you into all truth.* What a blessed promise! Jesus continues in John 16:13 with "for He shall not speak of Himself." Notice He did not say "about Himself." There are no less than 347 direct mentions of the Spirit in the Scriptures! Also, the Holy Spirit is implied multiple times in words, like "grace" (Spirit-enabling). Rather, Jesus said of the Spirit that *He shall not speak of Himself,* which means "from" Himself. The Spirit does not speak from Himself apart from the Father and the Son. Now let's continue: "but whatsoever He shall hear, that shall He speak." How does the Spirit do that? We will see the answer in verse 14. But verse 13 then ends with "and He will show you things to come." Certainly this could include the completion of the canon of Scripture. But I believe there is application also for us today. We know it cannot mean new revelation, for the Scripture prohibits adding to the Word of God. But is it not possible for the Spirit to guide you to a specific truth, so illuminating it and convincing you that you then have the foundation for faith? In that sense, knowing that the words of God provide the foundation of the works of God, He has shown you things to come!

Jesus further emphasizes in John 16:14, "He shall glorify me." How? "For He shall receive of Mine, and shall show it unto you." How does the Spirit receive of Christ and show it unto us? We have already noted the oneness between the incarnate Word (Christ) and the inscribed Word (the Scriptures). So when the Spirit illumines the words of God, thus giving them the weight, honor, and glory that is due them, He is taking of Christ, the living Word, and showing it unto us. Thus, He gives Christ the weight, the honor, and the glory that is due Him!

Let me illustrate. Have you ever read through a portion of Scripture and the thought occurs to you that you did not understand what you just read? I'm sure that all of us can relate to this. When this happens, the Bible is not alive. It is more like a desert—dry and lifeless. It is not being given the weight that is due it as the Word of God. What do you do? Do you sigh and finish your reading for the day, unfed? Or do you stop and cry out with the Psalmist, "Open Thou mine eyes, that I may behold wondrous things out of Thy law"?

Now consider in those times when the Bible seemed to be a desert, yet you kept meditating on the Word, did you ever suddenly see a well-spring in that desert? Has the Bible suddenly come alive to you? It is almost as if the words leap off the page and speak to you! What is that? That is the Spirit taking of Christ and showing Him unto you. It is the Spirit of truth guiding into truth. Now instead of mere facts, you understand the realities which relate to those facts. He is glorifying Christ by giving the Word the weight which is due it.

When the Spirit thus convinces of a promise, He is simply showing you things to come. For as you access that promise by faith, the words of God become the works of God. So look unto Jesus by looking at the Word, that the Spirit might author faith through convincement of the words, and finish faith by enabling, in accordance with the words on which you depend. This spiritual dynamic is not at all the same as the idea of "name it and claim it" and you demanding your will from God.

I believe it is this dynamic which allowed Peggy and Christine Smith to "know" revival was coming. As they sought God's face, the Spirit powerfully convinced them of the promise of Isaiah 44:3. In that sense, God showed them things to come. For these godly ladies knew that once they had the promise of the words of God, it was just a matter of time before they would experience the works of God if they depended on that promise.

## FOURTH PRINCIPLE:

# Dependence on the words of God for the works of God precedes dependence on the greater words of God for the greater works of God.

This is really a simple, yet often overlooked, truth. Dependence on the words of God for the works of God simply pictures the Spirit-filled life. For as we have seen through this book, the Spirit-filled life is the life of faith. Walking in the Spirit occurs through walking by faith (Colossians 2:6). In this life of God-dependence for Spirit-enabling, you learn to trust God for victory over sin, for victory over the tongue, for victory in patience, for victory in tithing and giving, for victory in home relationships, for victory in financial responsibilities (i.e., paying your bills on time), for victory in witnessing—in a word for victory in holiness and service. You are trusting God for this step, and the next step, and so forth. In other words, you are learning to trust God.

Now the Spirit can show you greater words for greater works. Without learning to trust the regular words, so to speak, you would never trust the greater words. For example, if you cannot trust God for individual harvests through personal witnessing, how will you ever trust God for a mass harvest through the outpouring of the Spirit? If you cannot trust God for the filling of the Spirit in daily living, how will you ever trust God for the outpouring of the Spirit in seasons of refreshing? Dependence on the words of God for the works of God precedes dependence on the greater words of God for the greater works of God.

## FIFTH PRINCIPLE:

# The expression of faith for greater works is God-dependent asking founded upon greater words.

After Jesus gives the promise of *greater works* in John 14:12, He then says "And whatsoever ye shall ask in My name, that will I do, that the Father may be glorified in the Son. If ye shall ask any thing in My name, I will do it" (John 14:13-14). Directly following the promise for *greater works*, twice He tells us to *ask*. Asking is emphasized.

What does Christ mean when He says *ask in My name*? What is His name in John 1? "The Word." Asking in His name, in a certain sense, includes asking according to His words. When you do, He promises the works *I will do it* based on those words.

This now leads us to categorizing the types of promises given in the Word of God. Generally speaking, there are two types of promises: present realities and future realities. The type of promise determines the expression of faith to access that promise.

## Present Realities: God-dependent Acting

The expression of faith for the promises which are stated as present realities is God-dependent acting upon those promises. For example, II Corinthians 12:9 states, "My grace is sufficient for thee." It does not say, "My grace will be sufficient." It says, *My grace is sufficient*. Therefore, in a certain sense you do not need to ask for grace; you need to act on it. Simply depend on the Spirit's enablement, for the supply is inexhaustible. You simply appropriate from the Bank of Heaven the life of Christ through the Spirit. When you draw money from your own bank account, you do not ask, beg, and plead for it, for it is already yours. You just appropriate from your account what is already yours. Likewise, draw upon what is already yours in Christ by appropriating it. Since His grace *is* sufficient, depend on it for the various areas of holiness and service, and you will find it to be so. Why? Because it says so!

The expression of faith for present realities is God-dependent acting. Not just acting, for acting apart from God-dependence is the futility of the flesh; rather, God-dependent acting upon promises of present reality. Other examples of such promises are "The harvest truly is plenteous" (not *will* be, it is) and "Christ liveth in me" (not *will* live, He does). Depend on present realities, and you will find them to be manifestly so.

## Future Realities: God-dependent Asking

The expression of faith for future realities is God-dependent asking. It is not God-dependent acting, for the promise is not "is" yet. It is God-dependent asking, or what has been called "believing prayer." It is not just asking, but God-dependent asking. The very fact that James 5 mentions the "prayer of faith" indicates there is a prayer of unbelief. This is simply the ritualism of the form of prayer without faith. Also, the very fact that James 1 says "ask in faith" indicates it is possible to ask in unbelief.

The promises of the outpouring of the Spirit are stated in the future tense. "Greater works than these **shall** he do" (John 14:12). "In the last days, saith God, I **will** pour out of My Spirit upon all flesh" (Acts 2:17). "For I **will** pour water upon him that is thirsty . . . I **will** pour My Spirit" (Isaiah 44:3). "Seek the LORD, **till** He come and rain righteousness upon you" (Hosea 10:12). "If my people . . . then **will** I" (II Chronicles 7:14).

Our responsibility is to ask for God to do what He promised. This is the expression of faith for future realities. Therefore, if we are not asking, we really do not believe. It is not enough to say, "I believe God can send revival." That by itself is still unbelief. It is no different than a lost man saying, "I believe God can save me" while he still depends on himself. Believing for revival is depending on God to send revival by asking Him to fulfill His promises.

The promises are there, but in order for us to come into union with their realities, we must depend on them. Consider a father who promises his children that, on his day off from work, he will take them out for ice cream. Yet on his day off, the day is quickly slipping by and so far—no ice cream. So his children come to him and say, "Daddy, you said on your day off you would take us out for ice cream. Daddy, will you take us for ice cream like you promised?" Of course, a good father will keep his word.

Just so, God has promised revival. He is waiting for His children to say, "Father, You said . . ." And God, our heavenly Father, is a good Father and will be true to His Word. O that we would allow the Spirit to convince us of revival promises and then plead for God to fulfill them. In His perfect timing—for He knows what sins are still separating between us and Him, what wrong motives must be purged, what soil still must be cultivated—He will be true to His Word. For every covenant which the Spirit convinces you of, there must be a covenant engagement. God gives covenants, not to be held accountable like a man, but to show us what He desires us to do. When the Spirit convinces you of one of God's promises, ask for it! If we give up asking, we really do not believe in the promises. For if you depend on the promises of future realities, you will keep asking until you receive. Who will set aside some time to intercede for revival? As we fulfill our daily responsibilities, may we make time to seek the Lord for a fresh manifestation of His presence.

Another example of these five principles comes from the latter part of the Lewis Awakening. Duncan Campbell had gone to Northern Ireland to speak at the Bangor Convention. Campbell's biographer tells us the story:

> "But Duncan, you can't possible go! You're booked to speak at the closing meeting. The people will be disappointed."

It was Easter Monday, 1952. Duncan had just given an address . . . when he was suddenly arrested by a conviction that he should leave at once and go to Berneray, a small island off the coast of Harris with a population of about 400 people. Sitting in the pulpit he tried to fight off the insistent urge but the urgency only increased.

Eventually turning to the chairman he said: "I must leave the Convention and go to Harris immediately." Objections were valid enough . . . but Duncan was unrelenting: "I'm sorry, I must obey the promptings of the Spirit and go at once."

He left the pulpit to pack his case and the following morning flew from Belfast to Scotland. On Thursday morning he reached Harris and took the ferry to Berneray. He had never been there before and knew no one on the island. The first person he met was a sixteen-year-old boy. "Could you direct me to the manse, please?"

"The manse is vacant," the lad replied. "We have no minister just now. The men (the elders) take the services," and pointing to a house on the hill, added, "One lives up there."

Duncan glanced from the hill to his suitcase, then back to the boy. "Could you please go and tell him that Mr. Campbell has arrived on the island. If he asks what Mr. Campbell, tell him it's the minister who was in Lewis."

Ten minutes later the boy came back to say that the elder was expecting him, accommodation had been arranged and a service already intimated for nine o'clock that night! God had gone before.

Three days earlier when Duncan was in the pulpit at Bangor, this man was praying in the barn. He had been there most of the day. God had given him a promise: "I will be as the dew unto Israel," which he had laid hold of in faith, assured that revival was going to sweep the island.

More than that, he was confident that God would send Duncan Campbell. His wife could hear him in the barn: "Lord, I don't know where he is, but You know and with You all things are possible. You send him to the island." So convinced was he that God would bring him in three days time that he made the necessary arrangements for a mission [meeting].

The first few services were uninspiring. Duncan felt tired and spiritually out of breath, but the elder adamantly affirmed that revival was at hand.

One evening as they were preparing to leave the church the old man suddenly took his hat off, pointing excitedly in the direction of the congregation which had just left the service: "Mr. Campbell, see what's happening! He has come! He has come!" The Spirit of God had fallen upon the people as they moved down towards the main road and in a few minutes they were so gripped with the subduing presence of God that no one could move any further. Amid sighs and groans from sin-burdened souls prayer ascended to God on the hillside. The entire island was shaken into a new awareness of God as many lives were saved and transformed during the following days. In this movement . . . the results were . . . deep and abiding.[12]

The man on the island was Hector McKennon. He was burdened about the condition of the church on this little island south of Harris, the southern part of Lewis. Undoubtedly, the news of the Lewis Awakening had stirred his heart to seek God. After spending the day in prayer and apparently fasting, the Spirit bore witness with his spirit, convincing him of the words of Hosea 14:5, "I will be as the dew unto Israel." "About 10:00 that evening, he was possessed of the conviction that God had heard his cry."[13] After the first few services in which about 80 people attended, which is considerable since the island population was only about 400 people, God came down. In Duncan Campbell's account, he says, "Soon the whole island was in the grip of a mighty movement of the Spirit, bringing deep conviction of sin and hunger for God. . . . Perhaps the most outstanding feature was the awe-inspiring sense of the presence of God that came over the whole island."[14]

This is going from greater words to greater works! Who will walk by faith so that when the Spirit reveals "greater words," they will have the eye of faith to see the promise? Who, then, will intercede in faith persevering until the measure of faith is full and move from greater words to greater works?

---

[1]Andrew A. Woolsey, *Channel of Revival: A Biography of Duncan Campbell* (Edinburgh: The Faith Mission, reprint 1982), p. 112.

[2]Ibid., p. 113.

[3]Ibid., pp. 113-14.

[4]Ibid., p. 114.

[5]Duncan Campbell, *The Price and Power of Revival* (Vinton, Va.: Christ Life Publications, reprint n.d.), p. 31.

[6]Woolsey, pp. 114-15.

[7]Duncan Campbell, *The Lewis Awakening* in *Heritage of Revival* by Colin N. Peckham (Edinburgh: The Faith Mission, 1986), p. 165.

[8]Campbell, *The Price and Power of Revival*, p. 31.

[9]Woolsey, pp. 115-16.

[10]Ibid., pp. 117-18.

[11]Ibid., p. 118.

[12]Ibid., pp. 139-41.

[13]Duncan Campbell, *The Nature of a God-Sent Revival* (Vinton, Va.: Christ Life Publications, reprint n.d.), p. 9.

[14]Campbell, *The Lewis Awakening*, pp. 174-75.

CHAPTER FOURTEEN

# WHEN GOD COMES DOWN

The culmination of our study in "The Wind of the Spirit for Personal and Corporate Revival" is the truth in this chapter. We have learned that as salvation is by faith, so sanctification and service are also by faith. Beyond that, as the Spirit-filled life of sanctification and service is by faith, so the outpouring of the Spirit is also by faith. May the Spirit of Revival stir us to faith and grant us seasons of refreshing from the presence of the Lord. O for the reviving rain of righteousness when God comes down!

# ISAIAH 64:1-5

We are living in a nation that has largely turned its back on God. Though I understand our agitation at the wickedness of worldlings around us, yet we as Bible-believers must accept our share of responsibility in this. Because it is our lack of power to reach the lost that has allowed such degeneration. Our lack of power indicates that we have largely turned our backs on the Holy Spirit. In a sense, there has been an apostasy from the Holy Spirit. Life without the Spirit is life without God! We need God to come back into our midst in manifest power. Revival is the powerful, spiritual manifestation of the presence of God that leads believers to a restoration of the Spirit-filled life for holiness and service and leads unbelievers to a convincement of sin, righteousness, and judgment for salvation. When Jesus ascended to the throne and sent the Spirit, He launched the age of the Spirit—the age of power! If we as the body of Christ are anemic, we can either defend our anemic condition and continue powerless or we can pray for the power of God to clothe us in manifest reality.

"When God comes down" is the imagery of the inspired prophet in Isaiah 64:1-5: "Oh that Thou wouldest rend the heavens, that Thou wouldest come down, that the mountains might flow down at Thy presence, As when the melting fire burneth, the fire causeth the waters to boil, to make Thy name known to thine adversaries, that the nations may tremble at Thy presence! When Thou didst terrible things which we looked not for, Thou camest down, the mountains flowed down at Thy presence. For since the beginning of the world men have not heard, nor perceived by the ear, neither hath the eye seen, O God, beside Thee, what He hath prepared for him that waiteth for Him. Thou meetest him that rejoiceth and worketh righteousness, those that remember thee in Thy ways." Notice how God coming down is equated to His manifest presence: *Thou wouldest come down . . . Thy presence* (v. 1); *Thy presence* (v. 2); *Thou camest down . . . Thy presence* (v. 3); God coming down is simply God manifesting His presence. It is the outpouring of the Spirit in revival. O for a fresh manifestation of the presence of God. **The desperate need of the hour is for God to come down!** What's involved in God coming down once again? In our text we see three dynamics involved in God manifesting His presence again in our midst.

## INTERCESSION FOR THE PRESENT

Verses 1-2 record an intercessory prayer for revival: *Oh that Thou wouldest rend the heavens, that Thou wouldest come down, that the mountains might flow down at Thy presence, As when the melting fire burneth, the fire causeth the waters to boil, to make Thy name known to Thine adversaries, that the nations may tremble at Thy presence!* When God comes down notice two man-ward results and one God-ward result.

# Man-ward Results

### Mountains Melt

*That the mountains might flow down at Thy presence.* Mountains in Scripture often represent the objects of man's confidences, which are deceitful false confidences. How many look to the mountain of worldliness for getting something out of life only to be sadly disappointed? How many look to the mountain of materialism for happiness and satisfaction only to come up empty of that for which they grasped? How many churches today look to the mountain of marketing a fleshly appeal to bring people in instead of looking to God to make Christ appealing? How many look to the mountain of isolationism which is a false separation and false security? O when God comes down, the mountains of worldliness, materialism, marketing carnality, isolation, and so forth melt at His mighty and powerful presence! "Truly in vain is salvation hoped for from the hills, and from the multitude of mountains: truly in the Lord our God is the salvation of Israel" (Jeremiah 3:23). O how we need revival among the saints! For when God comes down, "The hills melted like wax at the presence of the Lord" (Psalm 97:5).

### Masses Move

*That the nations may tremble at Thy presence.* God's manifest presence beyond the people of God powerfully affects the lost. When God comes down and saturates a community, the awareness of God's presence awakens the sleeping lost to their need of Christ. Duncan Campbell tells of the outpouring of the Spirit in the village of Arnol during the Lewis Awakening. The meeting was opposed by one of the village churches. Few from the village attended. But during a prayer meeting at night God came down upon the interceding saints. Campbell said that after he pronounced the benediction he "walked out to find the community alive with an awareness of God." The convicting presence of God was so real that as the meeting continued "men and women were carrying stools and chairs and asking, 'Is there room for us in the church?'"[1] Have we not all seen this same dynamic of conviction on an individual basis where someone is smitten before the Lord's presence? In this small village thirty came to the Savior. This was fifteen percent of the village population. Imagine that in a large city!

When God comes down, mountains of man's confidences melt and masses of lost people move!

## God-ward Result

When mountains melt and masses move, God is glorified. *To make Thy name known to Thine adversaries* indicates God is magnified even to His enemies which ultimately lie in the spiritual realm. When God comes down manifesting His presence, mountains melt and masses move, but ultimately the name of God is vindicated! People and the enemies of God will know that there is a God in heaven! God is given the weight, the honor, the glory that is due Him. Ultimately, revival glorifies God. God's glory is at stake.

R. B. Jones, one of the preachers in the Welsh Revival of 1904, testifies of God's glory in the revival:

> The writer will never forget one outstanding experience of this sense of an atmosphere laden with the power of God's realized presence. He was conducting meetings in Amlwch, Anglesey, in the first months of 1905. Revival had even then reached the northernmost point in Wales, and the meetings were the culmination of several weeks' worth in that island called "the Mother of Wales." The "capel mawr" (big chapel) was crowded. The memory of that meeting, even after more than a quarter of a century, is well nigh overwhelming. It was easily the greatest meeting the writer ever was in. The theme of the message was Isaiah, Chapter Six. The light of God's holiness was turned upon the hearts and lives of those present. Conviction of sin and of its terrible desert was so crushing that a feeling almost of despair grew over all hearts. So grievous a thing was sin; so richly and inevitably did it deserve the severest judgment of God, that hearts

questioned, Could God forgive? Then came the word about the altar, the tongs, and the live coal touching the confessedly vile lips, and the gracious and complete removal of their vileness. After all, there was hope! God was forgiving, and He had cleansing for the worst. When the rapt listeners realized all this the effect was—well, "electrifying" is far too weak a word; it was absolutely beyond any metaphor to describe it. As one man, first with a sigh of relief, and then, with a delirious shout of joy, the whole huge audience sprang to their feet. The vision had completely overwhelmed them and, one is not ashamed to tell it, for a moment they were beside themselves with heavenly joy. The speaker never realized anything like it anywhere. The whole place at that moment was so awful with the glory of God—one uses the word "awful" deliberately; the holy presence of God was so manifested that the speaker himself was overwhelmed; the pulpit where he stood was so filled with the light of God that he had to withdraw! There; let us leave it at that. Words cannot but mock such an experience.[2]

True revival glorifies God. O that this generation might know the glory of God!

Another account of God being marvelously glorified comes from the 1859 revival in Wales:

> A noted minister—the Rev. Thomas John, Cilber-ran—after the meeting, was found alone in deep meditation in a field. Said one who drew near to him, "Mr. John, was not the sight of the thousands as they silently prayed a most impressive one? Did you ever see anything to compare with it?" "I never saw one of them," was the answer, "I saw no one but God!"[3]

May we intercede by the Spirit for the present and cry out: "*Oh that Thou wouldest rend the heavens, that Thou wouldest come down, that the mountains might flow down at Thy presence, As when the melting fire burneth, the fire causeth the waters to boil, to make Thy name known to Thine adversaries, that the nations may tremble at Thy presence!*" (Isaiah 64:1-2)

## INSPIRATION FROM THE PAST

*When Thou didst terrible things . . . Thou camest down, the mountains flowed down at Thy presence.* That God has done it before ought to inspire us today with the confidence that God can do it again. We must take inspiration from the past.

# Inspiration from Scripture

My first appeal is to the authority of Scripture. Let's consider New Testament examples of God coming down.

In Acts 2, on the Day of Pentecost, God poured out His Spirit. As a result the interceding saints "were all filled with the Holy Spirit" (2:4) and "about three thousand souls" through the Spirit-filled preaching "received [the] word" and "were added unto them" (2:41). This was a day of God's power! Acts 2:17 explains "in the last days, saith God, I will pour out of My Spirit upon all flesh." Notice the promise from Joel 2 referring to a future literal fulfillment is here applied as a partial fulfillment during the period known as *the last days.* The wording is different from the timing of the wording in Joel 2. We are still in *the last days.* Was the display of God's power to stop after the Day of Pentecost? Was it to be the end of God's power *in the last days?*

In Acts 4, we read "many of them which heard the word believed; and the number of the men was about five thousand" (4:4). God is still mightily working in Acts 4. When was the last time you heard of 5000 people believing? We read "and when they had prayed, the place was shaken where they were assembled together; and they were all filled with the Holy Spirit, and they spake the word of God with boldness" (4:31).

In Acts 5 we read "and believers were the more added to the Lord, multitudes both of men and women" (5:14). *Multitudes—added to the Lord*—is this not the power of God? We also read of persecution. Whenever the Wicked One's turf is threatened, opposition can be expected.

In Acts 6 we read "the word of God increased . . . the disciples multiplied . . . greatly; and a great company of the priests were obedient to the faith" (6:7). Notice the superlative words *increased, multiplied, greatly,* and *great.* Is this not an example of mountains melting and masses moving?

In Acts 7 Stephen is stoned. More opposition from the hosts of evil. A price is paid.

In Acts 8 "the people" of Samaria "gave heed" to Philip's preaching (8:5-6) so that "there was great joy in that city" (8:8). Also we read that the Spirit fell on them (8:14-17). Incidently, Philip was not an apostle. He was an evangelist.

In Acts 9 Saul is saved (9:1-22). We also read that "all that dwelt at Lydda and Saron . . . turned to the Lord" (9:35). Two whole towns! Can you imagine two whole towns in your area turning to Christ? This is the display of God's power beyond the Day of Pentecost. Later we read that in the town of Joppa "many believed" (9:42).

In Acts 10 we read that "the Holy Spirit fell on all them which heard the word" (10:44) further explained as "on the Gentiles also was poured out the gift of the Holy Spirit" (10:45). Is this not another outpouring of the Spirit beyond Acts 2?

In Acts 11 we read that in Antioch "a great number believed and turned unto the Lord" (11:21) and "much people was added unto the Lord" (11:24). More mountains melt and masses tremble. God is glorified as "the disciples were called Christians first in Antioch" (11:26).

In Acts 12 James is martyred. More opposition. "But the word of God grew and multiplied" (12:24).

In Acts 13 we read of the first missionary journey that at Pisidian Antioch "came almost the whole city together to hear the word of God" (13:44) and "many . . . believed" and that they "glorified the word of the Lord" (13:48). Can you imagine reading this about Detroit, Milwaukee, or Chicago? It should be noted here that there is no record of signs and wonders. That is not to say that God cannot do great physical miracles today, but that the powerful, spiritual manifestation of His presence is the real issue. When God comes down, His manifested presence alone melts mountains and moves masses!

In Acts 14 at Iconium we read "a great multitude . . . believed" (14:1). Again no mention is made of signs and wonders.

In Acts 16 we read that the "churches . . . increased in number daily" (16:5). Can you imagine daily increase at your church? O the power of God to again be manifested for His glory! We also read of a riot at Philippi, but the jailer gets saved. More opposition, yet more blessing.

In Acts 17 Paul and company came to Thessalonica. For "three Sabbath days" Paul "reasoned with them out of the Scriptures" (17:2). As a result we read "And some of them [Jews] believed . . . and of the devout Greeks a great multitude" (17:4). Although there is no mention of signs and wonders, yet more mountains melt and masses move. Then we read of another riot. When God manifests His presence, the results are radical one way or the other. We must be prepared for both. However, we then read the accusation which is really a testimony: "These that have turned the world upside down" (17:6). We also read that at Berea "many of them believed" (17:12). Then there is another riot or near riot. But at Athens "certain men . . . believed" (17:34).

In Acts 18 we then read "many of the Corinthians . . . believed" (18:8). Also "then spake the Lord to Paul . . . I have much people in this city" (18:9-10). Does not Christ's promise "The harvest truly is plenteous" still apply today? Surely it does!

In Acts 19 at Ephesus we read "the Holy Spirit came on them" (19:6). Also we read "All they which dwelt in Asia heard the word of the Lord Jesus" (19:10), "the name of the Lord Jesus was magnified (19:17), and "so mightily grew the word of God and prevailed" (19:20). More mountains melt and masses move. Then we read of another riot. More opposition.

In Acts 20-28 we read of Paul's persecution, yet in Acts 28:28 Paul declares under inspiration "the salvation of God is sent unto the Gentiles, and that they will hear it." What a promise for today—*they will hear it*!

Acts 2-28 records a phenomenal fifty-year period of God's manifest presence and power! Pentecostal power continued for an entire generation! The epistles speak often of *dunamis* power—miraculous power—as the standard for New Testament Christianity. This inspiration from the scriptural account of the past ought to move us to cry out for God to once again rend the heavens and come down so that this generation may also see God exalted and glorified.

## Inspiration from History

Our first appeal was to the scriptural record. However Psalm 78:4 speaks of "shewing to the generation to come the praises of the Lord, and His strength, and His wonderful works that He hath done." Psalm 145:4 states "One generation shall praise Thy works to another, and shall declare Thy mighty acts." These psalms teach us that it is right for one generation to praise God to the next. Therefore it follows that it is right for us to be inspired by God's mighty works among previous generations.

Did God's power cease with the apostles' generation? Quite the contrary, for the early church historian, Eusebius, writes: "There were many . . . who occupied the first place among the successors of the apostles . . . they themselves went on again to other countries and nations, with the grace and the cooperation of God. For a great many wonderful works were done through them by the power of the divine Spirit, so that at the first hearing whole multitudes of men eagerly embraced the religion of the Creator of the universe . . . in the age immediately succeeding the apostles."[4] Book of Acts type of power continued into the generation which followed the Book of Acts! "Whole multitudes" in pagan cultures with idolatry and superstition believing "at the first hearing" demands the powerful, spiritual manifestation of the presence of God. O when God comes down, mountains melt and masses move!

Justin Martyr testified at the end of the first century: "For there is not one single race of men, whether barbarians, or Greeks, or whatever they may be called, nomads, or vagrants, or herdsmen living in tents, among whom prayers and giving of thanks are not offered through the name of the crucified Jesus."[5] Is this not "the demonstration of the Spirit and of power"?

We could continue into the pages of church history of the accounts of God's "wonderful works." As long as God's people believed, God enabled. When unbelief set in and error was embraced, eventually we read of the dark ages. Yet I'm sure God's history books record revivals we know nothing of yet. Certainly the light began to shine with fearless preachers like John Hus. The early reformers unquestionably saw the mighty hand of God. However, for our purposes let's jump ahead to a few chapters in revival history from the seventeenth century through the twentieth century.

In 1630 a page of history records a mighty example of God coming down and manifesting His presence. At a gathering of thousands of people in an outside setting in Kilsyth, Scotland, John Livingstone had been asked to preach. The young preacher was relatively unknown. "The night before he was to speak he could not sleep, and so he spent the whole intervening hours in mighty intercession, with an overwhelming sense of his utter weakness." But he did face the crowd the next day. Near the conclusion of his sermon a light rain began to fall. A few people left to take cover. He then cried out, "'If a few drops of rain so easily upset you, then what will you do in the day of judgment when God rains down fire and brimstone upon the Christ-rejectors?' He then pleaded with them to flee to Christ, 'the city of refuge'. John Livingstone never finished his sermon! The power of God came down upon the multitude. They were literally slain as on the field of battle. Hundreds cried out in great soul agony, as if the very day of judgment had come. Five hundred were converted on the spot."[6] What a precious record of a divine visitation. Does this not resound with echoes from the Book of Acts?

In August of 1727 God came down among the Moravians. Within thirty-three years they had sent out no less than 226 missionaries.[7] Does not this remind one of the church in Jerusalem?

The First Great Awakening in the colonies during 1740-41 and the years following is a powerful example of the power of God. At times George Whitefield preached to crowds of 30,000 people. Does this not read just like the Book of Acts when nearly a "whole city" came to hear the Word of God?

The Second Great Awakening went from 1798 to 1830. This powerful revival spread through the new United States, covering many states. I believe it was this awakening more than any other which made the United States a "Christian" nation. Over a quarter of a century God gloriously manifested His power. We are here simply skimming through volumes of the records of that generation which saw firsthand the "wonderful works" of God. Literally thousands were brought to Christ in this day of God's power!

In the 1839 revival of Scotland, God used the preaching of a 24-year-old named William Burns, a young man who had interceded even entire nights for the outpouring of the Spirit on Scotland. On Tuesday, July 23, 1839, William Burns preached in Kilsyth, Scotland on the text from Psalm 110, "Thy people shall be willing in the day of Thy power." The presence of God became powerfully real. William Burns's brother recounts as an key witness, "As to the scene itself which followed, I can think of no better description than the account of the day of Pentecost, in the second chapter of the Acts, of which both in its immediate features and in its after results, and in everything except the miraculous gift of tongues, it seems to me to have been an exact counterpart."[8] For months heaven came down. The revival spread to Dundee, at Robert Murray McCheyne's church, and to Perth.

The Third Great Awakening of 1857-58 began in New York City through a prayer meeting. It spread from city to city. Multiplied thousands came to Christ in this visitation from on high. The awakening then spread to England, Wales, and Ulster in 1859. South Africa saw revival in 1860 with Andrew Murray. It should be noted that from 1762 to 1862 Wales averaged an awakening somewhere in the country every seven years.[9] Does this not exemplify "times [seasons] of refreshing . . . from the presence of the Lord"?

The 1904 Welsh Awakening started many fires of revival around the world. Kassia Hills, India saw revival in 1906, Korea in 1907, Manchuria with Jonathan Goforth in 1908.[10] As God's people realized God is not a respector of persons and sought God's face, God came down. Space does not allow for the detailing of the intercessors and the manifestations of God's presence.

The 1921 revival in East Anglia, England and northeast Scotland is another special page from revivals past. After two years of intercession at a Baptist church in Lowestoft, England, Douglas Brown was invited to come for a mission (meeting). The third night is described as a "cloudburst" when nearly seventy people "passed from death unto life."[11] Within eleven weeks over a thousand conversions were recorded.[12] But it must be noted that conversions among the lost, as blessed as that is, was not the only blessing. True revival restores the saints to the Spirit-filled life. As in other records of revival, the revival in East Anglia touched the saints with heaven. One preacher even "felt the greatest work had been done among Christians."[13] The revival spread to nearby towns and continued into 1922. Jock Troup was mightily used of God at this time in Scotland and W. P. Nicholson in Ulster.

John Sung, the Chinese evangelist "from 1933 to 1936, the great Holy Ghost time . . . had something over 100,000 converts."[14] God mightily poured out His Spirit repeatedly. The stories stir the depths of one's heart.

The Shantung Revival of China lasted fifteen years from 1933 to 1947. A four-year preparation time in the lives of C. L. Culpepper and others led up to this great time of revival. A great harvest was reaped before the communist take over.[15]

The Lewis Awakening began in December of 1949 and continued into 1953 in the Hebrides Islands of Scotland. Here God's intercessors interceded for at least eighteen months. What a blessed time of revival! Saints were quickened and the lost were converted.

North Uist, another island in the Hebrides of Scotland, saw revival in 1957 to 1958. Again, villages were moved by the Spirit. It was another blessed season of refreshing.

How about the Congo revival of the 1950s? The list could easily include far more than what has been mentioned here. These we have mentioned point up a few pages in God's history book of revivals. In each case, mountains melted and masses moved. Ultimately, God was glorified! May we absorb inspiration from the past. *Thou camest down, the mountains flowed down at Thy presence.* This leads us to a third dynamic involved in God coming down.

## INTERSECTION WITH THE PROMISE

Imagine with me a farmer who has plenty of state-of-the-art machinery. He has ample man-power. But he does not have any seed or access to water. Will he reap a harvest with his machinery and man-power without seed and water? Obviously not. This pictures flesh-dependence in the ministry. If we rely on "machinery" and "manpower" without the seed of God's Word and the water of God's Spirit, we will not reap a harvest for Christ.

However, imagine with me a second farmer. He sees the futility of the first farmer's endeavors, so he decides to go the opposite direction. He says he believes strongly in the "sovereignty of God." Yet his view of God's sovereignty is not accurate. So occasionally he walks to the edge of his field, not having cultivated the soil, nor having planted any seed, and he prays for a harvest. Will he reap a harvest? Again, obviously not. This pictures fatalism in the ministry. This often leads people to "blaming" God for the lack of a harvest.

Both extremes ignore the need for the seed and water. The laws of the physical harvest demand that seed be planted and that that seed be watered. These are laws or "means" for a harvest. However, the nature of these means or laws is simply an expression of God-dependence. For it is God who makes it all work. It is God who gives the harvest—but not without someone applying the laws of the harvest.

The same principles apply to the spiritual harvest. Spiritually, the seed is the Word of God (Luke 8:11) and the water is the Spirit (John 7:38-39). The laws of the spiritual harvest demand that seed be planted (God-dependence on the promises) and that that seed be watered (Spirit-enabling in accordance to the promises). These are laws or "means" for a spiritual harvest. However, the nature of these means or laws is simply an expression of God-dependence. For it is God who makes it all work. It is God who gives the harvest—but not without someone applying the laws of the spiritual harvest.

What then are the laws or expressions of God-dependence for the Acts 1:8 type of harvest? As you consider the conditions of God's promises, sometimes you see four conditions, sometimes three, two, or even one. Our text in Isaiah delineates two "laws" of the harvest.

## Intercession

Isaiah 64:4 *For since the beginning of the world men have not heard, nor perceived by the ear, neither hath the eye seen, O God, beside thee, what He hath prepared for **him that waiteth for Him***. God delights in *him*, just one, who *waits for Him*. This is the intercessor pleading the promises of God, thus *waiting for Him*. This is the cry for "water," the work of the Spirit, based on the promises of God, which is the "seed." This is a vital law of the mass spiritual harvest which comes when God pours out His Spirit.

## The Spirit-Filled Life

Isaiah 64:5a **Thou meetest him** *that rejoiceth and worketh righteousness, those that remember Thee in Thy ways*. One cannot rejoice in and work righteousness remembering God in His ways apart from the Spirit-filled life. So the intercession must be from the platform of the Spirit-filled life. The Spirit-filled life is the life of faith. Walking in the Spirit is simply walking by faith. The point is simple. You will never have faith for a mass harvest if you do not learn and practice faith for individual harvests. The law of intercession, so to speak, must be applied in conjunction with the law of the Spirit-filled life, or life of faith. So the intercession is from a life of faith.

Now, note God's promise to *him that waiteth for Him* and *rejoiceth and worketh righteousness*—**Thou meetest Him**! This is the intersection with the promise. We are still *in the last days*. God's promise for the powerful, spiritual manifestation of His presence is still true. In fact the longer we continue *in the last days* which began on the Day of Pentecost according to Acts 2, the greater the prospects. *For... men have not heard, nor perceived by the ear, neither hath the eye seen, O God, beside Thee, what He hath prepared for him that waiteth for Him.* If eye has not seen, nor ear heard what God will do for those who intersect with the promise, then God's greatest works must still be ahead! For we have heard what God has done in the past. Therefore God intends for revivals to increase in their greatness. Since God "is able to do exceeding abundantly above all that we ask or think," then God desires to do *greater works* than what He has already done!

O may we cry out in faith O *that Thou wouldest rend the heavens, that Thou wouldest come down!* For the promise states *Thou meetest him.* When God comes down, He *meets* with His people. This is the manifest *presence* of God among His people. O to experience God coming down and glorifying His name so that we can declare to the next generation the *wonderful works that He hath done.* May God teach us to intersect with the promise. For the desperate need of the hour is for God to come down!

---

[1] Duncan Campbell, *The Price and Power of Revival* (Vinton, Va.: Christ Life Publications, reprint, n.d.), p. 35.

[2] R. B. Jones, *Rent Heavens* (Asheville, N.C.: Revival Literature, 1963), p. 43.

[3] Ibid., p. 43.

[4] J. Philip Schaff and Henry Wace, eds. *The Nicene and Post-Nicene Fathers*, Second Series, Vol. 1, "The Church History of Eusebius" Book 3, chapter 37 (Peabody, Mass.: Hendrickson, reprint 1979), p. 169.

[5] Alexander Roberts and James Donaldson, eds. *Anti-Nicene Fathers: Translations of the Fathers Down to A.D. 325*, Vol. 1, "Dialogue with Trypho, a Jew" chapter CXVII (Grand Rapids: Wm. B. Eerdmans Publishing Company, 1979), p. 258.

[6] James A. Stewart, *William Chalmers Burns* (Asheville, N.C.: Revival Literature, 1963), pp. 24-26.

[7] "A Christian History Time Line," *Christian History*, ed. W. Carey Moore, vol. 1, no. 1 (Worcester, Penn.: Christian History Magazine, 1982), p. 12.

[8] Stewart, pp. 28-29.

[9] Eifion Evans, *Revival Comes to Wales* (Bryntirion, Bridgend, Mid Glamorgan, Wales: Evangelical Press of Wales, reprint 1995), p. 10.

[10] Jonathan Goforth, *By My Spirit* (Elkhart, Ind.: Bethel Publishing, reprint 1983).

[11] Stanley C. Griffin, *A Forgotten Revival* (Bromley, Kent, England: Day One Publications, 1992), pp. 20-22.

[12] Ibid., p. 39.

[13] Ibid., p. 50.

[14] William E. Schubert, *I Remember John Sung* (Singapore: Far Eastern Bible College Press, 1976), p. 40.

[15] C. L. Culpepper, *The Shantung Revival* (Atlanta: Home Mission Board, 1971, reprint 1993).

# POSTSCRIPT

A few final thoughts come to mind as we conclude this study:

## To the glory of God

By way of testimony to God's gracious dealings, since I have begun to preach on these truths I have received many more testimonial letters than ever before of personal revivals. Often these letters are sent months later, indicating a true and lasting work of God. Also, God has manifested Himself on several occasions affecting whole groups of people simultaneously. An honest appraisal must describe these occasions as localized revivals. In these times of meeting with God, several hours have seemed like a mere fifteen minutes. This is the outpouring of the Spirit. God was made real, and lives have been forever changed. God's Word is still true—"Draw nigh to God, and He will draw nigh to you" (James 4:8).

## Walking in the Light

As walking in the Spirit keeps from sin, so walking in the light deals with sin. This is simply the right response to God's light. I John 1:7 and 9 teach that when sin brings a cloud between you and God, that sin needs to be immediately confessed to God by agreeing totally with the light of truth. God promises to then immediately forgive your sin. He releases you from what you owe! God promises to cleanse you. You cannot be in a more right relationship with God than what the blood of Jesus truly makes you when you call sin what it is: sin! Therefore, God also promises that you are back in fellowship with Him. You do not have to wait a few days to be used of God. That would be meritorious thinking. Rather you are back in a right relationship with God. Walking in the light is not sinless perfection, it is immediate confession. This allows for perpetual revival!

## Essentials to Revival

Reading the details of various revival accounts can sometimes be confusing because the "manifestations" in revival vary. Many of the manifestations are incidental, yet people seem to gravitate toward the sensational. We may note three essentials to revival. First, revival preaching is God's plan. God uses the "foolishness of preaching." Revival preaching is Spirit-filled, sin-confronting, Savior-exalting preaching as on the Day of Pentecost. Second, revival praying is also necessary. Revival praying is prayer with the unction of the Spirit and a unity of faith as in the ten-day prayer meeting before Pentecost. Third, revival Presence is the very essence of the outpouring of the Spirit in revival. This is God coming down as on the Day of Pentecost. This is God meeting with His people. This is seeing Jesus!

Revival preaching without revival praying is powerless. Revival praying without revival preaching lacks detonation. Revival praying with revival preaching is explosive! In the last several years I have seen on a few occasions the reality of all three essentials. Groups of believers were restored to spiritual life. Preaching and even praying became a delight. Oh there is nothing to compare with the manifestation of the presence of God!

## Jesus is Everything!

Jesus is the Door in John 10. In John 14 Jesus is the Way. So He is the entrance to life and the enablement of life. However, He is also the End. In John 14:6 Jesus says, "I am the way . . . no man cometh unto the Father but by Me." So the Father is the "end" of the way. Then three verses later, Jesus says, "he that hath seen Me hath seen the Father." Therefore, Jesus is the Way and the End! Romans 10:4 says, "Christ is the end of the law for righteousness [right-relatatedness-to God] to everyone that believeth." Christ is the end of the struggle for justification, sanctification, peace, victory, service, and revival. Christ is all! He is everything! He is not just the way to redemption; He is our redemption. He is not just the way to victory; He is our victory, and so forth. Only Jesus satisfies. If our end is victory, power in service, or even revival blessings, all of which are good and right, we will still not be satisfied. These are the wrong ends. God often holds back blessing because our end is wrong, which often reveals wrong motives of selfish interest on our part. However, if our end is Christ, we will be satisfied, and then God can grant the blessings as well. All prayer for revival must be so others can see Jesus as everything! Seeing Jesus as the Door, the Way, the End—as everything—and resting in Him, enjoying Him, and being satisfied in Him is revival!

# APPENDIX A

# REVIVAL TESTIMONIES

Psalm 78:1-8—"Give ear, O my people, to my law: incline your ears to the words of my mouth. I will open my mouth in a parable: I will utter dark sayings of old: Which we have heard and known, and our fathers have told us. We will not hide them from their children, shewing to the generation to come the praises of the LORD, and his strength, and his wonderful works that he hath done. For he established a testimony in Jacob, and appointed a law in Israel, which he commanded our fathers, that they should make them known to their children: That the generation to come might know them, even the children which should be born; who should arise and declare them to their children: That they might set their hope in God, and not forget the works of God, but keep His commandments: And might not be as their fathers, a stubborn and rebellious generation; a generation that set not their heart aright, and whose spirit was not stedfast with God."

Testimony of God's *wonderful works* encourages others along in the same path. Several chapters in this book record many of God's blessings during the age of grace. Yet to the present reader, these stories are in the past. Perhaps it would encourage some to read of God's workings at the present time. This appendix, therefore, includes a sampling of letters, e-mails, and written testimonies of "personal revivals" as well as a few corporate touches of the Spirit from the last two years at the time of this writing.

Personally, since the Lord burdened my heart to preach on the truths emphasized in this book (which has been since 1999), we have received a marked increase of testimonial letters. Not only has there been an increase of letters, but also what is testified cannot be articulated unless the Holy Spirit has opened one's eyes. This has been most encouraging. Often the letters come months after our contact with an individual, indicating a lasting work of God.

Also, in the last two years the Lord has begun to move in several corporate settings of which I am aware. In some of these churches I have had little or no ministry, but others who preach the same truths of the

Spirit have. The issue is not a man or men, but the ministry of the Holy Spirit.

Typographical errors have been corrected, as well as abbreviations given in full. Very minor editorial adjustments have been made for a smooth flow.

# Personal Revival

After a Spiritual Awakening Conference, in Avoca, Ireland, a preacher wrote:

> The fullness of Christ, having sin confessed, being filled with the Holy Spirit, is such a joy. I almost feel like I got saved all over again. I am looking forward to serving Christ, not doing it for Him, but now allowing Him to live His life through me, which is true ministry.
>
> There were many things that are sticking out in my mind that the Lord used at the conference which were such blessings. I have just finished reading *Victory in Christ* a second time (I read it once after the July conference). But this time I took in so much more. I see clearly that the key to the victorious life is very simply CHRIST. He is all. I see this so much more plainly. He is the victory.

He later wrote:

> It's been three weeks since we left [the conference], and I must say that they have been the best three weeks of my life. I am enjoying my walk with the Lord so much. God is so good to have done in my heart what He did. He has given me victory in so many areas of my life; He has given me peace and joy in my heart; confidence and boldness in my preaching and assurance in my prayers. . . .
>
> Sometimes I just think back on the messages, the songs, the prayer meetings, and my decision to be filled with the Holy Spirit. My heart cannot contain the joy that fills me. Truly, that [conference], for me, was definitely my Peniel (Genesis 32:30) and El-bethel (35:7). My walk and worship will never (by His grace) be the same again! God met with me, and I don't ever want to go back to the flesh.

Nearly a month later he again wrote:

> Again, I'm just rejoicing in the truths the Lord taught us at [the conference]. Today I was listening to the first message . . . on Acts 2. Wow, being baptized with the Holy Spirit, the Spirit of Christ being in me. Amazing! What a position.
>
> Well, I'm not finished with the tape yet. Now, having experienced Him so much more intimately, and going through the tapes more slowly, it is all a wonderful feast. When you dig down deep and

discover what really happened at salvation, and understand Who it is that lives, dwells, abides in us, it is almost too wonderful to really grasp. No wonder we'll have all eternity to praise Him; we'll need that much time, and more!

After the same conference, another preacher wrote:

We were in the sin of unbelief—I didn't understand what it was until last week. We came back from the conference different people. Pray that we continue to abide in Christ.

Weeks later he wrote again:

PRAISE THE LORD, God is continuing His work in my heart. I have been studying your book *Engine Truths* and presenting the "truths" on Sunday morning. God is working in the people's heart. I have been studying again the chapter on The Overcoming Life. . . . It has really revealed truth to me that I did not understand. To tell the truth, the whole book has opened my eyes to the Spirit-filled life. It started at the conference and continued as [my wife] and I returned home and began to study out the truths that were preached during the meetings. I have to say it has totally changed my life. I am over-flowing with joy. Thank you again for your faithful preaching of these truths.

A teen, who had attended these conferences on the Spirit-filled life, wrote:

I just wanted to drop you a quick line and tell you how things are going with me. Well, unlike all the other false starts in the Christian race I've had, this watershed point in my life has set me constantly climbing, and this joy and zeal for His work that the Lord has graciously given shows no signs of letting up! I've discovered that I needed to give my problems with discipline to the Spirit and let Him correct them. And in so many miraculous ways He has! The Lord gave me a passage that really helps me: "Let thy hand be upon the man of thy right hand, upon the son of man who thou madest strong for thyself. So will not we go back from thee: quicken us, and we will call upon thy name. Turn us again, O Lord God of hosts, cause thy face to shine; and we shall be saved" (Psalm 80:17-19).

David knew that GOD makes us strong, when HE so wills and sustains us by HIS power. As I realize this, everything that I've ever struggled with seems to be falling effortlessly into place. I wake at 6:00 A.M. every morning and spend time with God (that is so important). My schoolwork is 100% improved, my relations with the family are wonderful, and I am giving out 40-50 tracts a day and waiting for opportunities to witness. I think my greatest strength is that I have less fleshly character than most people and my life is physically, as well as spiritually, impossible when I am not in dependence on the Spirit! ("My grace is sufficient for thee: for my strength is made perfect in weakness. Most gladly therefore will I rather glory in my infirmities, that the power of Christ may rest upon me" II Corinthians 12:9). I am just rejoicing in the Lord and getting closer to Him everyday, and life has never ever been better!

A church lady wrote who also attended two conferences. The letter came about ten months following the first conference and over four months following the second:

> Just a note to say we were doing fine in the Lord and keeping well. . . . The Lord is answering our prayers and cleansing and purging us. . . . I want to thank you for bringing the message of the Holy Spirit's power to us. He (the Holy Spirit) has changed our lives (the church), and I know my life has been hugely changed since summer last year, as I look back to last year and see where I was then and compare it to now. The Lord is good! The Netcasters course is excellent, and the notes have all these references to the Holy Spirit power that were never there before! . . . I am doing fairly well, in general, in sensing His presence missing and making things right immediately. The Lord is giving the divine appointments. My trouble comes right at that time when a huge blast of fear comes sweeping in. I am gaining the victory (slowly) in relaxing and yielding at that point, but I would appreciate prayers for this if the Lord lays it on your heart.

Here is a letter from a preacher in Myanmar (Burma) after a Spiritual Awakening Conference. The language barrier will be slightly noticeable, but the sense clearly comes through:

> I am overjoy for the Tahan Ministers' Conference result. People got saved, and preachers' lives and church leaders' lives are changed. Now some churches have already formed prayer groups for REVIVAL. Not only that some got the truth from especially Christian victorious life. I myself came to know the real truth of how to have a powerful life and victory. I pray, I control myself, I discipline myself, I control my will and etc. This time I came to know that Jesus Christ is sufficient, He is my life, not He helps me, but He lives and He is life, victory. Brother, now I took rest. God sent you for me and others also. The book that you gave me, *Victory in Christ* by Charles G. Trumbull, is wonderful. I read and read and read and think. This small book is full of truth. Many people (Christians) do not know this truth. They are trying their level best to live like Christ as I used to do . . . I wish my people read this truth. Wonderful . . . wonderful Christ is all in all, for all.

This comes from a church lady in the States:

I have, through my entire life, always felt very fortunate. I'm an American (that is a huge blessing!), I have great parents, I've gotten to travel, I received a very good education, I have a great job, I live in a beautiful house, I've met tons of people, have great friends. Further, I'm a member of Ann Arbor Baptist Church, I get to hear strong preaching, we have good Christian examples, I'm involved in the church orchestra, choir, sign language program as well as Friday School. Having all these advantages, and doing the things the Bible says we should . . . I still felt a real lack in my Christian life.

This summer when John Van Gelderen was here, he really challenged all of us about the state of our Christianity, on the spiritual life, on depending on the Lord, and a last message to us that particularly stood out to me was about "speaking Christ." I was blessed and stirred by those messages, and thought that I understood. On a Wednesday night, close to my birthday, I was with my boss in a series of meetings that lasted most of the afternoon. We went from place to place meeting with different people.

Toward evening, he got a phone call to meet someone at a restaurant downtown, so we went. I was completely unsuspecting, but when we arrived many of my co-workers were there for a birthday party. They all know I go to church on Wednesday nights, but that night not only did I not "speak Christ," I didn't stand up for what I know is right. I didn't leave when I should have, and I missed church. I was completely undone by my lack of character. This group of people I wanted to see saved—but when I had opportunity I dishonored my Lord and, in fact, made my friends more important than Him. I was sick—and knew that I could not live the Christian life.

I was completely incapable even though I had the best church, the best preaching, the best of everything . . . I couldn't do it.

My sister came over a few days after this, and through the course of conversation said, "We act like we're saved by grace—and sanctified by struggle." That statement hit me so hard, I burst into tears. She began to share with me some of the truths of dependence that her husband had learned, and that she was also learning. A few days later, I attended special meetings nearby and heard John repeat what he had preached before, but it took on new life. Not only did I understand (head knowledge), but saw my error (sin!) and what the Lord really wanted from me and for me. I began to realize that the reason I could not live the Christian life was because I was trying to live it. I thought, "If I pray more, if I read more, if I have more faith, if I do more, etc." The problem was the "I." I found that the resource for the Christian life is just Jesus Christ. I had known Christ as an external Savior who did a saving work for me and who was ready to come along side in times of trouble. However, Galatians 2:20 and Philippians 1:21 show a much different relationship to Christ. Jesus Christ is in me, and better, I am in Him. He doesn't want to be my helper . . . He wants to be my life. He wants me to let Him do His work through me. Everything we need is provided. Christ does not require my struggle to succeed. His victory is won! What He requires of me is absolute surrender of my will, my way, and my work. And, by faith, He will do it. Christ cannot fail. His life was completely victorious!

Now, when I go back and read passages like John 15:4-5, John 7:37-38, I understand! And, what a thrill!

The result of this has been several-fold. First, the crushing weight of Christian service is gone. There is a freedom to obey and to serve that is entirely new. Second, to live Christ's life requires that I know Christ.

Reading and studying the Bible, instead of being a chore, has taken on a freshness and life that it has never had before. Third, is the practice of the presence of Christ. Fourth is the ability and desire to show Christ to others.

I remember Dr. Wayne Van Gelderen, Sr. preaching a message during one of his last times at our church. He said that he knew when he got to heaven and saw the Savior's face, he would recognize it as a face he'd seen before, and His touch as one he'd felt before. As I listened, I so wanted to be that one that could show him Christ. Now I understand more of what he meant, and I understand the extreme privilege and responsibility of showing Christ to others.

She also wrote at a later time:

I just wanted to tell you an answer to prayer. I have really been praying for witnessing, in light of depending completely on the Holy Spirit. I am able to witness, in that I've taken the class, know the verses, etc. What I mean is that I can force myself to do it because I know it's right. But tonight (and actually this afternoon, too) I actually enjoyed it! I am in awe! I really claimed the verse, "For me to live IS Christ," and went calling, knowing that if I depended on myself at all, I would completely fail, be miserable and defeated. However, depending on Christ, and showing His life through me made calling a whole new experience . . . I offered a tract to a South African man who very politely refused it, walked about twenty steps, and came back and asked me if he could please have the material! I talked with him for a moment in the full realization that what drew him back is Christ living in me. Was wonderful.

Another lady in the States wrote:

Thank you for the soul-stirring messages; these meetings on the filling and outpouring of the Spirit have touched my life to greater depths of Spirit-dependence. I have received many *rhemas* from Scripture this week to confirm your messages. I have been awed of how God has worked to accomplish in me greater dependence on His greater words. O how great is our God. O how marvelous the work of the Spirit. My life will never be the same.

A teen wrote:

There is one service that really impressed me and helped me. It was the service when John Van Gelderen came and preached on the filling of the Holy Spirit . . . and how that we need His help to do right. We can never do it on our own, and this truth really just came home to me: "the lights clicked on," you might say. We, in the strength of our flesh, can never do anything; however, "if we walk in the Spirit, we will not fulfill the lusts of the flesh." This truth of Spirit-enabling to do what we cannot has become very real to me. Through it I have found true victory, and the answer to my struggling, both personally and with my family, not only not to do wrong but not to even want to.

A preacher in South Africa wrote:

I really enjoyed the Netcasters Seminar and the revival meeting in August. I am trying to share everything with everybody I can. I want you to know that this is a great milestone in my life and has encouraged me greatly and revived me also in bringing new zeal and hope in my ministry of pastoring and evangelizing.

A church member in the States wrote the following testimony. The length of it and the organization of it with headings makes it especially helpful.

I had been saved when I was about 20 years of age. Shortly after I was saved, I entered and completed Bible College and have continued to serve the Lord through Ann Arbor Baptist Church for more than 20 years. I have been quite busy overseeing the church's music ministry, the jail ministry, working on staff, and working a secular job while at the same time raising a growing family. My wife and I have had the privilege of attending the Holiness Conferences at Falls Baptist Church from the time they first began.

*Awakening to My Need*

There has been an emphasis on the Spirit-filled life in the Holiness Conferences over these past few years and also in other preaching that I had heard by John Van Gelderen. However, I had kept myself busy with much church work and hadn't fully understood what was being presented.

I understand now that the Lord had to first awaken me to my need. The focus of the conference seemed to be faith, and I assumed that if I just exercised more diligent faith the Lord would use me more. After the conference I tried to do just that, but was frustrated with hardly seeing the Lord do anything! So I simply went on as I was, plunging back into a busy schedule, but in the back of my mind I knew there was something more that I needed. I continued to see some spiritual results, but also failures and disappointments. It wasn't until July that things slowed down enough where I could start thinking deeply about the Spirit-filled life again. I listened to the tapes from the conference, playing them over and over again, trying to grasp and apply what they taught. I also read some of the books that I had purchased at the conference. One book that was especially helpful at this time was Charles Trumbull's book entitled *Victory in Christ*.

### Struggling to Understand It

I was painfully aware that in my spiritual life I felt like I was just barely staying above water. What I heard from the tapes and read in Charles Trumbull's book was a spiritual plane that I could easily picture, but I could not stay at that level for long. Was this just a more earnest Christianity that I could obtain by more Bible study, prayer, and service for the Lord, or was it something altogether different? Was I just a feeble believer, and this type of life was only for the spiritual giants? I made a list of what I, at that time, understood to be the key characteristics of having and not having the victorious Christian life.

1. Great fluctuations from spiritual heights to spiritual depths (the defeated life)
2. Failure in habitual sins (the defeated life)
3. Spiritual power that works changes in other men's lives (the victorious life)
4. Continuous consciousness of Christ (the victorious life)
5. A dramatic change in life—a conversion—that cannot be forgotten just as our salvation cannot be forgotten and it will not be lost.

In honestly examining my life I realized that this list was totally foreign to my own experience. I simply did not have what this list suggested. Rather, I had the great fluctuations and failure in habitual sin. A statement by Charles Trumbull described my experiences perfectly:

> A strong, arousing convention, a stirring, searching address from some consecrated, victorious Christian leader of men; a searching, Spirit-filled book, or the obligation to do a difficult piece of Christian service myself, with the preparation in prayer that it involved, would lift me up. . . . But it wouldn't last. Sometimes by some single failure before temptation, sometimes by a gradual downhill process, my best experiences would be lost, and I would find myself back on the lower levels (*Victory in Christ*, p. 18).

This is not to say that my life was fruitless or that I didn't have seasons of rejoicing in the Lord or times of communion with Him. I often did. I was seeing some fruit but not what I ought to see. I would see a few people saved at the door every year, but they would rarely come to church, and not one had stayed. I would see dozens saved through the jail ministry but soon lose track of them. I wanted to see people saved, come to church, get baptized, and live for the Lord, but I personally was just not seeing it.

On one of the Sunday nights after John Van Gelderen had preached in our church, I approached him with some questions about what he had been preaching. My first question was, essentially, are these things really true? Is there really another spiritual plane that I haven't known, or is this just another explanation of what I've always known? My second question was how can we say that by doing this we've attained? Is there not spiritual growth and learning in the Christian life? These questions revealed that I did not grasp what was being said. His answer was, of course, that these things are wonderfully true!

However, there still needs to be spiritual growth. It is not that the believer has attained to anything, but these things are rather the means of spiritual growth. It is with these things the believer is really able to grow. To this I immediately objected. How can we say something more is needed before we can grow? A new convert usually experiences a large amount of growth and excitement about his newfound life in Christ. And in my own life I know that I have grown considerably from when I first was saved. His response to this was that the new child in Christ naturally depends upon the Lord to work and, as a result, grows. We grow every time we depend upon the Lord and only when we depend upon the Lord. It is because we have turned away from that child-like dependence that we have stopped growing. I thought I understood dependence, but I know I didn't understand the plane of the higher spiritual life.

*Road to Receiving It*

I now had become greatly burdened to have this life if indeed it was true. The next day I took some time off work to get alone with the Lord to read, pray, and work these things out. I asked the Lord to reveal to me what this really was. I looked up Bible passages. I prayed. I read again the sentences I had underlined in Charles Trumbull's book. I considered the things that John had said. I wanted to know, and, as I did, the light began to slowly dawn.

The Lord began showing me several areas in my life that were not surrendered to Him. As I considered these specific areas, I also felt a strong resistance in my heart. I simply did not want to surrender them and did not think that I would be able to really give these things up.

I spent some time struggling with them, but I could not get past them. I had to face them. Finally, I yielded them all to Him in sweet submission, and the burden was gone! I now saw clearly that I had been trying to live the Christian life in my own effort. I would do this no more. Christ's death was not only to take away the punishment of our sin, but to take away the power of our sin. Since He has done this for us, why was I not trusting Him to do so in my life?

With nothing between my soul and my Savior, I looked to Him and accepted by faith that He would be with me, guiding me in the way, constantly filling me with His Holy Spirit, enabling me with His grace so that I would be victorious over sin in every situation, using me in His service, and causing me to be an influence to others both for salvation and spiritual needs. I immediately experienced the great joy of the Lord's presence. I had unhindered communion with Him. I knew that I was accepted by Him, that He was going to work because He was faithful, and that I was now truly resting in Him. The years of dry, barren living were now replaced with that overflowing fountain of God—His love and His fullness!

This moment was like a conversion in many ways. It is a moment that I don't think I'll ever forget. It was a time of personal revival—a fresh start and a new beginning!

*The Unexpected*

I knew that God was now going to work, but there were many wonderful things that I had not expected or even looked for. I now have a lasting, inner joy; a constant, delightful looking to Jesus; the love, joy, and peace of Galatians 5; the flowing rivers of living water of John 7; the abiding of John 15; and the rest of Hebrews 4. Where previously reading God's Word and praying would many times be difficult and labored, I now have a new desire and longing for prayer and the reading of God's Word. Where previously I was often hindered from being a daily Witness because of fear, I now have a new desire and boldness to witness and pass out tracts.

Not everyone I talk to gets saved, but I often have a heart-to-heart talk with people where I know that God is working through me. There is a greater realization of sin in my life. There are still occasional failures, but immediate victory. There is a new appreciation for the cross and the blood that cleanses us from all sin. Previously when I thought about the cross I always looked back to my salvation. Now I also appreciate its forgiving and enabling power in my life right now.

*Four Promises*

There are four promises that I have discovered and am now claiming for God to work:

1. Victory over sin—I Corinthians 15:57

God promises us victory over sin. The Christian life is meant to be a victorious life, not a defeated one. For an example of one of the ways that I was able to apply this in my life, I need to explain that it was well known that I have had the habit of being late. Now I come by this honestly as I learned it from a child. In fact, I acquired it from our family. We call it "[last name] time." The time for a family event is usually announced to take place one hour before the real event to accommodate those who will be late. Even then, it's not unusual for some of my siblings to come even after that time! If you bend a sapling while it's young, when it becomes a full-grown tree it will have so hardened as to be impossible to straighten. But all things are possible with God! When I needed to get to places on time, I used to rush, break the speed limit, drive under freshly-red lights, and put myself in great anxiety wondering if I'll be on time or not. Now I look to the Lord claiming I Corinthians 15:57, drive the speed limit, stop for red lights, let other cars go first, and I am rarely late! But I can occasionally be surprised by defeat. After returning from a family trip one Saturday, I needed to attend a deacon's meeting at our church and realized when we were about an hour away that I was going to be late.

My wife asked, "What are you going to tell them? You haven't been late to anything in the last two months!" I didn't have an answer, but how much more did I appreciate that the blood of Jesus Christ cleanses us from all sin!

2. Power over weakness—II Corinthians 12:9

The Lord not only gives us victory over known sin but also over weaknesses in our life. For example, by His grace I have been able to consistently get up early in the morning, which I had not been able to do before, at least for more than a few days at a time.

### 3. Boldness to witness—II Corinthians 2:14

I am seeing more people saved when I go out calling. Though I'm not seeing people saved daily or even weekly, I am seeing the Lord use me daily in witnessing to people and giving out tracts. The first Thursday calling I was earnestly looking to the Lord to see what He would do.

While knocking at doors, we came across a middle-aged man who listened intently to what we had to say, even among constant distractions. The phone rang several times, the doorbell rang several times, and children kept interrupting with questions and needs. While all this was going on, the man bowed his head and trusted the Lord as his Savior! As soon as he did, the distractions immediately stopped! When he came to church with a friend, my wife led her to the Lord after the service. The lives of both of these have been noticeably changing. At another service he brought some of the neighborhood children, and one young man trusted the Lord after the service. This is nothing other than the working of God!

### 4. Overcoming in the battle—Romans 8:37

This promise is that the Lord will cause us to be conquerors in persecution and reproaches.

### A Noticed Change

It's one thing for me to say the Lord has changed me, but it's another thing altogether for someone else to say this. And it's even more for your wife of almost seven years who knows you better than anyone else to observe this! I hadn't asked my wife—it hadn't even occurred to me to do so—but one night she came to me and she was perplexed. She had noticed a lasting change in me and was wondering what was going on. She had been angry because God was working in her heart also and she knew that I was praying for her to have the same thing I had, but she was not understanding it. She said that she could understand how an unsaved spouse would feel betrayed when her husband got saved. She had noticed that I had been different; that I had been happier; that I had been getting up earlier in the morning which I was never able to do before, at least for more than a few days; that I had been kinder to the children, though I had been giving them more spankings. She wanted to have the same thing I had. We talked, and she began seeking the Lord that night. A short while after that she also came to the full understanding of it. The Lord was working!

### What I've Learned

There are a number of truths that I have learned that helps to understand what this plane of spiritual living is and what it is not.

Some object to this way saying that it will cause passivity. Though I'm sure this is possible, I have found the exact opposite to be true! Victory comes by looking to Jesus to bring it. You can't trust the Lord to do something if you're not looking to Him to do it. This brings a looking to Jesus in every aspect of our lives. My spiritual life has become much more active in every area.

This does not mean that you become a Hudson Taylor, a Charles Spurgeon, a Duncan Campbell, or a Walter Wilson. You become the person God has created you to be. Rather, you now have the key to grow into the person God wants you to be.

This is primarily for our relationship with God—to know His love and to love Him, and then it's for holiness and service. God left our old nature in us so that He could daily show us His power to give us victory.

This spiritual plane of living by faith can be lost if we turn back to flesh-dependence. This is not likely to happen, and does not ever need to happen, but it can, especially under wrong teaching. It happened to the Galatians! An entire book of the Bible is devoted to the theme of restoring believers who have fallen back into flesh-dependence.

This is a tool to overcome known sin. It is important, therefore, to have sin exposed and our understanding enlightened in order to grow spiritually. Placed in the wrong context, a person may not grow very much. For example, some people get saved (justification by faith) and continue to live in dead, unscriptural churches. They are truly saved, but their spiritual growth is greatly oppressed. Likewise, some can have this sanctification by faith and continue in new evangelical churches or liberal churches. Their spiritual life will likewise be greatly oppressed.

This closely parallels salvation. Justification is by faith and sanctification is by faith. Just as a person may struggle to obtain justification by faith, they may struggle to obtain sanctification by faith. The struggle for salvation is not to save yourself. That work, of course, has already been done. The struggle is to accept that it is true and to fully surrender to it so that you can trust Christ to save you. Sanctification by faith may come only after a similar struggle.

We don't struggle for victory because that work has already been done for us by Christ on the cross. But we may need to struggle over accepting that it is true and surrendering to the Lord so that we can trust Christ to give us the victory.

Some may object thinking that we need to build character by struggling against something, and overcoming it and the Christian life is to be one of struggle. But the victory over sin has already been won on the cross! The struggle in spiritual warfare is to be against the enemy, not our own flesh. A soldier who is always fighting himself is not very useful in the battle.

*Conclusion*

How can salvation be wonderful, and glorification wonderful, but sanctification miserable? God desires for everyone to have a victorious Christian life. He died upon the cross to give it to us.

God desires for us to know Him and to daily walk in fellowship with Him. It is there for everyone who will simply take God at His word and trust Him by faith. I am so thankful that I have left the path of self-powered Christianity and have learned to walk by faith. "The just shall live by faith!"

# Corporate Revival

As to some corporate touches of the Spirit, this letter comes from Pastor Mark Irmler in Fresno, California, who attended the Seeking Revival Conference:

> Please continue to pray for us as I am "Seeking the Lord" in a personal way as well as some of our people here at church.
>
> The Lord seized hold of some hearts last night during our prayer time after our midweek service as the Lord crushed two young men with an agony of soul over sin and for reviving.
>
> Most of the church folks excused themselves from the auditorium as these two young men continued to cry out to the Lord.
>
> Two of our deacons and another teen boy and myself remained in the auditorium for the next two hours and, in silence, prayed as these two young men lifted up their hearts to the Lord in confession and confidence in God to hear.
>
> The Lord gave the six of us a sweet time of instruction and united prayer as we asked God to continue this work in our own lives.
>
> When our prayer time ended, it was a full three hours after the regular service was dismissed. The comment of one of the deacons was: "It's 11:20, it's 11:20—How can it be 11:20?" All consciousness of time was removed for those precious hours as God dealt with our need.
>
> Would you lift us up in your prayers as we have so much fallow ground in our hearts?

These two excerpts come from Pastor Byron Herchenroder in Deltona, Florida, who I had been with for a meeting, which focused on the ministry of the Holy Spirit. He then attended the Seeking Revival Conference.

> We have some more encouraging things that are transpiring here. Upon returning from the conference, I began to ask the Lord

just how to begin dealing with the issues burning in my heart. He moved in the direction of preaching from Romans 12:1 on the "presentation." The first week, after preaching, I asked the people not to respond for presentation just yet as the series would give fuller view of the scriptural concept. At the invitation, two adults moved quickly and said they could not wait for the series to end before making their "presentation" to the Lord. Sunday last the same thing happened! Our neighbor across the street, who is of Lutheran background but saved, stepped from his seat before the invitation was really begun and, with tears, declared that he could no longer wrestle with God. Another of our regular ladies burst down to the front for "presentation." I had asked no one to move unless the Holy Spirit compelled and they could not resist, assuring them that if they had to present themselves before the Lord moved me to call for a special service of presentation that the Lord probably would understand! Sunday will be the fourth in the series, and we may have a special presentation service then or perhaps on Easter Sunday as the Lord moves. That would certainly be an unusual experience for someone who might be a "Christmas and Easter" attender of church!

The presence of the Lord is strong, and there is, of course, much opposition by our adversary. This kind of moving is dangerous to his evil kingdom, so we do ask you to pray much right now for the brethren here.

A later email said:

Just a note to report on our Easter Sunday—The Lord pressed on me the need to call for decisions concerning "presentation" of bodies to God for those who had never done so. It was the culmination of a month-long preaching on Romans 12:1-2, and Easter Sunday morning would not have been my choice to have such a service, but the Lord seemed to be driving for that time. At the invitation, I called first for those who, at some point, had previously offered their bodies to God and would be willing to walk forward in encouragement to others who needed to do the same. Approximately 60-70 adults instantly responded, flooding the front on one side. The next appeal was for those who had never presented their bodies to the Lord with no strings attached. Thirty-seven adults quickly came forward, and God's Spirit was openly moving in our midst! It is doubtful that there has ever been such open willingness at one particular time within our church.

Please pray much as you know the perils of such an hour. I am neither capable nor worthy of leading our people at such a time as this. It certainly must be "not I but Christ."

The following comes from Pastor Paul Alexander whom I have not been with yet. In our correspondence, he indicated he had been reading many of the old books as I had, that point one to the promise and power of God. He wrote:

> Who says God won't do it again???
>
> Just want to share what God did in our church this past Sunday as an encouragement to others to "not be weary in well-doing."
>
> "Last Sunday, Oct. 7, 2001, I had the service all planned out — the songs, the announcements, of course the message, invitation, etc. We sang an opening chorus, "Nothing Is Impossible," and then "Springs of Living Water." The last verse says, "Oh sinner, won't you come today to Calvary?" We had an opening prayer followed by announcements as usual, and that's where our well-planned "program" ended, and God took over. I had no sooner started announcements when Cindy, a middle-aged Catholic lady who has attended a few times, stood up and declared, "Preacher, I need to get saved!" I was completely surprised, but quickly asked Tammy if she would take her to a room to talk with her. After she left, we had prayer for her. I had just said 'Amen' when the door at the back of the church opened, and a man I had never seen came in. He was recognized and greeted by Tommy, our deacon, so I asked Tommy to introduce him. Gary was a man with whom Tommy had worked with several years before at a local factory. We found out later that Gary didn't know Tommy went to this church. It was just "coincidence." He was driving by and felt overwhelmed with the problems in his life and hoped he could find some answers at our church. After Gary was introduced and seated, we sang another song. The first one that came to my mind was "Revive Us Again." When we had sung the last verse, I gave an impromptu invitation, and Gary raised his hand for salvation. I asked him to look up at me if he wanted to be saved right now. To my surprise, he did, so I asked Tommy to take him to another quiet place. (I still hadn't even preached yet!)
>
> By now there wasn't a dry eye in the whole church. A couple of men led in another time of prayer, we sang another song, had another invitation, and many of our faithful raised hands that they needed to get things right with God. After some testimonies and another song or two, Cindy and Gary had rejoined us, so I tried to preach for a few minutes. (Anything I could possibly say seemed so anticlimactic.) I just shared part of what I had prepared: "Redeem the time because the days are evil." (That's where we are on a study through Ephesians.) "Redeem" in this passage means to buy for one's advantage and use; "time" means age or season, (i.e., Seize the opportunity of the season). The season of soul winning; the

season of salvation; a season is short. A harvest left in the field after the season is lost forever. After another invitation marked by a spontaneous testimony from the congregation that encouraged several more to repent of sin, we had a time of prayer down front. Nearly every man in the church came immediately to pray. There was no singing of a dozen verses of "Just As I Am." In fact, we didn't sing or plead at all. As we prepared to dismiss, someone suggested we sing "Victory in Jesus," and since many didn't seem anxious to leave, we just took a break so those who needed to, could go. Then we had a prayer meeting, more confession, and a great time of unity—It was like the kinship of a team after winning the championship game. When that seemed to be drawing to a close, Cindy said she wanted to be baptized. I was starting to go through the usual routine of setting up an appointment to go over the details of baptism, line up the baptismal in another church since we don't have one, and so forth. But she refused to be put off. It had to be today. So we announced to everyone that we were holding a baptism service at our house in our above ground pool right away. Nearly everybody came. The pool was cold. (I had told our kids I would only get in when it was 90 or above last summer. We have not lost our thin Florida blood.) One interesting note: Our pool had gotten algae and was unusable for the past month. Last Wednesday Tammy and the kids had just drained and cleaned it, so it was perfectly clean and ready for a baptism. Finally, about 3:30 P.M., people trickled back to their homes. A couple of hours later we had a great time of sharing and testimonies and prayer at the evening service. Many testified that they had grown up in church and had never seen anything like what happened that morning, and they had never thought they would.

God is still working in our congregation. Every day this week people are meeting together to pray for more souls and for God to keep working. We know that no plan or program or person had anything to do with what happened Sunday. We have had a long drought of souls—several months since anyone had been saved, and only two adults had been saved in two years. Some people blame the area and the hardness of people, but we don't accept that. Knowing God is still real, the Holy Spirit is still convicting, and Jesus still saves, several have been burdened to pray and fast for souls for the past two months. During this time many in the church had begun quietly getting things right with God. We are excited now about keeping right with God, ridding our lives of sin, winning souls, prayer and fasting, and anticipating what God will do next, if He so chooses, and we don't hinder. Actually many were scared of what might happen if they continued in sin any longer. We were reminded of Ananias and Sapphira.

This week, two key words keep coming to mind: "Helpless"—my total inability to accomplish anything for God in my flesh; and "Holiness"—God's demand of every believer so that He can freely accomplish all that He wants to do.

I share this as a reminder that old-fashioned Bible revival can still happen, that fasting and persevering prayer still work, and that God doesn't need our plans, programs, promotions, praise music, pumping people's emotions, or even preachers to send a mighty outpouring of His Spirit.

The following is a brief testimony from Evangelist Mike Redick who serves the Lord primarily in Southeast Asia:

## MERCY DROPS

Even now as I write these words, the storm clouds are forming outside my window, soon to bless the earth with much needed refreshing. I'm reminded of that great hymn of the faith "There shall be showers of blessing." The chorus reads: "Showers of blessing, showers of blessing we need; mercy drops round us are falling, but for the showers we plead." In the last eighteen months my wife and I, while in the midst of our busy evangelistic schedule, have had the privilege of being a part of the work of the Lord in Gospel Light Christian Church in Singapore. In this short period of time we have witnessed "mercy drops" of the Holy Spirit's working.

From June to November 2000, through the pulpit ministry and special meetings, the Holy Spirit began convincing and convicting God's people of the absolute necessity and importance of living a God-dependent life. As this truth was unfolded, God's people began to enthrone the Spirit as Lord and leader of their lives, and the Spirit was given His rightful place as both administrator and builder of the Church. The result of the Spirit's enthronement has been beautiful to behold.

Without any special push or announcement, the unsaved began to come into the church. At times there would be over 50 unsaved present (This is significant in a church of less than 300 people). From December 2000 through May 2001, the church saw well over 500 conversions, averaging 15-20 a week. Nearly 140 of these converts went through a new believers class, and, to date, over 90 have been baptized. The Wednesday night Bible study was soon packed to capacity (200 people), and the Friday night prayer meeting quickly doubled in size. Some 160 people would gather together, and from 8:30 P.M. to 11:30 P.M. they would pray (In Singapore, Saturday is still a work day). Before long a second worship service was added to hold the crowd; then God gave birth to an Indonesian service. In all there are five services on Sunday: two English services, a Chinese service, a

Filipino, and an Indonesian service. In this short period of time the church has grown from 300 to nearly 600 on Sunday mornings.

In addition to the increase in size, a new power and zeal has possessed the people. In prayer people often weep for the lost and sin is dealt with. Thirteen people have surrendered for full-time service and there is a real desire to serve the Lord. Gospel Light today has nearly 600 people in attendance and, like any church, has a multitude of ministries and weekly activities, but uniquely no paid staff, not even the senior pastor. The work of the Lord is done willingly by God's people. Evangelism is the heartbeat with 100 people trained to be soul winners and many actively involved in various outreaches of the Church.

It is exciting to see what the Lord can do through a group of believers who are willing to give the reign of their lives and the rule of the church over to the Holy Spirit. The church has truly seen mercy drops, but it is entirely aware that God desires to do much, much more. "O for the showers we plead."

The following is a brief account by Pastor David O'Gorman of the Lord's work at Lifegate Bible Baptist Church in Dublin, Ireland:

Church camp 2000 has dramatically changed Lifegate Bible Baptist Church. We went to camp anticipating the usual time of challenge, fellowship, and fun, but returned having met with God. Evangelist John Van Gelderen's theme focused on knowing the Holy Spirit as a personal reality in the life of the believer. Each evening we had a prayer meeting given over to the control of the Holy Spirit. There was no human leader; the people could pray, begin a chorus, or testify, but only as the Holy Spirit led. Those were wonderful times of waiting on and communing with God. There were many tears as 'Christ in you' became a reality. The spiritual warfare was intense, and several desired to leave during that week. No one did, however, and one by one the Holy Spirit met with them and ushered them into a new reality in their relationships with God. When the week was over, no one wanted to leave. There was the fear that this new intimacy with God would be left at camp. However, that was not to be.

We returned from camp on Saturday. On Sunday night we had an after-meeting (prayer meeting), and God met with us wonderfully. Our usually very reserved deacon burst into tears at one point, overcome by the plight of the lost. After about two hours I closed the meeting, but again no one wanted to leave.

Evangelist John Van Gelderen left on Tuesday morning early. He and I had misgivings about his leaving, but the schedule required it. That evening was calling night and believing that we had spent to much time "doing our own thing" as far as evangelism was concerned, we decided to wait on God until the Holy Spirit directed us to go to a specific person. Our meeting room is upstairs and by way of a challenge I said, "God was able to bring someone up those stairs if He wanted to." He did, and about thirty minutes later a young man walked up the stairs. While one of our young men spoke with him, I was able to lead his girlfriend to the Lord on a bench at the front of the church.

The next day John Van Gelderen returned, both of us believing that God's work was not finished. During the next week God moved with regard to faith for revival. We began to have prayer meetings, and since that time fifteen months ago we have had at least four prayer meetings per week and often more. They have continued with varying degrees of power but with a constant attendance and a growing expectation of revival in Ireland.

There have been many blessings since of that time. One of them concerns a 20-year-old called Leighton Kelly who came back to church after eight years. He had been on fire at first but then got away from the Lord and into drugs (heroine) and the wicked life that goes with it. He kept dreaming about being a pastor!!!! And wanted to know could he after being on drugs and what would he have to do. The Lord led us to take him into our home. He came off all drugs and went to Scotland to a rehabilitation program. That was more than a year ago. Today he has almost finished the program and believes the Lord would have him work with addicts.

Another young man called Liam found the "New Birth" tract on a building site where he worked. He had been searching, and, having read it, he put it away intending to phone the church. However, he didn't phone, and one week later he found the same tract on a dumpster. He knew God was speaking to him, and he phoned that day. He came to church one Sunday evening and accepted the Lord.

There have been many such stories, but the greatest work has been in the hearts of people as God has become real and His smile more important than anything in life. We are rejoicing in what God has done and anxiously anticipating His greater blessing in revival!

I trust that the testimonies recorded here will be, in God's manifold mercies, a light shower preceding greater showers of blessing yet to come.

# APPENDIX B

# SPIRITUAL WARFARE

Ephesians 6:10-18a—"Finally, my brethren, be strong in the Lord, and in the power of His might. Put on the whole armour of God, that ye may be able to stand against the wiles of the devil. For we wrestle not against flesh and blood, but against principalities, against powers, against the rulers of the darkness of this world, against spiritual wickedness in high places. Wherefore take unto you the whole armour of God, that ye may be able to withstand in the evil day, and having done all, to stand. Stand therefore, having your loins girt about with truth, and having on the breastplate of righteousness; And your feet shod with the preparation of the gospel of peace; Above all, taking the shield of faith, wherewith ye shall be able to quench all the fiery darts of the wicked. And take the helmet of salvation, and the sword of the Spirit, which is the word of God: Praying always with all prayer and supplication in the Spirit."

It is of utmost importance that the believer, by faith, depends on the victory of Christ to win the battle against sin, so that he can, by faith, depend on the victory of Christ to win the real battle—the battle against Satan. The real wrestling match is in the spiritual realm. After listing the armor, which is primarily defensive, our text emphasizes two spiritual weapons: *The sword of the Spirit* and *praying . . . in the Spirit.*

The real battle for souls is won on our knees in the spiritual realm. Matthew 12:29 explains, "Or else how can one enter into a strong man's house, and spoil his goods, except he first bind the strong man? and then he will spoil his house." The context makes clear that Satan is the strong man who must be bound. The following are some *rhemas* of God, which provide a foundation of faith to bind the strong man:

Colossians 2:15—"And having spoiled principalities and powers, He [Christ] made a shew of them openly, triumphing over them in it [the cross]."

I John 3:8b—"For this purpose the Son of God was manifested, that He might destroy the works of the devil."

John 16:11—"The prince of this world is judged."

Revelation 12:11—"And they overcame him [Satan] by the blood of the Lamb, and by the word of their testimony; and they loved not their lives unto the death."

We have no power against Satan and his cohorts on our own. Rather, we must plead the victory of Christ over Satan, which took place at the cross to thus bind Satan, and then *spoil* [plunder] his house by seeing souls saved. The greatest means is through revival.

[NOTE: For further study on spiritual warfare, *War on the Saints* by Jessie Penn-Lewis with Evan Roberts is of great value. This book was written to deal with the attacks and counterfeits of Satan during the 1904 Welsh Revival. When the saints embrace counterfeits, the Spirit is grieved, and revival fires are quenched. This book seeks to instruct believers in this "war on the saints."

The book is heavy reading and perhaps not for every person. Also, the definitions given at the beginning of the book must be well taken in to understand the book. Many criticize the book today simply because they misunderstand what is meant (i.e., "possession"). But many fundamentalists prior to the Charismatic excess of the 1960s greatly appreciated the book.]

# APPENDIX C

## COUNTERFEITS OF THE SPIRIT TO THE SURRENDERED SAINT

Some have suggested, understandably so, that in the midst of the Welsh Revival of 1904–5, Satan sent his counterfeits. As counterfeits were embraced, the Spirit was grieved and quenched, and the revival ended. When a child of God is restored to spiritual life, the Evil One's turf is threatened. It should not surprise us, therefore, that the powers of darkness will be aroused against Spirit-empowered believers. However, we need not fear Satan; we need but to fear God. The Scripture says of the Evil One and his tactics, "We are not ignorant of his devices" (II Corinthians 2:11). One of the devil's greatest devices is deceit. Jesus said in John 8:44, "The Devil . . . is a liar, and the father of it."

"Seducing spirits and doctrines [teachings] of devils" (I Timothy 4:1) have caused many believers to embrace worldliness, or to think that life this side of heaven must of necessity be a defeated life. They are unsurrendered Christians. They may talk occasionally of surrender, but know little of it in reality.

However, it is possible to be surrendered but deceived. Some forget that the powers of darkness are in the supernatural realm. When Satan cannot keep a person unsurrendered and, therefore, apart from the power of the Spirit, he often tries to push the surrendered saint into error in the other direction, which will hurt the cause of Christ and also grieve away the Spirit.

Surrendered saints must discern between the genuine guidance of the Spirit and the counterfeit guidance of evil spirits. How can one truly know the difference between the two? The key is to first know what the real guidance is and then be aware of the false.

# GENUINE GUIDANCE OF THE SPIRIT

## Key Principles

### The Wisdom of the Spirit

First, there is the wisdom of the Spirit. Ephesians 1:17-18 says, "That the God of our Lord Jesus Christ, the Father of glory, may give unto you the Spirit of wisdom and revelation in the knowledge of Him: The eyes of your understanding being enlightened . . . " Notice the appeal is to your mind. The Spirit illumines the truth of Scripture to our minds and, thus, gives us knowledge of Christ. The key to discerning all error is to know the truth. Jesus said in John 17:17, "Thy Word is truth."

### The Witness of the Spirit

Second, there is the witness of the Spirit. Romans 8:16 says, "The Spirit itself [Himself] beareth witness with our spirit." Notice here the appeal is to your spirit.

Several considerations must be kept in mind: First, this witness is a knowledge, not a feeling. Romans 8:16 goes on to say "that we are [not feel like] the children of God." Second, the Spirit's witness is always in harmony with the laws of God as revealed in Scripture. The Spirit is "the Spirit of truth" (John 14:17) and will not violate the Word, which is truth (John 17:17). Third, sometimes both the wisdom of the Spirit and the witness of the Spirit are given as a matter of guidance. Fourth, sometimes there is no witness of the Spirit in a given situation. Otherwise what need is there of the mind? In such cases, we must simply follow the wisdom of the Spirit. In other words, we must use the light God has already given to the mind. Finally, it must be remembered that the Spirit never bypasses our faculties—in this case, the mind. Rather, He uses our faculties.

## Key Pictures

How do you know the difference between your own whims and the real leading of the Holy Spirit? When people follow their own human whims, many ridiculous actions that follow are blamed on God's leading. Some people, because they so desire something, mistake their own whim for the Holy Spirit's leading. The result is foolishness.

We need to understand biblical principles of how the Holy Spirit leads. Obviously, the Spirit never leads contrary to Scripture. How does the Holy Spirit lead? Let's look at three principles from God's Word that enlighten this subject.

### Light

When the Holy Spirit leads, there is light with no darkness. I John 1:5 declares, "God is light, and in Him is no darkness at all." When the Spirit leads, there is not any confusion as to what to do because that is darkness. When God leads, there is light. God gives clarity, not confusion, as to what direction to take.

### Life

The Spirit gives life with no deadness. II Corinthians 3:6 says, "For the letter killeth, but the Spirit giveth life." When the Holy Spirit is in a matter, He gives life to it, not deadness. When He leads, there is not a sense of drudgery or staleness. No, there is a sense of life.

### Liberty

When the Holy Spirit guides, there is liberty with no duress. II Corinthians 3:17 states, "Now the Lord is that Spirit: and where the Spirit of the Lord is, there is liberty." Liberty is the freedom to do God's will through the power of the Spirit. When God leads, He gives liberty, not duress or a sense of being forced into something. When the Holy Spirit leads, there is a sense of freedom.

For example, when a preacher studies what to preach, and the message seems like dry bones, the Holy Spirit is probably leading him to preach something else. It is darkness, deadness, and duress if he tries to preach what is dry to him. When the Holy Spirit leads, there is light, life, and liberty. The message will be full of life and the sense that this will meet the need of the hour.

# COUNTERFEIT GUIDANCE OF EVIL SPIRITS

## External Appeals

"The Spirit itself [Himself] beareth witness with our spirit" (Romans 8:16). This reveals an inner man appeal, not an outer man appeal. For example, if the body senses are directly appealed to, then you have an appeal to the outer man, not the inner man. This is physical, not spiritual. Audible voices and physical manifestations appeal to the outer man and are, therefore, signs of counterfeit.

This is different from spiritual hearing or seeing. For example, Elisha prayed that God would open the eyes of his servant to see "the horses and chariots of fire" (II Kings 6:15-17), and God opened his eyes. Up to that point, all the servant saw was the enemy. Therefore, the horses and chariots of God were not physical; otherwise, the servant would have seen them. They were spiritual.

# Internal Promptings

Satan can feign himself as "an angel of light" (II Corinthians 11:14) to deceive God's people.

## Counterfeit Voices

Generally speaking, there are three ways to discern counterfeits. First, when an internal prompting is from your "circumference," it is a sign of counterfeit. As already noted, the Spirit bears witness with our spirit (Romans 8:16). He communicates with our innermost being, not our outer being.

Second is "compulsion." When the prompting is such that you must follow it without being able to think about it, you have a sign of counterfeit. I John 4:1 says, "Try the spirits whether they are of God." If you have no time to test the spirits, the prompting is not of God. When the Spirit speaks, there will be a growing conviction (convincement).

Again, the Holy Spirit uses our faculties, whereas evil spirits bypass our faculties. God has so fixed it that not only does He not violate the human will, neither does He let evil spirits violate the human will. Therefore it is when believers will their minds or bodies to be in a passive state that the powers of darkness do their work. In contrast, the Holy Spirit uses our minds and bodies, which is partnership, not passivity.

Third, "confusion" is another sign of counterfeit. "God is not the author of confusion" (I Corinthians 14:33). If a prompting leads you this way, then as you follow, another prompting leads you that way and so forth, you have a sign of counterfeit. This haphazard leading is irritating and can be used of the Evil One to keep a believer off the poise and peace of resting in Christ.

## Counterfeit Texts

Satan misused Scripture in the temptation of Christ. He will do the same with the followers of Christ. How can we know counterfeit "texts"?

First, when a "text" supposedly leads you to violate another text, you have a misuse of Scripture. Christ answered Satan with Scripture.

Second, a "text" is counterfeit when it flashes across the mind, demanding instant obedience before you can think about it and, thus, negates the real use of the mind. We are not automatons. Again, the Spirit uses our faculties.

Third, when a "text" leads you to pride, thinking you are especially led of God, you have a sign of counterfeit. God does not lead us to pride.

Fourth, when a "text" leads you to despair by so crushing and condemning you, you also have a sign of counterfeit. The Spirit uses the Word to bring about a serious-dealing with God Himself. This is ultimately encouraging, not discouraging or crushing.

### Counterfeit Peace

Any "peace" that contradicts God's words or ways is a false peace. Proverbs 28:26 says, "He that trusteth in his own heart is a fool." Also, true peace is a knowledge, not a feeling, as seen earlier with the concept of light, life, and liberty. It is inner man (spiritual), not outer man (physical).

# Conclusion

How do you get delivered from deception? Recognize the possibility of deception. Recognize the possibility that you have been deceived. Depend on the Holy Spirit for the discernment of any deception in your life, based on the Word of truth. Discover where you have been deceived. Confess the embracing of deception as sin. Refuse the deception. Finally, embrace the truth.

[NOTE: See note at end of Appendix B.]

# APPENDIX D

# FIERY DARTS

*"Above all, taking the shield of faith, wherewith ye shall be able to quench all the fiery darts of the wicked [one]"*
*(Ephesians 6:16).*

## Discerning the Fiery Darts

First, if an "attack" seems to have no reasonable or apparent cause, you may know you are dealing with a fiery dart. For example, discouragement is never of God. In fact, discouragement is always sin, for the scriptural command is "Be careful [anxious] for nothing" (Philippians 4:6). If something occurs that is potentially discouraging, then the temptation to be discouraged has a reason or apparent cause, even though we should not give in to it. If, however, a feeling of discouragement comes when there is no reasonable or apparent cause, you are facing a fiery dart.

Second, when temptation to sin arises, and the faith choice based on Galatians 2:20 truth does not seem to work, you may know you are dealing with a fiery dart. The reason for this is that you are not actually dealing with the flesh and the world but, rather, the powers of darkness directly. It is not a Galatians 2:20 or Romans 6 issue. The powers of darkness often use the world or our flesh to tempt us to sin. However, trusting the victory of Christ over the world and the flesh is promised, based on Romans 6 and Galatians 2:20. So if the victory does not come, it indicates that the attack is not the world or the flesh, but directly from the powers of darkness.

## Deliverance from Fiery Darts

When you discern fiery darts, then use the shield of faith by simply asking God to quench or destroy the fiery darts. If you have given ground by giving into the fiery darts for a time, then confess that as sin, refuse the ground (even verbally, if possible), and ask God to destroy the fiery darts. Ephesians 6:16 promises the shield of faith is able to quench all the fiery darts of the wicked one. As you trust in God, the fiery darts will be quenched and you will sense a lift in your spirit. If you have given ground for a while, evil spirits will not give up easily. You may have to apply these principles repeatedly until the evil spirits know they have been exposed.

[NOTE: See note at end of Appendix B.]

# APPENDIX E

## FANATICISM

"Another hindrance [to receiving power from the Holy Spirit] is fear of fanaticism. Instinctive revulsion from fleshly excesses and foolish undisciplined conduct on the part of some who profess lofty spiritual attainments has closed the door to a life of power for many of God's true children . . .

"They have made the mistake of putting all teaching concerning the Holy Spirit in the same category, and consequently will have nothing to do with any of it. This is as much to be regretted as it is easy to understand.

"Such victims must be taught that the Holy Spirit is the Spirit of Jesus, and is as gracious and beautiful as the Saviour Himself. Paul's words should be kept in mind, 'For God hath not given us the spirit of fear; but of power, and of love, and of a sound mind' (2 Timothy 1:7).

"The Holy Spirit is the cure for fanaticism, not the cause of it."[1]

---

[1] A. W. Tozer, *Tozer on the Holy Spirit*, comp. Marilynne E. Foster (Camp Hill, Penn.: Christian Publications, Inc., 2000), March 24.

# APPENDIX F

## THE WONDER OF INTERCESSION

by Mark Gillmore

*And He saw that there was no man, and wondered that there was no intercessor (Isaiah 59:16).*

God can work great spiritual deliverance . . . whenever He finds a faithful intercessor. What a wonderful truth!

The story of the Telegue Mission in India is a thrilling one. The Canadian Baptist Missionary Society had only one station, right away by itself, and so it was called "The Lone Star Mission." The missionary who labored there found himself alone because of a shortage of workers, and it was resolved by the Mission Board that instead of giving him a helper they would close down the station. Boldly and bluntly the missionary told the Board that he would carry on alone, if only to leave his bones there as a witness to Christ. Touched by his impassioned earnestness, the Board resolved to make one more attempt, and a helper was sent. The lonely laborer definitely claimed and believed, on the authority of the Word of God, that a mighty movement of the Spirit was coming. Before long their prayers were answered, and the good news was flashed back to the thousands of praying saints in North America that God had performed a miracle. As strong an authority as Dr. A. T. Pierson has left on record: "Probably the largest number of people baptized at one time since the Day of Pentecost took place at the Lone Star Mission. Two thousand two hundred and twenty-two converts were baptized in a single day!"[1]

Praise the Lord, in Telegue, India, God found an intercessor!

> Pastor Harms, of Hermannsberg, Germany, when appointed to his pastorate, felt discouraged because it seemed an impossible task given him. The church in the village was small and the testimony weak. His parish, ten miles square, was overgrown with unbelief and formalism. There was no concern among the unsaved. But as he fasted and prayed he received a mighty enduement of the Spirit, whereby he was able to receive definite promises from God's Word, definite passages of Scripture which revealed to him that the whole neighborhood would be transformed. With a little band of believers he prayed through on these promises, and very soon the desert began to blossom like a rose. Large numbers flocked to hear the Word. No year passed without new awakenings. Thousands were brought into the fellowship of the Church, and so great was their depths of spirituality, and so great was their missionary spirit, that it has been said by deep mature spiritual minds that very few evangelical churches in any part of the world could equal the village church of Hermannsberg.[2]

Praise the Lord, in Hermannsberg, Germany, God found an intercessor!

However, Isaiah 59:16 reveals an utterly appalling reality: God's work of deliverance is wholly compromised whenever a faithful intercessor cannot be found. Such absence of intercession literally shocks the heart of God ("wondered") and leaves Him with only a recourse of judgment upon the sinning, rather than a display of mercy and grace. Ezekiel 22:30-31 echoes this same reality: "And I sought for a man among them, that should make up the hedge, and stand in the gap before me for the land, that I should not destroy it: but I found none. Therefore have I poured out mine indignation upon them; I have consumed them with the fire of my wrath. . . ."

It is appalling when, in the face of spiritual desolation all around, God can find no intercessor. Does no one care? Does no one believe that God could and would deliver? If God could but find an intercessor, He could send mercy instead of judgment. How tragic that judgment must fall when deliverance is but a prayer away. The challenge is that God would find in our hearts and in our churches the intercession He is looking for, the intercession that accesses God's mighty revival power. *God's people must surrender to God's means of intercession if they are to obtain the deliverance so desperately needed in our churches and in the world today.*

Moses provides an outstanding example of God's plan to deliver through intercession. We find that (1) God placed Israel in need of deliverance, (2) God chose a man through whom to work His deliverance, and (3) God turned that man into an intercessor.

## Deliverance out of a Great Need

*Israel was in great need of deliverance,* but did the Israelites' need for deliverance catch God by surprise? No. In fact, it was God who had sent Joseph and his father Jacob and all that they had down to Egypt years before (Genesis 46:3-4). It was God who raised up the opposition of Pharaoh for the express purpose of displaying God's power to deliver (Exodus 9:16). All along God had planned a mighty deliverance in accordance with His own supernatural power and desire to bless abundantly in the Promised Land (Exodus 3:8).

As we come face to face with the desperate spiritual needs that are in the lives of those around us (or even in our own lives), we tend to forget that such humanly staggering needs have not caught God by surprise. He has allowed them to exist because He wants to manifest before our eyes His power to overcome. We tremble and shake in unbelief when we should confidently rest in our God's will and power to deliver. The fact that the need exists, rather than driving us to despair, should drive us to wholehearted dependence upon our God through intercession. God's will is to deliver!

Take, for instance, the need of born-again believers to comprehend the victory that is in Christ and to walk by faith in the fulness of the Spirit. Think of the need for saved teenagers and adults to fall in love with Jesus as their wonderful Lord and Savior, to love serving God, to love doing right, to love God's Word, to love prayer, to love witnessing—not just merely doing what is right, but truly enjoying what is right. Is not this the biblical standard of God's law written on our hearts? Cannot our God make such a glorious standard a reality in our churches? Absolutely, if we would recognize our unbelief on this point and ask God to grant deliverance to our fellow-believers.

One day a Sunday school teacher, a man of about thirty who was incredibly wealthy, powerful, and educated, became burdened about his class of nine junior-aged girls, ages ten to thirteen. The girls were always present and proper, but in their hearts he could not find a single trace of love for Jesus. They did all that he asked them to do, but when he talked about the love of the Lord Jesus Christ, nothing seemed to stir in their hearts. He went to prayer and poured out his soul in great heart-affecting prayer, accompanied by a flood of tears, interceding for the spiritual deadness of his junior girls. Praise the Lord, he saw the need and believed that God could deliver! God did answer, and every one of those girls was gloriously born again and fell in love with Jesus. Who was the Sunday school teacher? The man was the German Count Zinzendorf, and the year was early in 1727, just months before God poured out his spirit in one of the greatest revivals of the church age. Zinzendorf saw the great spiritual need and believed God would deliver through prayer.

Think of the six billion souls alive today on planet earth. Do we think that the vast worldwide need is too great for God? That sin has become too pervasive for God to overcome? That somehow God has made more souls than He can effectively reach? Or do we remember that He has made each one in His image and is not willing that any should perish and has died once and for all for the sins of the whole world? The mighty Spirit of Christ has been given to empower believers to go to the ends of the earth preaching the gospel to every creature. In our unbelief have we forgotten God's power to deliver the lost?

Let us take heart! The need for deliverance is all part of God's plan to display His almighty power to overcome the opposition, whether it be of Satan, the world, or the flesh. God can do it! In Christ we are more than conquerors.

## Deliverance through a Chosen Man

In the face of such a need among the Israelites, *God chose a man through whom to work his deliverance,* and that man was Moses. What a man Moses was—a "goodly" and "proper" child, "exceeding fair" (Exodus 2:2; Hebrews 11:23; Acts 7:20). Moses was blessed with extraordinary natural abilities along with the best education the world had to offer. He had godly parents and a social position of immense power and wealth in the courts of Pharaoh. He was a natural-born leader, mighty in words and deeds (Acts 7:22) People just looked at Moses and they immediately concluded, "This man is going to make it. He has it all together. Let's follow him."

At some point Moses became aware that God had called him to be the deliverer of his people the Israelites (Acts 7:25). He saw the desperate need they faced as the bondage and slavery grew more severe, and he knew that God had called him to bring deliverance. What a calling! With Moses' power with people and his position in Egypt, certainly he was the perfect man for the job.

Yet what a tragedy occurred the first time Moses stepped out to do what he knew God had called him to do. He utterly failed! (Exodus 2:11-15) His decision to forsake the world and identify with the people of God was admirable and right (Hebrews 11:24-26), but his dependence upon the arm of the flesh backfired. After he slew the Egyptian taskmaster, his own people turned against him, and he was in danger of losing his own life. Something went horribly wrong, and now Moses was the one who stood in need of deliverance.

What shall we learn from this stage in Moses' life? First of all, we must realize that God does not work a divine deliverance apart from choosing a human deliverer through whom to work His deliverance. This is God's plan in His relationship with man—He *always* forms a deliverer, a human channel through whom He can work, always. Even in Christ we find this pattern of God's plan, for Christ our Savior did not deliverer us apart from becoming a man Himself. There never has been a random deliverance or spontaneous revival in which God has not prepared some person or persons through whom He intended to channel His mighty power. Matthew Henry said, "When God intends great mercy for His people, the first thing He does is set them a praying." In other words, before God delivers, He always forms His human intercessors.

At the age of seventeen, William Burns sat down in an alley-way within the bustling city of Glasgow, Scotland. In great agony of soul, tears were streaming down his face. His surprised mother exclaimed, "Willie, my boy, what ails you? Are you ill?" "O Mither! Mither!" he cried, "The thud of these Christless feet on the way to hell breaks my heart!" The great crowds of lost humanity had stirred him to his deepest depths. One morning a couple years later, he approached his mother at breakfast time and told her that through the night he had prayed, and he said, "Tonight, God gave me Scotland." Soon revival fires burst aflame, and a great spiritual deliverance swept through the land of Scotland. God had found and formed His deliverer, and He turned him into an intercessor.

God is at work today forming channels of His power through whom He can send great deliverance. In fact, each New Testament believer has a greater position, a greater calling, and a greater opportunity than Moses himself ever had. We stand complete in Christ (Colossians 2:10), fellowcitizens in the household of God (Ephesians 2:19), potentially filled with all the fulness of God (Epesians 3:19). Our calling is greater than any of the Old Testament saints, for the least of us is greater than John the Baptist, and he was the greatest of the Old Testament saints, including Moses (Matthew 11:11). What an opportunity! We tend to look at Moses and wish that we had the same type of opportunity to serve the Lord as he did, but the Bible truth is that every New Testament believer has a *greater* opportunity than Moses ever had. The commission of the gospel worldwide and the New Testament filling of the Spirit, on the basis of the completed work of Christ and Word of God, place us in a position far superior to that of Moses.

Why then do we seem to be so utterly failing? What has gone wrong? If God wants to work great spiritual deliverance through us, why hasn't He done it? Why does revival tarry?

Our problem is the same one Moses had: We are depending on the arm of the flesh. We know that God's plan is to deliver, and we know that God has called us to be deliverers, but we are expecting God to deliver our way. We are depending on our natural strengths, abilities, resources, and position to accomplish God's great will, and we are failing. Will we wake up to this cause for our wilderness experience, our spiritual fruitlessness, our lack of revival power in our churches? We must let God bring us to the end of ourselves, to the point where we abhor our flesh-dependence and fear its consequence, to the point where we cast our dependence utterly upon God in the face of humanly impossible spiritual opposition. Revelation 3:17 characterizes the flesh dependence that permeates our Christianity: "Thou sayest, I am rich, and increased with goods, and have need of nothing; and knowest not that thou art wretched, and miserable, and poor, and blind, and naked." What a tragedy!

# Deliverance through a Humble Intercessor

Thankfully, God can use the wilderness experience to deal within our souls and change us into a vessel He can use. *God turned Moses, His deliverer, into an intercessor. First of all, an intercessor must wholly and humbly identify with the people for whom he is interceding.* After forty years in the wilderness, Moses was no longer separate in his identity from the people of Israel; he, too, had become a shepherd of sheep (which, by the way, was an abominable employment to the Egyptians). After forty years in the wilderness, Moses was no longer superior to the people of Israel; he who had been "mighty in words" (Acts 7:22) no longer felt he could even speak (Exodus 4:10). God had taught Moses his complete inability to produce the deliverance. Moses said, "Who am I, that I should go unto Pharaoh, and that I should bring forth the children of Israel out of Egypt?" (Exodus 3:11)

As intercessors, these are lessons we must learn. God must teach us our own absolute inability, and He must enable us to wholly identify with those who are in desperate need. Exodus 32:32 reveals just how completely Moses had selflessly united himself with the people of Israel. In light of the judgment they deserved for their idolatry at Mount Sinai, he prayed, "Yet now, if thou wilt forgive their sin—; and if not, blot me, I pray thee, out of thy book which thou hast written." Moses loved the people more than he loved himself to the point of offering himself in exchange for their forgiveness. What humility! What love! Truly, this is the heart of an intercessor.

Have we gotten to the point where we pray, "God, bless these people, grant them deliverance, or I die?" Have we put our own lives completely on the altar before God, that He might deliver the lost and backslidden around us? The apostle Paul knew this reality when he wrote, "death worketh in us, but life in you" (II Corinthians 4:12). Are we determined not to leave the throne of grace, not to leave the position of intercession, until God blesses the one with whom we have identified? This is the life of an intercessor. Sadly, our American Christianity typically falls far short of this inner reality, but it need not. We can be different by God's grace. For Moses it took God forty years, but it need not be that long for you and me.

At age twenty-two James Frazier abandoned himself to the gospel cause in China and became a missionary to the Lisu tribespeople of Yunnan province. Soon after beginning work among the Lisu people, he asked and believed God for a great work in their midst. He labored ceaselessly for nearly ten years, seeing very little fruit in the face of severe spiritual oppression and darkness. Yet he did not leave the people, nor did he stop believing God for a great deliverance. And then . . . the deliverance came. In a period of months thousands were converted and the people themselves became missionaries to villages James Frazier had never visited. God worked a great deliverance through the heart and life of His servant, whom He had formed into an intercessor.

Not only must an intercessor wholly and humbly identify with the people, he also must wholly and humbly depend upon God. God taught Moses that his main responsibility was not to fight for the people, nor even to teach the people, but rather to pray for the people. The advice he received was, "Be thou for the people to God-ward, that thou mayest bring the causes unto God: and thou shalt teach them. . . ." (Exodus 18:19-20) Moses' first priority was to be prayer, even before teaching the people. The prophet Samuel also testified, "As for me, God forbid that I should sin against the LORD in ceasing to pray for you: but I will teach you the good and the right way" (I Samuel 12:23). The same priority is found in the New Testament for pastoral leadership in the church: "We will give ourselves continually to prayer, and to the ministry of the word" (Acts 6:4).

James Frazier, mentioned above, wrote in his journal: "I used to think that prayer should have the first place and teaching the second. I now feel it would be truer to give prayer the first, second, and third places, and teaching the fourth."[3]

Intercession became the constant response of Moses in the face of his people's spiritual need. We may be well aware of Moses' prayer in Exodus 32:32 and the forty days of intercession that followed (Deuteronomy 9:18-19), but the Bible records numerous other occasions in which Moses prayed, as well. They provide an interesting and challenging study:

Numbers 11:1-2 (v. 2)—
Complaining in the wilderness

Numbers 12:1-15 (v. 13)—
Jealousy of Aaron and Miriam

Numbers 14 (vv. 5, 13-19)—
Uprising at Kadesh-Barnea

Numbers 16 (vv. 4, 22, 45b-48)—
Rebellion of Korah

Numbers 20 (v. 6)—
Murmurings in the desert of Zin

Numbers 21 (v. 7)—
Discouragement in the wilderness

We find in these situations a repeated cycle of (1) the people's rebellion, (2) God's impending judgment, (3) Moses' intercession, (4) God's glory/presence manifest, and (5) God's mercy bestowed. How this needs to become the pattern of our own ministries as well.

## Our Great Need—Learning How to Intercede

Before leaving Moses' example of intercession, there is a vital lesson we must learn from the well-known events of Exodus thirty-two to thirty-four. The great idolatry of the golden calf at the foot of Mount Sinai threatened to corrupt and destroy the great work that God had begun to do in and through the Israelites. God was preparing to destroy the rebellious people and make of Moses himself a great nation. In this crisis situation, Moses responded with prayer, specifically a series of four prayers.

**Prayer #1, Exodus 32:9-14.** In the first prayer, Moses revealed his true identification with the people when he selflessly turned down God's offer to make of Moses a great nation. (How would you respond if such an offer were made to you?) He then pleaded the name and reputation of God (vv. 11-12) and the promise of God (v. 13), and God heard and stopped the judgment that was about to fall. Moses' intercession was successful to a point, but he had only stopped the immediate wrath of God; he had not genuinely reconciled the people to their God. He knew there was more business to be done with God.

**Prayer #2, Exodus 32:30-35.** After confronting the people with their idolatry and shame and after dealing with those who refused to repent, Moses returned to the mount to speak with God, endeavoring to make atonement for the sin of the people. This is one of the remarkable prayers of Scripture, and in it we understand just how far Moses had gone in selflessly identifying with the people he was seeking to deliver. He prayed, "Yet now, if thou wilt forgive their sin—; and if not, blot me, I pray thee, out of thy book which thou hast written." Literally, Moses cared more about his people's destiny than his own. What humility and love! Can we say that God has gotten us to this point? That we are more concerned about the spiritual destiny of our church members, of our class members, of the lost in our community than we are about our own selves? This is the heart of a true intercessor.

Notice, however, God's response to Moses' prayer. In verse 33, God did not accept Moses' offer to substitute himself as atonement for others' sins; and in verse 34, God did not promise to return His presence to His people, but instead God would send an angel to go before the people. This was not good news, as the response of the people in Exodus 33:4 reveals. An angel could in no way replace the very presence of God that Moses—and now the people—knew they desperately needed. The situation was critical. Moses had to return to God and speak with Him a third time.

In light of this second prayer, we must understand that while complete selfless identification with those who are in spiritual need is absolutely vital to the work of intercession, it is wholly inadequate in its ultimate power to deliver. If we depend upon our ability to selflessly identify with another, than who are we really depending on to earn the right for deliverance from God? Ourselves! If we are not careful, we can become self-dependent upon our effort to selflessly identify with the needy. If such is the case, we will fail, and deliverance will be lost. Moses realized this, and so he moved to the next step in his intercession for the rebellious people.

**Prayer #3, Exodus 33:12-18.** Thank God Moses knew what was so desperately needed in this critical moment of spiritual life or death for the people of God. Moses prayed, "If thy presence go not with me, carry us not up hence. For wherein shall it be known here that I and thy people have found grace in thy sight? is it not in that thou goest with us? so shall we be separated, I and thy people, from all the people that are upon the face of the earth . . . I beseech thee, shew me thy glory." There was only one solution to meet the spiritual crisis of the moment and of the coming years—Moses had to have God's presence and know His glory. There was no other option. Moses had to have it. The formerly strong and self-dependent Moses had truly come to the place where he was utterly convinced he could not lead these people alone (v. 12); he had to have the grace of God's presence manifest in the assembly of people (vv. 13-15). Otherwise, he would fail.

Herein is the power of intercession—the pleading for the power of the presence of God. Oh, how this truth has been neglected. We have denied the personal, powerful presence of the mighty Spirit of God. We have refused to see our need of Him, to understand the promise of His coming, to cast our dependence upon Him, to desperately plead for His very presence manifest in our midst, in our meetings, in our ministry. If Moses had to have God's presence manifest, how much more do we?

The power of intercession is not just coming to the end of ourselves, although that is a necessary prerequisite. The power of intercession is the dependence upon the very presence of the fulness of God by His Spirit. This is our desperate need in this hour and in every hour. Daily we ought to cry, "If thy presence go not with us, carry us not up hence." We ought to fear lest we grieve or quench the Spirit and step outside of His blessed presence, failing of that command to be literally filled with His presence (Ephesians 5:18).

It was on the basis of this heart cry of Moses that God did indeed reveal Himself and prepare Moses to pray the wonderful fourth prayer which was gloriously answered. God revealed Himself in spirit (Exodus 34:5) and in word (Exodus 34:6-7), showing Moses that the very character of God is one of abundant mercy, lovingkindness, and undeserved favor. God is faithful to judge sin, but He is longsuffering and willing rather to forgive iniquity and remember it no more. This proclamation stands out as one of the greatest self-revelations of God, repeated numerous times throughout the Old Testament.

**Prayer #4, Exodus 34:9.** When Moses received this wonderful personal revelation, he fell on his face before God and worshipped Him. Moses no longer needed to plead his own will that the people be delivered; he now could plead the very character and will of God as the basis for his intercession. Our God is a God who pardons sin on the basis of His own plan to reveal Himself in mercy and grace. What a basis for powerful, successful intercession! In the following verse (v. 10), God speaks, and He renews the covenant with the people of Israel, promising in effect to restore His chosen people to Himself and once again to manifest His presence among them. For a second forty days and forty nights Moses is alone with God (v. 28) and returns with the glory of God shining upon his face.

Oh, this is what we need today—men and women of God who get alone in the presence of God, in His Word and in prayer, and who, in dependence upon the blessed Spirit of God, plead the promises and character of God as the basis for their intercession for those they love around them, in their homes, in their churches, in their communities, and in their world. What revival we would know if we would get desperate enough for God's presence that we would spend much time alone with Him that He might be manifest when we stand before those we long to reach for His glory. May we learn the lesson Moses learned: If we are to be successful as intercessors, it is the blessed presence of the Spirit of God that we need more than anything else. He alone can empower us to know, plead, and experience the promises and character of God as we ought. Oh, may we moment by moment and meeting by meeting depend on Him for that reality.

The wonder of intercession is the glorious will of God to reveal Himself in mighty deliverance and mercy in answer to the selfless prayers of His children who see the need in the lives of those around them. God longs to deliver. He has done so in the past; He will do so in the future. It is His very nature to do so. May God not stand in wonder because He can find no intercessor. Rather, may we stand in wonder over the mighty works that God will do in response to those who learn to intercede.

**Note:** For further challenge and instruction concerning intercessory prayer, may I encourage you to purchase the book *The Ministry of Intercessory Prayer* by Andrew Murray. It can be ordered through Preach the Word Ministries by calling 1-800-656-PTWM.

---

[1]James A. Stewart, *Opened Windows* (Asheville, N.C.: Revival Literature), pp. 112-13.

[2]Ibid., pp. 111-12.

[3]James O. Frazier, *The Prayer of Faith* (Singapore: Overseas Missionary Fellowship, 1958), p. 27.
53

# APPENDIX G

## MR. FACT, MR. FAITH,
## MR. FEELING

Evan Hopkins, quoted in a book by Steven Barabas, gives the following instruction and illustration:

> In proportion as we fix our eye upon God's fact, and enter into God's reckoning, and act upon it, just in that proportion are we brought into the blessed experience of deliverance. Deliverance from the power of sin is not an attainment, any more than the pardon of sins is. It is a gift of God's grace. Deliverance is not attained by struggle and painful effort, by earnest resolutions and self-denial, but through the cross. It is stepped into by simple faith . . .
>
> Do not wait for feeling . . . I used to put it before my working-men, in Richmond, in this way. Here are three men walking in procession—"Mr. Fact goes first, Mr. Faith follows him, and Mr. Feeling follows Mr. Faith. Supposing the middle man turns around and looks at Mr. Feeling, everything goes wrong. His business is to fix his eye upon Mr. Fact, and Mr. Feeling follows him. Get hold of the fact, first of all—free in Christ, free on the cross. There is the fact. Do not reverse the order.[1]

---

[1] Steven Barabas, *So Great Salvation* (Westwood, N.J.: Fleming H. Revell Company, 1952), pp. 90-91.

# APPENDIX H

## DIAGRAMS

Some people understand truth better with the aid of pictures. The following diagrams are designed to aid one's understanding of the old man and new man, and flesh and Spirit type of concepts. The order is designed as well to aid in understanding.

### Diagram One

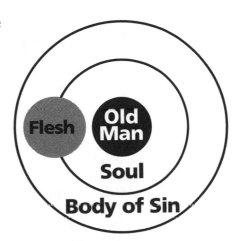

### Observations

Body of Sin = physical realm for the action of sin
Soul = mind, affections, will (personality/self)
Old Man = unregenerate spirit
    Dead to God, alive to sin
        **Note:** Ephesians 2:1 says "dead in trespasses and sins." The old man is reveling in trespasses and sins. He is not dead in the sense of being annihilated or nonexistent. Rather he is dead in the sense of being separated from God. He is dead to God, but very alive to sin.
    Separated from God
Flesh—represented in both the soul and body of sin levels
Soul—pressured to do evil from both the old man and the body of sin

### Summary

This diagram pictures the unsaved or unregenerate man. Even the noblest efforts of this man are merely the "filthy rags" of man's righteousness (Isaiah 64:6). This man, therefore, actually possesses no true acts of righteousness.

## Diagram Two

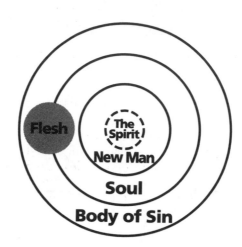

### Observations

Body of Sin = physical realm for the action of sin

Soul = mind, affections, will (personality/self)

Old man—died with Christ; new man was raised with Christ (This is a change of center.)

New man = regenerate spirit

>   Alive to God, dead to sin—Ephesians 2:5 "[God] hath quickened [made alive] us together with Christ."
>
>   Something of the nature of God implanted – I John 3:9 "for His seed [*sperma*] remaineth in him"
>
>   New creation—II Corinthians 5:17 "Therefore if any man be in Christ, he is a new creature [creation]."
>
>   Perfect—Ephesians 4:24 "new man, which after God is created in righteousness and true holiness"
>
>   Capable of growth—II Corinthians 3:18 "changed into the same image from glory to glory"
>
>   Growth occurs through faith – John 6:35 "I am the bread of life: he that cometh to Me shall never hunger; and he that believeth on Me shall never thirst."
>
>   Dwelling place of the Spirit of the glorified Christ—Colossians 1:27 "Christ in you"
>
>   Union with God—I Corinthians 6:17 "But he that is joined unto the Lord is one spirit."
>
>   Union with the eternal life—John 17:3 "And this is life eternal, that they might know Thee, the only true God, and Jesus Christ whom Thou hast sent."

Seated with Christ in the heavenlies—Ephesians 2:6 "And
hath raised us up together, and made us sit together in
heavenly places in Christ Jesus."
Life flows from God—II Corinthians 5:18 "all things are of
[out of] God"
Divine life available for holiness [being] – John 4:14 "the water
that I shall give him shall be in him a well of water
springing up"
Divine life available for service [doing]—John 7:38-39 "Out of
his belly [heart, innermost being] shall flow rivers of living
water. (But this spake He of the Spirit . . . "
Seat of communion with God—II Corinthians 13:14
"communion of the Holy Spirit"
Body—seat of world-consciousness (through the five senses)
Soul—seat of self-consciousness
New Man (Spirit)—seat of God-consciousness
Flesh—represented in both the soul and body of sin levels
Soul—pressured to do evil through the body of sin, and pressured to
do right through the Spirit in the new man

## Summary

If the new man were in a new body, there would be no pressure or
tendency to sin. The soul of the regenerated man this side of heaven has
a choice of focus. James 1:8 warns against being double-souled. Walking
in the flesh occurs as the soul yields to the body of sin or depends merely
on the soulish level to do right. Flesh-dependence is depending on the
body of sin to do right or depending on the soulish level of intellect
(merely man's reasonings), emotions (merely subjectivity) or volition
(merely willpower) for Christian experience. Therefore, flesh dependence is either self (soul)-dependence or (body)-dependence. Walking
in the Spirit occurs as the soul yields to the Spirit. Then the Spirit
counteracts and overcomes the body of sin. The will of the soul is the
doorway to either flesh-dominance or Spirit-dominance.

Imagine taking the outer edge (body of sin) of the diagram and lifting it up to a position of dominance. This next diagram pictures this
fleshly or carnal Christian.

## Diagram Three

### Observations

> Soul—yielding to flesh
> Body of sin—leading and dominating
> New man and the Spirit—ignored

### Summary

This pictures the carnal believer who is yielding to his flesh. However, thinking back to Diagram Two, if we were to lift up the center (the Spirit in the new man) to a place of dominance, it would look like the following diagram.

## Diagram Four

### Observations

> Soul—yielding to the Spirit
> New man and the Spirit—leading and dominating
> Body of sin—counteracted

## Summary

The old man died with Christ and was raised a new man. But the body of sin must be mortified or made to die. This occurs as choices are made to depend on the power of the new life, which came through death and resurrection with Christ. As the single-souled believer looks to the Spirit in the new man, the Spirit leads and dominates. This pictures the spiritual man as one who is rightly related to the Spirit. As the believer cooperates with the Spirit's leadership and depends on the Spirit's enablement, the Spirit through the new man counteracts and overcomes the body of sin, deprives the body of sin of earthly life, and replaces old acquired habits with new acquired habits. Thus bad character is replaced with good character by the dynamic of divine life. This spiritual growth occurs only as one depends—choice by choice—on the life of the Spirit based on God's promises. Therefore, if one does not recognize and honor the Spirit, he has no hope of victory. But the one who honors the Spirit, yielding to His leadership and power, accesses the promises of victory. This is not the Spirit instead of the believer, but the Spirit through the believer who actively cooperates.

The picture is not the old man and the new man in a contest. The old man died with Christ. He is gone! The picture is a battle between the Spirit and the flesh. When one realizes this, if he but yields to the Spirit, the contest is over. For the flesh is no match for the Spirit.

## Diagram Five

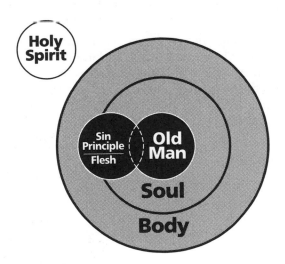

## Observations

The old man (unregenerated spirit) is dead to God and alive to sin. The old man is separated from God and united to sin.

## Summary

This pictures the unsaved man.

# Diagram Six

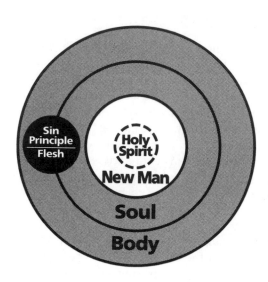

## Observations

The new man (regenerated spirit) is dead to sin and alive to God.
The new man is separated from sin and united to God.

## Summary

This pictures the saved man. Notice the radical change of center. The innermost being is now separated from sin and in union with the Holy Spirit. As long as the believer realizes his union with God, the battle with the flesh will easily be won. The flesh and the Spirit are not equal entities. The key is to keep yielding to and depending on the Holy Spirit. [This is explained at the end of chapter 6.]

## Significant Bible Passages

Romans 6:6—"Knowing this, that our old man is crucified with Him, that the body of sin might be destroyed [cancelled or counteracted], that henceforth we should not serve sin."

Romans 8:2—"For the law of the Spirit of life in Christ Jesus hath made me free from [counteracted] the law of sin and death."

Romans 8:5—"For they that are after [live according to] the flesh do mind [set their minds on] the things of the flesh; but they that are after [live according to] the Spirit [set their minds on] the things of the Spirit."

Romans 8:11—"But if the Spirit of Him that raised up Jesus from the dead dwell in you, He that raised up Christ from the dead shall also quicken [give life to] your mortal bodies by His Spirit that dwelleth in you." [This is the principle of counteraction.]

Romans 8:13—"For if you live after [according to] the flesh, ye shall die: but if ye through the Spirit do mortify [put to death] the deeds of the body, ye shall live." [This is the principle of counteraction accessed through dependence on the Spirit. Notice it is the deeds of the body of sin which must be put to death. The old man already died with Christ.]

Galatians 2:20—"I am crucified with Christ: nevertheless I live; yet not I, but Christ liveth in me: and the life which I now live in the flesh I live by the faith of the Son of God, who loved me, and gave himself for me." [Notice the change of center from the old man (*I am crucified with Christ*) to the new man (*nevertheless I live*) which is indwelt by the Spirit (*yet not I, but Christ lives in me*).]

Galatians 5:16–18—"This I say then, Walk in the Spirit, and ye shall not fulfil the lust of the flesh. For the flesh lusteth against the Spirit, and the Spirit against the flesh: and these are contrary the one to the other: so that ye cannot do the things that ye would. But if ye be led of [yield to] the Spirit, ye are not under the law [of sin]." [When you follow the leadership of the Spirit, the battle is over!]

Ephesians 4:20–24—"But ye have not so learned Christ; If so be that ye have heard Him, and have been taught by Him, as the truth is in Jesus: That ye put off [infinitive, aorist tense, middle voice—have put off] concerning the former conversation [conduct] the old man, which is corrupt [participle, present tense, passive voice—which allowed itself to be growing corrupt] according to the deceitful lusts; And be renewed [infinitive, present tense, passive voice—allowing yourself to being renewed] in the spirit of your mind; And that ye put on [infinitive, aorist tense, middle voice—have put on] the new man, which after God is created in righteousness and true holiness." [The new man, or new creation, is perfect yet capable of growth.]

Colossians 3:1–14—"If ye then be risen with Christ, seek those things which are above, where Christ sitteth on the right hand of God. Set your affection [mind, soul] on things above, not on things on the earth. For ye are dead, and your life is hid with Christ in God. When Christ, who is our life, shall appear, then shall ye also appear with Him in glory. Mortify [imperative, aorist tense, active voice—put to death by Christ's life] therefore your [lit., the] members which are upon the earth; fornication, uncleanness, inordinate affection, evil concupiscence, and covetousness, which is idolatry: For which things' sake the wrath of God cometh on the children of disobedience: In the which ye also walked some time, when ye lived in them. But now ye also put off [imperative, aorist tense, middle voice—to take off from oneself] all these; anger, wrath, malice, blasphemy, filthy communication out of your mouth. Lie not one to another, seeing that ye have put off [participle, aorist tense, middle deponent—to take off completely] the old man with his deeds; And have put on [participle, aorist tense, middle voice] the new man, which is renewed in knowledge after the image of Him that created him: Where there is neither Greek nor Jew, circumcision nor uncircumcision, Barbarian, Scythian, bond nor free: but Christ is all, and in all. Put on [imperative, aorist tense, middle voice] therefore, as the elect of God, holy and beloved, bowels of mercies, kindness, humbleness of mind, meekness, longsuffering; Forbearing one another, and forgiving one another, if any man have a quarrel against any: even as Christ forgave you, so also do ye. And above all these things put on charity, which is the bond of perfectness. [Lesson: Put off the ways of the old man (v. 8), since you have put off the old man (v. 9); since you have put on the new man (v. 10), put on the ways of the new man (v. 12). The key to this is depending on the Spirit to take the old ways to the cross for the application of Christ's victory.]

Hebrews 4:12—"For the word of God is quick, and powerful, and sharper than any twoedged sword, piercing even to the dividing asunder of soul and spirit, and of the joints and marrow, and is a discerner of the thoughts and intents of the heart." [The spirit which sunk down into the soul at the fall of man is raised to a position of dominance as one depends on the words of God and accesses God's promises. Therefore the Word of God truly is *dividing asunder* between *soul and spirit.*]

# BIBLIOGRAPHY

Arndt, William F., and Gingrich, F. Wilbur. *A Greek-English Lexicon of the New Testament*. Chicago: University of Chicago Press, 1979.

Barabas, Steven. *So Great Salvation*. Westwood, N.J.: Fleming H. Revell Company, 1952.

Campbell, Duncan. *The Lewis Awakening* in *Heritage of Revival* by Colin N. Peckham. Edinburgh: The Faith Mission, 1986.

Campbell, Duncan. *The Nature of a God-Sent Revival*. Vinton, Va.: Christ Life Publications, n.d.

Campbell, Duncan. *The Price and Power of Revival*. Vinton, Va.: Christ Life Publications, n.d.

Carré, E. G. ed. *Praying Hyde*. Asheville, N.C.: Revival Literature, n.d.

Carson, D. A. *Exegetical Fallacies*. Grand Rapids: Baker Book House, 1984.

Culpepper, C. L. *The Shantung Revival*. Atlanta: Home Mission Board, 1993.

Custer, Stewart. *A Treasury of New Testament Synonyms*. Greenville, S.C.: Bob Jones University Press, 1975.

Custer, Stewart. *Witness to Christ: A Commentary on Acts*. Greenville, S.C.: Bob Jones University Press, 2000.

Edwards, Jonathan. *The Works of Jonathan Edwards*. Edinburgh: Banner of Truth, 1974.

Evans, Eifion. *Revival Comes to Wales*. Bridgend, Wales: The Evangelical Press of Wales, 1995.

Evans, Eifion. *The Welsh Revival of 1904*. Bridgend, Wales: The Evangelical Press of Wales, 1997.

Frazier, James O. *The Prayer of Faith*. Singapore: Overseas Missionary Fellowship, 1958.

Goforth, Jonathan. *By My Spirit*. Elkhart, Ind.: Bethel Publishing, 1983.

Goforth, Jonathan. *When the Spirit's Fire Swept Korea*. Elkhart, Ind.: Bethel Publishing, 1984.

Goforth, Rosland. *Climbing*. Elkhart, Ind.: Bethel Publishing, n.d.

Goforth, Rosalind. *Goforth of China*. Minneapolis: Bethany House Publishers, 1937.

Greenfield, John. *When the Spirit Came*. Minneapolis: Bethany Fellowship, 1967.

Griffin, Stanley C. *A Forgotten Revival*. Bromley, Kent, England: Day One Publications, 1992.

Jones, R. B. *Rent Heavens*. Asherville, N.C.: Revival Literature, 1963.

Lloyd-Jones, D. Martyn. *Revival*. Wheaton: Crossway Books, 1992.

Moore, W. Carey, ed. *Christian History*. Worcester, Penn.: Christian History Magazine, 1982.

Morgan, G. Campbell. *The Spirit of God*. Grand Rapids: Baker Book House, 1983.

Moule, Handley G. C. *Studies in Romans*. Grand Rapids: Kregel Publications, 1977.

Moule, Handley G. C. *The Holy Spirit*. Great Britain: Christian Focus Publications, 1999.

Murray, Iain. *Revival and Revivalism*. Edinburgh: Banner of Truth, 1994. [The historical information in this book is a blessing. Yet, although the author shows a heart for revival, his conclusions seem to be fatalistic.]

Paxson, Ruth. *Rivers of Living Water*. Chicago: Moody Press, 1930.

Phillips, Thomas. *The Welsh Revival*. Edinburgh: Banner of Truth, 1998.

Pierson, A. T. *The Acts of the Holy Spirit*. Harrisburg, Penn.: Christian Publications, Inc., 1980.

Pollock, J. C. *The Keswick Story*. Chicago: Moody Press, 1964.

Rienecker, Fritz, and Rogers, Cleon L. *Linguistic Key to the Greek New Testament*. Grand Rapids: Zondervan, 1980.

Roberts, Alexander, and Donaldson, James, eds. *Anti-Nicence Fathers: Translations of the Fathers Down to A.D. 325*. Grand Rapids: Wm. B. Eerdmans Publishing Company, 1979.

Schaff, Philip, and Wace, Henry, eds. *The Nicene and Post-Nicene Fathers*. Peabody, Mass.: Hendrickson, 1979.

Schubert, William E. *I Remember John Sung*. Singapore: Far Eastern Bible College Press, 1976.

Spurgeon, C. H. *Power for You*. New Kensington, Penn.: Whitaker House, 1996.